Negotiating Respect

UNIVERSITY PRESS OF FLORIDA

Florida A&M University, Tallahassee
Florida Atlantic University, Boca Raton
Florida Gulf Coast University, Ft. Myers
Florida International University, Miami
Florida State University, Tallahassee
New College of Florida, Sarasota
University of Central Florida, Orlando
University of Florida, Gainesville
University of North Florida, Jacksonville
University of South Florida, Tampa
University of West Florida, Pensacola

NEGOTIATING RESPECT

Pentecostalism, Masculinity, and
the Politics of Spiritual Authority
in the Dominican Republic

Brendan Jamal Thornton

University Press of Florida
Gainesville · Tallahassee · Tampa · Boca Raton · Pensacola
Orlando · Miami · Jacksonville · Ft. Myers · Sarasota

Chapter 6 was previously published as "Residual Masculinity and the Cultivation of Negative-Charisma in a Caribbean Pentecostal Community" in *The Anthropology of Religious Charisma: Ecstasies and Institutions*, edited by Charles Lindholm, 2013, Palgrave Macmillan, reproduced with permission of Palgrave Macmillan.

This book may be available in an electronic edition.

First cloth printing, 2016
First paperback printing, 2020

25 24 23 22 21 20   6 5 4 3 2 1

A record of cataloging-in-publication data is available from the Library of Congress.
ISBN 978-0-8130-6168-9 (cloth)
ISBN 978-0-8130-6449-9 (pbk.)

The University Press of Florida is the scholarly publishing agency for the State University System of Florida, comprising Florida A&M University, Florida Atlantic University, Florida Gulf Coast University, Florida International University, Florida State University, New College of Florida, University of Central Florida, University of Florida, University of North Florida, University of South Florida, and University of West Florida.

University Press of Florida
2046 NE Waldo Road
Suite 2100
Gainesville, FL 32609
http://upress.ufl.edu

This book is a part of the Latin American and Caribbean Arts and Culture publication initiative, funded by a grant from the Andrew W. Mellon Foundation.

For Mom and Dad

Contents

Acknowledgments

Of course it is impossible to acknowledge everyone who has contributed in one way or another to the birth, development, and completion of this project. I could not have done it alone, and it was with the support of professional colleagues, friends, family, and especially the residents of Villa Altagracia and the Dominican Republic that this book became a reality.

I would first and foremost like to express my deepest gratitude and extend my most heartfelt thank-you to the men and women of Villa Altagracia for inviting me into their lives with open arms and asking nothing in return. Their openness and selfless hospitality throughout my fieldwork, as well as their continued friendship to this day, has touched me in profound ways. While I might never be able to return to them everything that they have given to me both personally and professionally, I wish to acknowledge their fundamental contribution: *muchas gracias a todos!* I sincerely thank you all.

This project began under the early guidance of exceptional scholars who continue to inspire me to push my work further and to grow as an academic. I would like to thank Keith McNeal, who has been an indispensable resource even before I made my first trip to the Dominican Republic in 2006. His fastidious guidance combined with a keen intellect has generously supported and enriched this project from its inception. In this same vein I would also like to thank Joel Robbins for being a bountiful intellectual resource to me for many years; I have benefited greatly from his advice and rewarding feedback at every stage of this project. Thanks go to Nancy Postero and Sara Johnson for their inspiration and early support, and especially to Robin Derby, whose expertise and acumen contributed greatly to this study's depth and whose passionate enthusiasm for all things Dominican has been both infectious and motivating. I would also like to extend a special thanks to Mary McEntee. If I am a better writer today it is because of her influence.

I traveled to the Dominican Republic for the first time in the summer of 2006 and stayed for several months with the most delightful family in Ingenio Consuelo—the Abreus. They provided me with a kind and memorable introduction to the country. Thanks go to Miguel Abreu; Domingo Abreu and his wife, Antonia; and their children, Michael, Angie, and Mariela. Thanks also to Carlos, Victor, and especially Peter for their friendship and hospitality. From 2007 until 2009 I made Santo Domingo my home. I must thank my roommate, Lissette, with whom I lived for over a year; I could not have asked for a better housemate.

A number of people provided helpful comments on chapter drafts of the manuscript. I would like to express my sincere gratitude to Elizabeth Brusco and Jon Bialecki, who provided considered, challenging, and constructive feedback on the manuscript. I also received generous feedback on different parts of the book from Charles Lindholm, Lauren Leve, and Miguel La Serna.

I have had the good fortune over the past several years to present and receive feedback on my work at the annual meetings of the American Anthropological Association and the Caribbean Studies Association. I would like to thank panel organizers and discussants, especially William Dawley, Ruy Blanes, Annelin Eriksen, Naomi Haynes, and Stanley Brandes. I have also presented my work at different forums at the University of North Carolina at Chapel Hill (UNC); in particular, I am thankful to Louis Pérez for his invitation to speak at the Institute for the Study of the Americas in 2012 where I received a warm reception.

I am lucky to have had the support of many great people at UNC over the past few years, mainly my colleagues in the Department of Religious Studies, including Laurie Maffly-Kipp, Randall Styers, Jonathan Boyarin, Yaakov Ariel, and especially Todd Ochoa and Lauren Leve. All have offered helpful comments on my work at different points and have provided me with as supportive and as nourishing a work environment as anyone could ask for.

I made it through this project with the personal support of good friends. I would like to thank Robert Desmond White, Diego Ubiera, Robert Turner, Alyssa Peace, Thomas and NaEshia Freeman, and especially Miguel La Serna and Mario Marzan, two colleagues and close friends who kept me sane and grounded throughout the most difficult stages of writing while at the same time teaching me how to negotiate academia with grace and humor.

I wish that I could include here a special thank-you to everyone, but space and time do not permit. I want to thank the following people by name who helped in countless ways during my time in Santo Domingo (in no particular order), all of whom contributed in one way or another to the birth, development, and final completion of this project: Daniel Castellanos, Stéphanie Daviot, Alicia Sangro Blasco, Antonio de Moya, Martha Ellen Davis, Mariano Sanchez, Francisco Cueto Villamán, Eddy Tejeda, Sonia Pierre, Emildo Bueno, Miguel Hernandez, Guillermo Sterling, and Cristóbal Rodríguez. I benefited most from the friendship and aid of Liliana Gamboa. Without her enthusiastic support and tireless assistance throughout the data collection portion of this project, it simply would not have been completed. To her I owe a mountain of debt, and I consider myself most fortunate to have had her invaluable help throughout my fieldwork.

This book would not have been written had it not been for the financial support of UNC and a two-year postdoctoral fellowship that provided generous support to complete this book in a timely fashion. Subsequent follow-up trips were made possible by funding from the Department of Religious Studies here at UNC.

I would like to thank Erika Stevens and the rest of the University Press of Florida editorial staff for making it a reality. Thank you for your hard work and belief in this volume's potential. I would also like to acknowledge Robert Burchfield, the project's copy editor, for his fine work and attention to detail.

Finally, this book is dedicated to my mother and father, whose contributions cannot be measured. I would like to thank my mother, Frances Grace Thornton, for being my number one fan and for supporting me with unwavering confidence and love throughout this process. I would like to thank my father, Leslie James Thornton, for his confidence in me, for nurturing my intellectual curiosity at a young age, and for teaching me to question everything. Thank you both for giving me the opportunity to take this journey.

Introduction

Pentecostal Cultural Change

This book is about religion, identity, and culture. Through an ethnographic account of Pentecostal Christianity, I explore the dynamic intersection of these domains as they are lived in the context of urban poverty in the Dominican Republic. Based on over two years of anthropological fieldwork in a barrio of Villa Altagracia, I examine the everyday practices of Pentecostal community members and the complex ways in which they negotiate legitimacy, recognition, and spiritual authority within the constraints of religious pluralism and Catholic cultural supremacy. By focusing on the cultural politics of belief and the role religious identity plays in poor urban communities, this book looks to provide new insight into the social dynamics of Pentecostal culture and offer a fresh perspective on religious pluralism and the ever-evolving contours of contemporary religious and cultural change.

In order to highlight the cultural transformations attending Pentecostal entrenchment locally and to probe the character and social force of evangelical identity for believers and their communities, I ground my study in the demanding and uncertain environment of the urban barrio and with those who call it their home. In particular, I consider in detail the determinative role of the church in the lives of young male residents and the nuanced ways in which gender and masculinity are both remade and affirmed through charismatic conversion. Exploring the relationship between the church and competing social institutions like youth gangs and Dominican *vodú*,

I lay bare the significant and multiplex ways in which Pentecostal Christianity has become a meaningful feature of social and moral life in Dominican neighborhoods.

Today studies of Pentecostalism are on the rise following the veritable explosion of evangelical faith over the past fifty years (Martin 1990; Stoll 1990; Poewe 1994; Cox 1995; Jenkins 2002). Pentecostal charismatic forms of Christianity appear to be spreading the fastest, dramatically developing among the poor and popular classes of the global South (Jenkins 2002; Martin 2002). In Latin America, where Pentecostal growth began in earnest in the 1950s, it accounts for 80 to 90 percent of all Protestant growth (Jenkins 2002:80), making Pentecostalism the most popular version of Protestantism in Latin America (Stoll 1990).[1] Up from a smattering of followers in the United States just a hundred years ago, according to some generous estimates today there are close to 500 million adherents worldwide (Cleary 1997:1; Anderson 2004:1).[2] The exponential success of global Pentecostalism has prompted at least one observer to ask whether this is not the most successful social movement of the past century (Jenkins 2002:10). If not, by winning converts in seemly every populated corner of the planet, Pentecostalism is arguably the single most wide-ranging religious movement in the world today. Few other religions can claim the same spectacular success across continents as diverse as North America, Europe, Asia, Africa, and South America.

The growing social scientific literature focusing on the movement attests to the profound ways in which Pentecostal culture has transformed communities where it has become a prominent feature. Joel Robbins, in a review essay on the anthropology of Pentecostalism, refers to it as a "powerful driver of radical cultural change" and characterizes its effects among converts as "most akin, say, not to rearranging the cultural furniture but to moving that furniture to an altogether new house, one where even old familiar pieces look different than they did before" (2010:156). Pentecostalism is a unique cultural formation in that while it shares a variety of similarities and recognizable characteristics wherever it takes root, the ways in which it has been appropriated and put to use in local settings demonstrate dramatic variability. How people grapple and come to terms with Pentecostal charismatic Christian culture, especially when it seems apart from the traditional, taken-for-granted, and dominant culture of the times, is an ongoing concern of studies emerging within the anthropology of Christianity (Robbins 2004b:326).

My ethnographic concern to understand Pentecostal Christian culture and its effect on social relationships beyond the church positions this project's contribution within a new wave of anthropological scholarship on Christianity (see Robbins 2003a; Cannell 2006; Engelke and Tomlinson 2006; Bialecki, Haynes, and Robbins 2008; Haynes 2012). Haynes (2012:123) has noted that while plenty of studies to date have connected Pentecostalism to wider social contexts—such as those that link Pentecostal expansion to the rise of neoliberalism in the global South—there has been a "lack of detailed ethnographic engagement with the lives of local believers as they unfold outside the church." This may require putting aside for the time being the important question of "why people convert" in order to ask equally compelling and perhaps more revealing questions about the social and cultural implications of conversion, not solely for individual converts to the church but for their communities of origin as well.

Despite a few historical studies on the development of Protestantism in the Dominican Republic, meager scholarship exists on popular non-Catholic faith in the country, to say nothing of studies that trace the impact of Pentecostal Christianity on local culture and religion. I take this as my starting point by asking not just what evangelical Christian identity means to believers (in terms of their gender and social status, for instance), but asking what the "Pentecostalization" of Dominican society means at the local level and querying how this cultural transformation has informed the ways in which Dominicans negotiate religious difference and authority locally. I am hence less concerned here with *why* people convert and more concerned with the *consequences* of conversion or, as Cannell (2006:1) asks to open her introduction to *The Anthropology of Christianity*, with "what difference does Christianity make" for believers and the social worlds they inhabit. What does the existence of Pentecostal churches, their leaders, their congregations, their conventional rituals and beliefs, mean to everyday and spiritual life in the barrio? What social role does this unique form of Christianity play in poor urban contexts? By examining how converts manage prestige, gender, and authority (both spiritual and moral), my investigation centers on the strategic negotiations of churchgoers over power and identity in the community, showing how conversion shapes and is shaped by the social norms and values governing moral and religious life in Villa Altagracia.

This book is not about the origins of Pentecostalism or Protestantism in the Dominican Republic, its missionary history, or its historical expansion. That work has largely been done (see Wipfler 1966; Platt 1981; Lockward 1982; Alvarez Vega 1996). This is also not specifically a study about why Pentecostalism is popular or why people convert. This book *is* about Pentecostal cultural change, meaning making among evangelical converts, and the role of religious identity in shaping social realities for Dominican barrio residents. It is also therefore more generally about popular religion and how average Dominicans put (Protestant) religion to work in the twenty-first century.

The growth of Pentecostal religion in Latin America and the Caribbean over the past fifty years has been particularly acute despite having to contend with and find space beside established and powerful state churches like Roman Catholicism. The Dominican Republic is a case in point, as it has long been considered a staunch supporter of Catholic supremacy. However, despite having inhabited the margins of popular culture for years, today Pentecostal Christianity constitutes a common and in some cases inseparable feature of everyday culture and society in the country. Just fifty years ago Protestantism in the Dominican Republic was claimed by a mere 1.6 percent of the population (Damboriena 1963:153; Gonzalez 1969:82; Hurbon 2001b:126); today it has likely surpassed 15 percent, having grown at least tenfold since 1960.[3]

In centering my research on religious life at the local level with ordinary residents in a typical neighborhood, I offer evidence to dispel the myth that the Dominican Republic is somehow simply, or matter-of-factly, a Catholic country. In fact, to describe it as such is to ignore the distinct ways that evangelical culture has permeated important domains of meaning making for society's members, to say nothing about the actual cultural organization of social life in many if not most parts of the country. Even while the most conservative estimates suppose that only 10 percent of the population is Protestant, the influence of evangelical conversion is undeniably felt by nearly everyone. In the following pages I marshal evidence to suggest that evangelical forms of Christianity are deeply entrenched in the everyday social and symbolic worlds of Dominicans in complex ways, most profoundly so for the popular classes, and set out to explain its specific expressions and principal social correlates in a poor urban setting.

Unlike parts of Africa and Asia where Pentecostalism has found unprecedented growth without ever having to contend with a strong state church, both Latin America and the Caribbean, at least since the modern period, have always been Christian regions dominated by the Christian church. Pentecostalism in the Americas has caught fire not just among the "brush-wood of spirit cults," as Martin (1990:115) once wrote, but also among the dense timbers of Catholic and even mainline Protestant churches that have long shaped the social realities of New World societies. It is within the con-text of profoundly Christian worlds that Pentecostalism has been able to claim for itself not just acceptance but also, importantly, cultural legitimacy, a measure of spiritual authority, and nearly universal recognition as a viable religious alternative. *Negotiating Respect* interrogates the local politics of this recognition and the astonishing legitimacy that evangelical Christian cul-ture now enjoys as a dynamic aspect of contemporary Dominican culture and society.

It is my intention that the research presented here contributes to a better understanding of the diversity of Christian experience as well as a deeper appreciation for the experience of Christian diversity by exploring what it means to be a *cristiano* (an evangelical Protestant or Pentecostal Chris-tian) in the shadow of Roman Catholic supremacy. In many respects the emergence of Pentecostalism has reshaped Dominican society's ideas about what it means to be Christian. This is no small feat in a country that has claimed Catholicism as its cultural, political, and historical progeni-tor. What it means to be a certain type of Christian in a particular kind of Christian country is a central theme I explore throughout the book. For residents of Villa Altagracia, the question of *who* and *what* is a Christian is a contentious one and has far-reaching personal and social implications. Multiple Christian subjectivities such as *evangélico, católico, carismático*, and *adventista* vie for recognition and authority in a contentious religious field. These categories are not inconsequential and often express differing social locations and alternative ways of being-in-the-world no less than conflicting theological perspectives. As a result, what kind of Christian one claims to be carries potentially varied social consequences for religious actors.

With an analytic lens trained on local negotiations over the meaning and status of evangelical identity, I show how Dominican Pentecostals substan-tiate declarations of spiritual and moral authority and realize certain claims to authentic Christian identity. I focus on the processes and precepts by which Pentecostal converts and evangelicals as a community craft personal and group identities based on fidelity to what they call "true Christianity," a proposition constructed both with and against the dominant Catholic and African-derived traditions of the island. Under what conditions, for example, is evangelical religion rendered legitimate and recognized as a powerful and authentic spiritual authority? How did this once marginal "sect" come to be regarded by followers and many others as *the* exemplar of Christian faith? For many Dominicans, in order to be a true Christian, in order to truly serve God, it is believed that one must convert to a Pentecostal church—which begs the crucial question: why? Over the following pages I answer these and related questions to better understand the basis of evangelical popularity and to evaluate the transformative role of Pentecostalism in local settings.

Despite modernity's threat to behead religion with the sword of secularization, prophesies of the ultimate victory of secularism over the supernatural seem quaint today with the unquestionably apparent reaffirmation of the religious in contemporary life (see Taylor 2007). In much of the Western Hemisphere, specifically Christian themes continue to dominate public and private life with varying degrees of ferocity. Leading this charge in Latin America and the Caribbean are Pentecostal churches that seek to make sweeping cultural changes beginning at the grassroots level. In addition to promoting spiritual goals of sanctity and salvation, the church attempts to reform individuals from the inside out, to save society through the redemption of its members by means of moral transformation and a radical reformation of identity, inciting in believers not just novel worshipping styles but new modes of being that extend far beyond church walls. Alongside these personal transformations I examine the social and cultural changes occurring outside of the church as a result, carefully detailing how Pentecostalism shapes meaning in local communities one neighborhood at a time.

I understand this book's contribution to be situated alongside other important works on the crucial role of religion in shaping social status and identities. Specifically, a number of scholars have focused on the role of Pentecostalism in mediating the experience of ethnic, gender, and racial identity (see, for example, Brusco 1995; Austin-Broos 1997; Toulis 1997; Burdick 1998). The analysis offered here complements these studies with its emphasis on understanding converts' experiences of their Pentecostal identity as having both transcendental spiritual and practical social value. Addressing the issue of gender specifically, I contribute to an ongoing discussion in the literature on gender and Pentecostalism with a focus on men and masculinity, a second primary focus of this book, and how conversion mediates the performance of male gendered behavior. An analytic focus on gender dynamics as they relate to both men and women in the church contributes to studies of Pentecostalism that center on gender but which to this point have focused in the main on women alone.[4]

Little has been written about the culture of Pentecostal Christianity in the Dominican Republic today, let alone the Caribbean as a whole (notable exceptions are cited later). More often than not, Protestant faith is ignored in favor of more "exotic" religions like Haitian *vodou* and Cuban *santería*—syncretic African-derived or "Afro-Creole" religions that perhaps seem better suited to fit the "savage slot" of anthropological imagination (Trouillot 2003). Observers who continue to gloss countries throughout the region as simply "Catholic" uncritically recite historical and political affiliations that today seem difficult to reconcile with popular religious enthusiasm. At the same time, they reproduce stereotypes of the exotic Other that function to define the Caribbean region in terms of its imagined alterity, belying the salient cultural realities of a good majority of the region's people (besides denying them accurate representation).

It is astonishing how little international scholarly attention religion in the Dominican Republic has received. While a significant literature exists in English covering religious diversity in countries from Cuba (e.g., Ochoa 2010) to Trinidad (e.g., McNeal 2011), including even small islands like Saint Martin/Sint Maarten (Guadeloupe 2008) and St. Vincent (Zane 1999), to name just a few, popular religion and culture in the Dominican Republic have failed to draw serious attention from foreign scholars—indeed, a striking state of affairs for being the second largest country in the Caribbean! Religion in the Dominican Republic has, with few exceptions, all but been ignored. I have come to the opinion that the likely reason for this is twofold. First, the fascination with religion in Haiti, a legacy beginning with Melville Herskovits and the widespread study of African American culture and the search for Africanisms (Herskovits 1946), has created a blind spot over the Dominican Republic due to a myopic focus on what George Simpson called "black religions" of the New World (Simpson 1978). In comparison to Haiti, which is almost always considered somehow to be more "black" than anywhere else in the Caribbean, the Dominican Republic has consistently been viewed (however mistakenly) as too ordinary, too Christian, and much too orthodox and conventional to constitute an interesting subject for anthropological research on religion. Second, the widespread (mis)perception of the country as definitively Catholic and chiefly Hispanic at the expense of acknowledging its African heritage, to say nothing of its Haitian-derived traditions, has left an inaccurate picture of popular religion in the country with little basis in reality. This has meant that *vodú* in the Dominican Republic, as well as its rich folk Catholic tradition, has largely been ignored while studies on *vodou* in Haiti continue ad infinitum. Needless to say, when it comes to the study of Protestantism or Christianity more generally in the Caribbean, historically Catholic countries like Cuba, Puerto Rico, and the Dominican Republic seem always to be overlooked. Furthermore, the primacy of gatekeeping concepts like "race" and "nation" that dominate Caribbean studies has tended to steer scholarly discussions about Caribbean religion in directions that disregard or simply ignore the global cultural advance of Pentecostal Christianity. The reason for this may be due as much to the faith's conservatism and apolitical leanings as to its antisyncretic and patently antagonistic opposition toward traditional, African-derived creole religions. As a morally conservative, principally Anglo-American cultural export, Pentecostalism does not seem to fit expectations of the region as putatively syncretic and uniquely Afro-Creole. In this way Pentecostal Christian culture is perceived to be a challenging contradiction to the ideas of locality, mixture/hybridity, and diversity—indeed to the very idea of "creolization"—usually applied to the Caribbean and which constitute its master symbol (see Khan 2001 for an astute critique of the creolization concept). The tendency has been to study religions indigenous to the region and not necessarily those institutions that are the most widely embraced. While the Rastafari movement in Jamaica has more global exposure, for example, garnering more attention from foreign scholars, there are considerably more Pentecostals in Jamaica than there are Rastafarians (see Austin-Broos 1997:245). A provocative question to ask might be whether studying Jamaican Pentecostalism would tell us more about Jamaicans and Jamaican culture than studying Rastafari religion.[5]

By calling into question the presumed marginality of Pentecostal Christianity today, *Negotiating Respect* helps to reconceptualize the social and cultural organization of religious belief and authority in the Dominican Republic and to reorient the ways in which scholars think and talk about religious pluralism, Christian orthodoxy, and Catholic hegemony through a more nuanced and balanced view of the present-day religious field in light of the lived experiences and actual desires of contemporary believers.

In sum, *Negotiating Respect* is an ethnographic study of the role of evangelical modes of Christianity in shaping contemporary attitudes, orientations, affectivities, and identities within and toward local matrices of power, legitimacy, and authority. As such, this book is as much about the culturally constituted modalities of Christian personhood as they are made and remade through evangelical practice as it is about the cultural and sociological implications of evangelical belief in urban barrios with respect to power and status. By interrogating the politics of Christian identity locally and by focusing on the mechanisms by which Pentecostals bring such exchanges into being by asking what difference *Pentecostal* Christianity makes in the Dominican Republic, I hope to foster further discussion about the practice and place of Christianity in contemporary urban contexts, particularly in plural religious contexts marked by Christian hegemony, and to contribute a new direction of inquiry into the ways in which Pentecostalism is changing public ideas about what it means to be Christian, not only for converts but also for the communities and societies where the church has become more norm than exception, more local than foreign, more orthodox than heterodox, more accepted than disdained.

Chapter Summaries

Today in barrios across the Dominican Republic, no less in locales around the Caribbean and Latin America, Pentecostal culture has become an important and powerful cultural agency: in shaping religious exchange and mediating religious difference (chapter 3); in transforming Christian subjectivity and the practice of being Christian (chapter 4); for the sense people make of Christianity (chapter 5) and the sense people make of themselves as Christians (chapter 7); in shaping social roles and statuses as well as modes of religious authority (chapter 6); and in influencing the conceptual ways in which people experience Christian pluralism and the very possibilities of being Christian (Conclusion).

In order to contextualize contemporary Pentecostal religion in the country and to outline the historical constitution of Christianity and Christian subjectivities locally, chapter 1 offers a brief social history of Christian culture in the Dominican Republic. Christian orthodoxy has been the religion of status and power on the island since the establishment of the first colonies. This chapter traces the origins of Christian hegemony, rooted in over 500 years of Christian domination, and briefly plots the primary vertices of religious pluralism in the country.

In chapter 2 I introduce my field site, two small neighborhood Pentecostal churches and their local community in Villa Altagracia, San Cristóbal province. I give a brief description of my ethnographic methodology following a summary of the social-economic context of the barrio where I conducted research. Named after the country's revered patron saint, Villa Altagracia is an archetypal Dominican town. "Poor" and "traditional" by the cosmopolitan standards of the capital, Villa sits at the intersection of the decline of prosperous sugar production, the rise of export manufacturing, and trying economic transformations affecting Dominican society over the past quarter century. I chose Villa Altagracia as a field site not because it is exceptional but because it is ordinary, a town not unlike many others in the country that struggles to remain viable in uncertain economic times. Far removed from the tourist economies of the capital and beach towns (yet not entirely outside their influence), Villa Altagracia is a beloved place for residents though it is rarely a destination for visitors. It is, nevertheless, a culturally rich location, locally flavored and unmistakably Dominican in its sights, sounds, and spirit.

In chapter 3, the first of five ethnographic chapters, I consider the religious field as a whole and trace the dimensions of popular religion as they manifest in the local barrio. I advance the argument that the predominant religious institutions in barrio Francisco (a microcosm of the country's religious diversity) share basic cosmological assumptions and precepts that underlie religious meaning locally and establish the terms of cooperation and conflict—agreement and discord—across the religious continuum. It is within this implicit sharing that believers constitute themselves as effectual religious actors, prosecute their religious identities, and negotiate spiritual authority. In Villa Altagracia, meaningful interaction in the realm of the sacred is dependent upon the articulated practical and symbolic relations of agreement obtaining between local religions (primarily popular Catholicism, so-called Dominican *vodú*, and Protestant evangelical, namely Pentecostal, churches) within the context of Christian domination.

Efficacy across the religious spectrum in Villa is achieved as a result of the cosmological assumptions that religious institutions share at the local level. For example, conversion to Jesus Christ represents an effective means of removing initiates from compulsory service to the saints/spirits of Dominican *vodú*, just as the existence of these spirit entities is an acknowledged fact of the known universe for believers of all types locally. This is possible only within a context where diverse institutions agree on the rules of the game and in fact share in much more than they differ. Even while disparate religious actors may disagree on the relative merits of each other's beliefs, and despite at times fostering open hostilities, they abide by the same conceptual rules and acknowledge the same basic contours of a shared spiritual universe wherein a range of perspectives are accommodated. This implicit agreement or sharing structures the religious conflict and cooperation that proceed from living in plural religious contexts dominated by Christian hegemony and provides the bedrock upon which Pentecostals and others stake claims to religious authority.

In order to flesh out the nuances of this accord, I utilize a case study of a woman named Mariela, whose religious career has traversed all three major local religious horizons. As a representative example, her story illustrates the exceptional role of Pentecostalism in the everyday social drama and highlights the reciprocal relations of meaning that obtain between ostensibly disparate religious traditions, revealing the remarkable ways in which individuals and their communities navigate diverse religious environments and derive meaning, efficacy, and identity in plural, heterodox contexts.

Chapter 4 is about the process of being and becoming an evangelical Christian and the specific ways in which converts negotiate the politics of Christian identity on the ground. I explore the folk construction of *"cristiano"* as a public category of personhood and consider the practical strategies Pentecostals use to claim an orthodox or "true" Christian status. By looking specifically at the meanings that people attach to being Christian converts and by locating exactly how those meanings are mobilized for the validation (or rejection) of others, I outline a politics of Christian identity crucial to the practice of Dominican Pentecostalism in the urban barrio.

Accordingly, chapter 4 looks not just at *what* Pentecostalism does, but *how* it does it (e.g., Lindhardt 2011:7). I advance the argument that the core of Dominican Pentecostalism in urban barrios is the *performance* of piety and not personal conviction or belief per se. Converts ultimately constitute themselves as exceptional Christians, or Christians apart, through public rituals of personal affirmation—namely, the interrelated conventions of conversion (and adult baptism) and testimony, and the observance of behavioral prohibitions. Because being Christian in the context of the barrio is a continual process that is mediated publicly, and because it renders the rewards of fidelity based on a tenuous achieved status that must be renewed regularly, the role of personal belief or conviction becomes subordinate to the proper performance of piety and the successful courting of public approval. This chapter theorizes Pentecostal ritual practice as projects of identity formation that precede conviction and make belief possible, but not necessary.

Chapter 5 looks at the manner in which Pentecostalism has come to epitomize the ideal form of Christianity for countless barrio residents as it considers how the evangelical church is viewed publicly and the conditions under which it is deemed to be a Christian authority from the perspective of popular youth gangs. I explore the criteria by which individuals evaluate one another's conduct as "Christian" and show how, by authorizing evangelical themes and validating Pentecostal claims to sanctity, youth gangs contribute to the shaping of an evangelical exceptionalism wherein so-called true converts are recognized as special sanctified persons who are entitled to exceptions, exemptions, and immunities based on their verifiable commitment to serving God and their demonstrable fulfillment of a born-again lifestyle. This chapter considers the relationship between youth gangs and the church as an instantiation of Pentecostal cultural change.

Conversion to Pentecostal Christianity represents, in most cases, the only feasible way out of sworn lifelong allegiance to a gang. Once a male convert has left a gang for the church, he is no longer a participant in the reciprocal economy of violence that characterizes street life in the gang. Gang members "look after" Pentecostals, whom they see as exemplars of Christian faith and representatives of God on earth. As favored and respected neighbors, remarkable exceptions are made for converts, including absolution of preconversion transgressions, immunity from violence, and freedom from harassment and involvement in street life. Evangelical modes of Christian practice represent for youth gangs the embodiment of Christian morality, and, as such, Pentecostals are revered for their favor with God.

I attempt to understand this puzzling relationship between the church and youth gangs in terms of local moral hierarchies rooted in Christian cultural hegemony. The often-heard admonition that "one doesn't play around (or joke) with things of God" highlights the seriousness with which Christianity is regarded locally and the social status it enjoys as the preeminent moral authority in the barrio. By using the example of youth gangs, ostensibly the most unlikely ally of Pentecostal churches, I uncover in detail the considerable authority granted to evangelical Christianity in the public sphere and illustrate the unique and meaningful ways in which Pentecostal culture has both transformed and become a part of everyday life in the Dominican Republic.

Chapter 6 considers gender and religious authority in the church through an investigation of men, masculinity, and testimony. I argue that male converts in the Dominican Republic reconcile the apparent antinomy between Pentecostal Christianity and barrio masculinity by exploiting their former identities in the streets as admirable and exemplary machos. Through detailed narratives of sin and redemption grounded in the particulars of their preconversion lives as so-called *tígueres* (or "macho men"), converts articulate and assert their maleness at the same time they satisfy the esteemed conversion ideal of transformation from sinner to saint. Those converts who demonstrate the greatest reversals of fate, those who best exemplify a personal transformation from severe depravity to unquestioned righteousness, are often attributed the most prestige and recognized as charismatic exemplars and spiritual leaders in the faith community. This chapter explores the intersection of conversion, gender, and religious authority in order to learn what it means to be male and Pentecostal in Villa Altagracia. I am interested here in how local gender ideals are managed by converts who find in the church alternative but conflicting ways of being masculine.

In chapter 7 I am concerned with the ways in which Pentecostal converts experience their evangelical identities as symbolic capital in the form of prestige. Local Pentecostal churches make male and female converts "respectable" (by promoting cultural values of respectability) and, in so doing, furnish poor and otherwise marginalized men and women with access to forms of prestige from which they are typically excluded. I situate evangelical Christianity within the context of a moral order similar to that of Wilson's (1995) model of reputation and respectability in order to elaborate on the stakes of conversion and to show how the Pentecostal faithful earn respect from their peers by deftly navigating the dominant local value system. The evidence I provide in this chapter shows that Wilson's theory has comparative utility in the Dominican Republic and can help elucidate a deeper understanding of Dominican social relationships and the moral principles organizing barrio life, and, in turn, make sense of the enthusiastic reception of evangelical Christianity locally.

For the Pentecostal community in Villa Altagracia, "respect" is the most cited benefit of conversion and is the predominant idiom through which converts experience the positive social rewards of their adopted evangelical identity. This idea of respect is dynamic, referring both to the prestige one earns as a *cristiano* as well as to the experience of sanctity that converts cultivate as part of their personal transformation in Christ. I refer to this type of prestige as a form of Pentecostal social currency that is awarded on the basis of a convert's ability to embody time-honored cultural ideals associated with the "good Christian," such as "the benevolent and sacrificing neighbor," "the reformed and redeemed sinner," and "the dutiful and loving wife." Through an economy of respect, Pentecostal converts transform their ascetic religious commitments into prestige or, in other words, real social value leading to tangible experiences of the enigmatic promise of salvation following repentance.

I conclude with an examination of Christian identity politics: the complex of relations relating to and concerned with the definition, status, and reckoning of Christian identity. I understand this production as following from the establishment of Pentecostal culture in local communities and enlivened where Christian pluralism and hegemony obtain. I consider here how this unique complex shapes the meaning and experience of Christianity locally, as well as the possibilities and closures it sponsors as a result of its unfolding in everyday interaction.

In the context of Catholic hegemony, Pentecostal rhetoric about truthfulness, validity, seriousness, and sincerity opens up conceptual possibilities in everyday life to be "more" or "less" Christian, to be a "true" or "false" believer, in ways that are narrowly possible in places where Catholicism enjoys absolute supremacy. The establishment of Pentecostal and other evangelical churches in barrios across the Dominican Republic creates the opportunity in local communities for people to choose what kind of Christian they want to be, along with providing a language to distinguish between them, moral criteria with which to evaluate them, and license to recognize or refute them. In addition to igniting contest over the meaning of Christianity and inciting competition between faiths, Pentecostal culture opens the door to public debate about how Christians should act and what they should believe, essentially altering the terms of public debate about what it means to be Christian and shaping the public's view of conversion, Christian morality, and Christian identity par excellence.

1 Orthodoxy and Christian Culture in the Dominican Republic

The Birth of Christian Culture on Hispaniola

An important feature part and parcel of Dominican culture and society today, Christianity constitutes the primary referent for interrelated Dominican moral and religious worlds. The culture of Christianity in the Dominican Republic is as old as the country itself, the Roman Catholic Church a primordial agent in the birth of the nation and precipitating stimulus of the modern age. Implicated in virtually every significant historical period in the country, from Spanish discovery and colonization (Todorov 1982:3–13), to the republic's struggle for independence (Martínez-Fernández 1995:71–74), to political reform and rhetoric today, Christian culture and its dominant symbols have for over 500 years been the principal moral frame within which the Dominican Republic has realized its national identity and progressive historical development.

Even before the first colonial government was established on the island of Hispaniola (known as Quisqueya or Ayiti by its original Taíno inhabitants, but christened "Little Spain" by none other than Christopher Columbus himself), the Roman Catholic Church sought to be a major player in power politics in the New World. Conquest of the Americas was itself construed as an evangelizing mission, providing the moral and religious pretext for Europe's manifest destiny in the Western Hemisphere. It is clear from

Columbus's own journal writings that the apparent motive of his journey across the Atlantic, that which impelled him to set forth on a voyage of discovery, was not something as banal as greed or want for gold but rather that of crusade and the desire to execute the universal victory of Christianity (Todorov 1982:8–10, 3–13). Citing a letter Columbus authored to Pope Alexander VI in February 1502, Todorov (1982:10) reports the admiral's true heart's desire: "His future voyage will be 'to the glory of the Holy Trinity and to that of the holy Christian religion,' and for this he 'hopes for the victory of God the Eternal, as He has ever granted it to me in the past'; what he does is 'great and magnifying for the glory and growth of the Holy Christian religion.' This, then, is his goal: 'I hope in Our Lord to be able to propagate His holy name and His Gospel throughout the universe.'"

The Catholic monarchs of Spain, Queen Isabella I of Castile and King Ferdinand II of Aragon, who together had commissioned the admiral's western voyage, understood his travels in terms of conquest *and* crusade and made certain that the expansion of the Spanish empire throughout the newfound lands would go hand in hand with a mutual commitment to the Christianization of its inhabitants. King Ferdinand affirmed this mission when he wrote: "According to the obligation and charge which has made us Lord of the Indies and the states in the ocean, nothing do we wish more than the publication and the expansion of the Gospel Law and the conversion of the Indians to our Holy Catholic Faith" (quoted in Bayle 1946, cited in González 1969:15n.4).[1]

The diffusion of Roman Catholicism in the New World was rapid (if partial and inconsistent) and furthered appreciably by the integrated role the church assumed in the subsequent colonial administration and governance of the region. This intimate liaison with secular technologies of power, coupled with lawful authority, ensured that the church would be an integral political and cultural figure in the structures of dominancy ordering colonial then later postcolonial Dominican society, making certain that Christianity would represent the religion of privilege and influence on the island for centuries to come.

The conjunction of church and state, the joining of spiritual/religious and administrative/political authority—God and government, as it were—while taken for granted in Spain, was guaranteed in the New World colonies by the *Patronato Real*, a system of royal patronage enacted by a series of papal edicts issued by Alexander VI that gave the Spanish Crown absolute authority over lands discovered or yet to be discovered west of the Azores archipelago (González 1969:16). While the bulls (such as the *Inter Caetera*, which was issued in May 1493) assured that the function of the Spanish Crown in the New World included a missionary charge, the extensive rights granted therein became a charter for expansion that lent the Spanish colonial enterprise divine rationale and religious sanction. Any responsibility for the suffering and dispossession that attended Spain's operations in the New World was absolved by the belief that it was God's will to spread the Christian message, by sword if necessary.

Through a ceremony called the *Requirement*, Spanish conquerors established the Christian terms of their authority by declaring in public hearings their divine right to rule as unequivocal Christian sovereigns. During these ceremonies, a formal speech was read before gatherings of indigenous people proclaiming that the conqueror's authority was derived from God and that any resistance to conversion would result in violence (Chidester 2000:355–356). This further served to transfer the blame for military aggression from the conquerors to their victims, effectively offering them a "Sophie's choice" of conversion or death. In 1511 King Ferdinand issued a decree authorizing the enslavement of the natives in the event that they rejected Christianity—a persecution backed by the Catholic Church (Lampe 1992:203). In this way, mass conversions were made alongside Spain's violent colonial regime, indeed brutal twin disciplinary procedures that served to conquer all aspects of corporeal and ideological life, disseminating through force Christian and Hispanic culture to native populations.[2]

Colonial administration on the island of Hispaniola was executed hand in hand with the institutionalization of the church. According to Armando Lampe (1992:203), the first joint ecclesiastical and political government was established in the Caribbean: "there were bishops who were also governors, and governors who intervened directly in church affairs." The church also maintained close links with sugar plantations and the slave economy, offering divine consent for the ruthless institution in exchange for financial support and continued social and political relevance. Although the interests of the church did not always coincide with those of the state, both relied on the support of the other as a matter of course—the church ensuring the ideological domination of the region as well as providing the religious justification for the submission of its inhabitants and defense of the colonial enterprise, while the political machine made sure the church remained a privileged cultural institution and could further its mission in the colonies unobstructed.

While it was more or less routine for enslaved Africans arriving in Hispaniola (the first arriving in 1502 along with Nicolás de Ovando, the colony's first governor [Pérez Memén 1984:117]) to be incorporated into the Catholic Church through baptism and other sacraments, according to Lampe (1992:204), "the Church had no real interest in evangelizing the blacks, mainly because it was too deeply involved in the slave system." Indeed, at that time there was no shortage of bishops and priests who owned sugar mills and large numbers of slaves (Lampe 1992:204). Laënnec Hurbon (1992:365) goes as far as to argue that the church was the "breeding ground" for the institution of slavery. Subordinated to the will of the Crown, the church was charged with founding parishes that consolidated the slave system. He posits further that it was within these churches that masters and slaves learned the rules of their correct social relationship. Evangelization became less about saving souls and more about making good colonial subjects by teaching slaves to accept their subordination as an unalterable fact of life (Pérez Memén 2008:88). This particular arrangement was likely antagonistic to the enslaved; the clergy's status as slave owners must have been a major handicap in their task of evangelization (Hurbon 1992:365).

At the same time slaves arriving from Africa were baptized, they were forbidden from practicing any of their ancestral beliefs. Rather than abandon those beliefs wholesale, many attempted to preserve them by publicly affirming Catholicism while continuing their traditional practices behind closed doors, drawing upon fragmented memories of their ancestral traditions in order to make ritual and cosmological sense of life in the New World. The result became a synthesis of Christian and African-inspired spiritual traditions that produced an Afro-Christian or Afro-Creole religious experience common throughout the Caribbean, a continuum of religious variation (Burton 1997:38) ranging from the orthodox Christianity of the European tradition to the more or less "creolized" or syncretic neo-African religious practices of *vodou* in Haiti and the Dominican Republic, Shango in Trinidad, Revival and Kumina in Jamaica, and *santería* in Cuba (to name just a few) (see Herskovits 1964; Bascom 1950; Bastide 1971; Simpson 1978; Fernandez Olmos and Paravisini-Gebert 2003).[3]

Independence and the Cross

The seeds of the now uneasy relationship between the Dominican Republic and Haiti (Wucker 1999; see note 11 below) were first sowed by the complex rivalry between Spain and France that kindled during the colonial period (González 1969:33). Thanks to the Treaty of Ryswick, in 1697 the island of Hispaniola was divided into the Spanish and French colonies of Santo Domingo and Saint-Domingue, respectively, and remained that way until 1795, when war with France led Spain to forsake the colony in favor of recovering its peninsular holdings with the Treaty of Basel, by which it effectively surrendered possession of the eastern region to French rule, thereby leaving its Dominican inhabitants to fend for themselves. On the other side of the island, a Haitian slave revolt beginning in 1791 culminated in successful rebellion for independence from France in 1804, and with it Saint-Domingue became the Republic of Haiti, the first independent nation in Latin America and the Caribbean and the only one to have won its independence as a direct result of a slave uprising. Subsequent to the Haitian Revolution, Dominicans won their independence three times: first in 1821 from Spain, most significantly again in 1844 from Haiti, and once again in 1865 after a brief four years of annexation to Spain. Santo Domingo, after being conquered by Toussaint Louverture in 1801 as part of his campaign against France, was recaptured again by the French a year later, in 1802. France controlled the former colony until 1809, when Dominican Juan Sánchez Ramírez repelled French forces and once again proclaimed Spanish sovereignty over the region (González 1969:73–74). This new arrangement with Spain lasted until a Dominican rebellion led by José Núñez de Cáceres declared the country's independence by expelling Spanish authorities from the island. Established as Spanish Haiti by constitutive act in December 1821, despite diplomatic efforts to place the new nation under the protection of Simon Bolivar's federation of Gran Colombia, independence could not be secured for long (González 1969:74; Moya Pons 1985:186). Too far removed from Bolivar's central government in Bogotá, Núñez de Cáceres failed to procure annexation to the young Colombian federation, leaving the nascent Dominican state fledgling and vulnerable (Matibag 2003:95).

Concerned with preserving Haitian independence and fearing yet another French invasion, an opportunistic Haiti, then led by President Jean Pierre Boyer, took advantage of the relatively weak Dominican military and its government's tenuous political stability by invading the region once more, successfully occupying it from 1822 until 1844. This, Moya Pons (1985:186) points out, "had been the third Haitian invasion of the eastern part [of the island] in [the span of] twenty years. The other two were in 1801 and in 1805, and on both occasions the Dominican population reacted by leaving the island en masse for fear of a massacre of the white people, as was believed to have happened in Haiti during and after the revolution" (see also Moya Pons 1978).

According to Lampe (1992:207), Haitian policy toward the Catholic Church in Santo Domingo during the occupation was one of persecution, "viewing the Church as part of the Spanish culture it was determined to stamp out." Martínez-Fernández (1995:70) submits that no other sector of Dominican society endured deeper losses during this time than the Catholic Church. In addition to nationalizing land belonging to the church and its religious orders, Boyer and the new Haitian regime openly scorned church leaders and stopped paying priests' salaries, which were previously financed under the *patronato real* (Martínez-Fernández 1995:70). Church buildings deteriorated due to neglect, and others were demolished by Haitian leaders to make room for secular construction projects (Martínez-Fernández 1995:71). Today *la dominación haitiana* (Moya Pons 1978) is remembered with bitter indignation—a period of the nation's history Dominicans caution themselves never to repeat. According to Martínez-Fernández (1995:75), the key difference fueling this resentment is that patriots fought for independence "not against Spain and by extension its official church but against French-speaking Haiti and its open hostility toward Dominican Catholicism."

During the middle decades of the nineteenth century "the Catholic Church remained a bastion of Dominican nationality, which it sought to define on the basis of religious purity, anti-Haitianism, and Europhilia" (Martínez-Fernández 1995:70). The underground Dominican independence movement itself found inspiration within Catholicism (Martínez-Fernández (1995:70–71), a contrastive detail that dovetails nicely with efforts to forge Manichaean differences with Haiti, whose revolutionary beginnings are rumored to have been initiated by a *vodou* ceremony at Bois Caïman. In consultation with extensive historical records, Martínez-Fernández (1995) proposes that the movement for Dominican independence was understood as "a great moral and religious revolution" and that it was the Dominican

Republic's "Christianness" that was to separate it from its neighbor and oppressor to the west. Pedro Santana, the country's first president, understood independence from Haiti in exactly these terms when he "publicly proclaimed that God Almighty had vanquished the Haitians whose rule [he] equated with demonic oppression" (Martínez-Fernández 1995:73). Martínez-Fernández (1995:73) cites evidence that "Dominicans thus defined their nationality in religious terms, juxtaposing it against that of Haiti. The 'Dominican Christian family' continued to contrast itself with its 'fetishist' and 'sacrilegious' neighbors even beyond independence because the threat of Haitian invasion persisted well into the late 1850s. Haitians were compared with the biblical Chaldeans and their occupation of Dominican territory was interpreted as a divine punishment from which God in his infinite mercy finally redeemed the Dominican people."

The Dominican Republic won its independence, definitively, not from Spain but from Haiti, a historical fact that today fuels the antagonistic hostilities of the Dominican people toward their western neighbors. For a good many Dominicans, the Haitian occupation is remembered as a shameful, utterly humiliating chapter in their nation's quest for self-determination. The resentment toward Haiti readily evident today, seemingly unabated 150 years after the fact, has not been extended to Spain, which by most appraisals is a celebrated cultural forebear. Potent Hispanophilia at the expense of an Afrocentric or Afrophilic worldview, coupled with a plainly racist disposition toward the self-consciously black nation of Haiti, has led the Dominican Republic to a mostly ambivalent view of its own racial history and complex relationship to blackness (see Torres-Saillant 1998). To this day the Dominican Republic has yet to develop a popular black consciousness movement that would challenge many of the harmful attitudes that underlie enduring structural and interpersonal racism endemic in the country and that might help recuperate the nation's African heritage.[4]

Hoetink (1970:117) writes that "few Dominicans have not judged the period of Haitian domination as a black page in the history of a people that would have liked to be white." In discussing the rhetorical role of the Haitian occupation, Hoetink wonders to what extent the discursive framing of Haitian domination as "a traumatic collective experience" serves the greater purpose of alleviating racial tensions internal to the Dominican Republic. Since this period, he argues, "it has been possible to attribute [black] traits in members of respectable families to the barbarian cruelty of the Haitian conquerors." Haitians, he argues further, "[were] and [are] the racial scapegoat and escape valve upon whom feelings of racial uneasiness can be projected." Ironically, by uniting a range of racial groups in the struggle for Dominican independence, the Haitian occupation had a cohesive effect on race relations in the Dominican Republic by bringing together even the darkest Dominicans alongside others to fight for liberation. In this instance, it would seem cultural identity served to be more salient than racial identity, at least in opposition to Haiti. Occasions like these have helped sustain the view that black Dominicans are somehow less "black" than those from Haiti or other Caribbean nations.

Much of this punitive dialectic remains in Dominican popular discourse today, stating that a fundamental moral difference exists between Haiti and the Dominican Republic—a difference purportedly revealed in religious observance. The Dominican nation is itself envisioned as staunchly Catholic (or Christian more generally) and categorically orthodox at official and formal levels. Allegedly, it is this orthodoxy that makes Dominican nationality (*dominicanidad*, or "Dominicanness") different from that of Haiti, which is construed in the Dominican popular imagination as pagan, sometimes demonic, but in any case emphatically *not* Christian.

Moreover, according to Martínez-Fernández (1995:74), "Dominican patriots made it clear that their movement was Catholic. The declaration of independence of 1844, alluding to Haitian abuses and excoriation of the Dominican clergy, promised that the church would be restored to its earlier splendor and would be declared the official church of the state." The exalted founding fathers, or *Padres de la Patria*—Juan Pablo Duarte, Francisco del Rosario Sánchez, and Ramón Matías Mella, referred to collectively as *la trinitaria*, or "the Trinity"—were the foremost agents in this initiative. As the story goes, *la trinitaria* was the name given to a secret society formed by Duarte in 1838 with the goal of destabilizing Haitian rule over Dominicans during the Haitian occupation. Their subversive efforts led to Dominican independence in 1844. *Dios, Patria, Libertad* (God, Fatherland, Freedom) was established as the national slogan and can be found prominently displayed on a banner adorning the national crest at the center of the national flag. The crest itself is an escutcheon similar to the flag design and features a Bible, a cross of gold, and six Dominican flags hanging from spears. The crest sits at the midpoint of a white cross dividing the flag into red and blue quadrants. The red and blue colors of the Dominican flag symbolize the struggle for independence and liberty, respectively, and the white cross a declaration of Christian fidelity from which the country is proclaimed to have emerged.

The nation's foremost national symbols invoke, to one degree or another, a Christian historical consciousness, no less an inalienable identification with the church. Posted in front of the Museo del Hombre Dominicano, the national museum of Dominican culture located in Santo Domingo, are anthropomorphic renderings of European, African, and indigenous Taíno beginnings, three large statues representing the ancestral wellsprings from whence Dominicans are alleged to have sprung forth. Foregrounded, and in the center, is Bartolomé de las Casas, a Spanish friar who became famous as a sixteenth-century social reformer on Hispaniola and who is revered today as a national hero. His likeness is flanked on either side by Enriquillo, an indigenous Taíno leader, and Lemba, an enslaved African remembered for his resistance to slavery.[5] Clutching by his side a Bible in his left hand and holding out a cross stretched out before him in his right, Las Casas is posed in ceremonial vestments standing resolutely ahead of the other statues in a scene that unambiguously proclaims Christianity as the chief guiding principle for the Dominican people. And, finally, perhaps the Dominican Republic's most gaudy monument, the Faro a Colón, a massive "lighthouse" located in Santo Domingo Este—purported to contain the remains of Christopher Columbus and built as part of the celebrations attending the 500th anniversary of the "Discovery of America"—is constructed in the shape of a cross and when activated projects a powerful beam of light that forms an impressive cross in the sky visible throughout the city. Engraved on the lighthouse is an inscription in the words of Columbus: "You shall set up Crosses on all roads and pathways, for as God be praised, this land belongs to Christians, and the remembrance of it must be preserved for all times" (quoted in Lundius and Lundahl 2000:334–335).[6]

The Church and Trujillo

The church's political relationship with the state was strengthened by a dubious partnership with Rafael Trujillo during his thirty-year dictatorial rule over the country. El Jefe ("The Boss," as he was known) took control of the Dominican Republic in 1930 after overthrowing then president Horacio Vasquez. For the next thirty years Trujillo ran what is considered by most accounts to have been an oppressive and tyrannical regime until his assassination in 1961. While the years of his dictatorship saw noticeable economic growth and a burgeoning middle class, nothing could overshadow the rampant corruption, scandal, and ultimate alienation from the international community that characterized his stint as ruler. Among countless human rights abuses, the most atrocious was the dictator's massacre of 2,000–15,000 ethnic Haitians living on the Dominican border in 1937—the devastating outcome of anti-Haitian nationalism and Trujillo's designs to consolidate political authority over the border region (Turits 2002; see also Derby and Turits 1993). Not long after assuming the presidency, Trujillo outlawed the practice of *vodú* and sought to eliminate threats to his power by suppressing popular religion and assassinating regional power figures (Adams 2006:14). Throughout the years that followed his ascent to power, the unspoken coalition between the church and the dictatorship was apparent (Wipfler 1966:94). Couching his political philosophy in moral and religious terms, Trujillo favored Catholicism and looked to consolidate his power by aligning his regime with the legitimacy of the church (Wiarda 1965:238). According to Wipfler (1966:94), the Catholic Church was expected to give the government spiritual backing in return for which the regime would provide considerable perks and material benefits: "The Church surrendered its responsibility to stand in judgment in the society, and entered with such vigor into its new role that it totally ignored the excesses of Trujillo and his government." Wipfler (1966:95) also notes that the material benefits amassed by the church during this time were phenomenal, with dozens of churches, rectories, schools, convents, and other buildings presented to the church, as well as a new seminary, several retreat centers, three cathedrals, and a palace for the Papal Nuncio. It could be argued that not since the original colonization of the island had the church enjoyed such extravagant favor. In 1954 a concordat was signed with the Vatican that increased the privileges enjoyed by the church and deepened its relationship to the state (Wipfler 1966:14).[7]

Catholicism Today

Following the U.S. military intervention in 1965 and the authoritarian regime of Joaquín Balaguer (1966–1978), who "was able to develop a stable relationship with the church, which became a factor of social and political cohesion," unlike other countries of Latin America during the 1970s and

1980s, the Dominican Republic did not develop a strong popular church movement within the Catholic ranks (Betances 2007:3). According to Betances (2007:3), "political mediation was a key aspect of church-state relationships during Balaguer's twelve years in power and subsequently became an enduring feature of the political system"; with transition to democracy in the 1980s, social pastoral programs became a mainstay of the church in building stronger relationships with the lower classes and boosting its credibility in society.

Today the Catholic Church continues to be an important figure in national politics and unquestionably foremost in dominant representations of Dominican culture. The church remains a powerful political institution, Christianity itself so much a part of the cultural fabric of the nation. Of course, the story of Catholicism and Christian orthodoxy is only one part of a larger, more complicated tale of religious life that includes popular forms of heterodoxy and Christian pluralism.

Religious Pluralism and the Syncretic Paradigm

The profound impression Christianity has made on the island of Hispaniola since 1492 cannot be overstated. Catholicism, the country's enduring alma mater and one of its principal cultural progenitors, in perpetual dialogue with African-derived beliefs and practices, along with and further influenced by Protestant, namely evangelical, forms of reformation Christianity, make up the three primary vertices of religious pluralism in the country and together constitute a vibrant field of religious possibilities generative of both cultural continuity and change, forming an undeniable locus of meaning and value for Dominican society at large.

While pervasively Christian, Dominican religiosity is also broadly characterized by the influence of African-derived beliefs and institutions, including those from neighboring Haiti. The influence of West African spirituality can be seen in widespread religious orientations toward spirit possession, magical healing, divination, polyrhythmic drumming, call-and-response singing and chanting, ecstatic and embodied modes of worship, and a local pantheon of African-, Dominican-, and Haitian-derived spirit entities.

Although dominated by Christian orthodoxy at the higher rungs of officialdom, several forms of heterodoxy flourish in the Dominican Republic, particularly among the popular classes—namely, versions of folk Catholicism, a variety of Protestant faiths, and a religious complex referred to by some as *vudú dominicano,* or "Dominican *vodú*" (Deive 1992; Patín Veloz 1975; Lizardo 1982; Davis 1987; Alegría-Pons 1993; Miniño 1985; Ripley 2002; Andújar 2007).[8]

Dominican *Vodú*

The use of the term *"vodú,"* or "voodoo," or related terms (*"vudú," "vodou," "vodoun,"* and so forth), to describe a domain of Dominican religiosity has been, and continues to be, controversial. The term is not used by Dominicans to describe their own practices and generally carries negative connotations owing to the stigma associated with "black magic" and possession cults in the country.[9] Throughout much of the island's history these practices have been outlawed or disdained, at times even meeting repression (Deive 1992; Laguerre 1989; Desmangles 1992; Hurbon 2001a; Mintz and Trouillot 1995; Lundius and Lundahl 2000:577–578). The Dominican Penal Code of 1943, for instance, established a law mandating two months to a year of prison time plus a fine for anyone convicted of participating in *vodú* ceremonies (Davis 1987:40). Even today, associated practices of magic or "witchcraft" are condemned, and practitioners are the unfortunate targets of stereotypes, ridicule, and violent threats. One need only follow the weekly news in Santo Domingo to find a fairly regular stream of stories regarding witchcraft and contempt for it around the country.[10] *Vodú* and associated practices of magic, divination, and spirit possession are condemned by popular discourse as variants of witchcraft and are denounced by the Catholic Church as evil and repugnant to Christian morality. Many people are therefore reluctant to admit to being party to or participants in related rites.

Despite this repudiation, popular magical beliefs can be found throughout the country and across the island, and it is not uncommon to see people of all classes consult a spirit medium (a *caballo, brujo, adivino, espiritista, mambo,* or *bokor/bocó*) for remedies or to see them attend the rites and ceremonies of so-called *voduistas,* practitioners of *vodú* (Deive 1992:16). However, conservative Dominican intellectuals, elites, and "guardians of Dominicanness" have consistently denied the existence of *vodú* in the country (Deive 1992:163; Torres-Saillant 1998:132). Even though folklorists in the Dominican Republic have argued for years that there exists a vibrant folk religion, particularly in the rural areas (Dominguez, Castillo, and Tejada 1978; Rosenberg 1979; Lizardo 1982; Miniño 1985; Davis 1987; Andújar 2006, 2007), and despite attempts to recognize and simultaneously defend such beliefs within the universe of folk tradition, it has yet to be legitimated by elites or raised to the status of "respectable" religion thanks to a particularly punitive Catholic orthodoxy. *Vodú*, with few exceptions, is practiced outside of the public gaze, if not in secret, in the main because of its contradistinction with Catholic orthodoxy and its putative association with Haiti and by extension stereotypes of barbarism, evil, and backwardness attributed to its people.

Much of the negative perception of *vodú* is attributable to the country's historical anti-Haitian sentiments, about which much has been written.[11] The argument goes something like this: the barbaric practices of *vodú* reflect the backward culture of Haiti; *vodú* is something that Haitians do, not what Dominicans do, and it is just another example of the corrupting—in fact, polluting—influences of the neighboring country to the west, whose black hordes have been threatening to cross the border for years in an attempt to reunite the island under pagan rule and drag the Dominican Republic back into the dark ages of the past. Obviously this pernicious myth has little basis in reality, but the fears are common enough to be used as markers of difference and to form the foundation upon which racism against Haitians in the Dominican Republic is built and from which such virulent ideas draw their legitimacy.

Scholarly recognition of *vodú* practices in the Dominican Republic were more or less nonexistent until 1946, when Enrique Patín Veloz published a series of five articles on the subject in the newspaper *La Nación* (Deive 1992:170). Later, in 1975, Carlos Deive published a thorough investigation of a specific matrix of beliefs and practices in the Dominican Republic that he called *vodú dominicano*, and others followed suit (e.g., Davis 1987; Lizardo 1982; Miniño 1985). Studies of *vodou* in Haiti have a much longer history (e.g., see Price-Mars 1983; Parsons 1928; Herskovits 1964; Hurston 2009; Simpson 1940, 1945, 1954; Deren 1953; Courlander 1960; Huxley 1966), and the subject itself has received far more international attention in academic treatments as well as more sensational popular accounts (e.g., Pritchard 1900; Seabrook 1929; Wirkus and Dudley 1931).

Dominican *vodú*, an ever-evolving complex syncretic amalgam of religious beliefs and practices first developing on the island during the colonial period, is a popular religion based upon the ritual and theological innovations of Haitian *vodou*, Espiritismo, traditional West African religion, and Roman Catholicism, and includes distinct religious ceremonies (such as *prille* or *maní*), festivals (for example, *gagá*), rituals, and rites. As well as favoring magical healing and harming, spirit possession, divination, herbalism, music, song, and dance, it holds that spirit beings—variously known as *santos, seres, misterios,* or *luases*—function as intermediaries between God and humans and can be communed with through possession and other rites. As a quintessential example of Afro-Dominican culture (Andújar 2007), *vodú* has been described as an important repository of popular Dominican history despite its unofficial status and exclusion from authorized versions of national culture (Adams 2006:57).

Evangelical Protestant Christianity

Protestants first arrived in small numbers to the region of what is today the Dominican Republic beginning in 1824 during the Haitian occupation under then president Jean Pierre Boyer, who encouraged the immigration of Protestant blacks from the United States to assist in "darkening" the racially whiter Dominican population and also, it would seem, to antagonize Dominican clergy already reeling from their significant demotion during Haitian rule (González 1969:77; Martínez-Fernández 1995:71; Lockward 1982; Aracena 2000:17). Enticed by the prospect of land, religious freedom, and full citizenship, the first group of Protestant immigrants to arrive settled in Samaná and Puerto Plata, later growing in number and spreading out to Santo Domingo and the rest of the country (Martínez-Fernández 1995:71; Lockward 1982). Significant missionary work, however, did not pick up speed until the Trujillo era, and the total number of Protestants would remain relatively meager until the 1980s.

Evangelical Protestantism established its contemporary roots in the country during the Trujillo dictatorship, during which time the four largest Pentecostal denominations—Assemblies of God, the Church of God (Cleveland, Tennessee), the Church of God of the Prophesy, and the Pentecostal Church of God—began their missionary work (Betances 2007:218). They would not challenge Catholicism's numerical dominance until the 1970s and 1980s, when their numbers began to grow exponentially (Betances 2007:220). According to Betances (2007:216–217), historical Protestant churches in the Dominican Republic struggled to make any significant growth prior to that because most of them conducted their missionary work in English and "apparently did not have the will or the funding to expand their operations." It was not until after the Trujillo regime that significant changes to the religious field began when evangelical churches took hold in the popular sectors, with domestic leaders taking the reins and propounding a religious message specially attuned to the concerns of the relatively impoverished Dominican masses. Betances (2007) credits the rapid growth of the evangelical movement in the Dominican Republic to profound socio-economic and cultural transformations following the Trujillo regime, particularly those imposed from abroad. Villamán (1993a) likens the growth in Pentecostalism to social insecurities following the country's rapid modernization after Balaguer that left much of the swelling urban population impoverished and without recourse to the new economy.

Ideas about what it means to be Christian in the Dominican Republic have changed since the expansion and entrenchment of evangelical forms of Protestant Christianity in the country. No longer the sole preserve of the Catholic Church, Christian authority is being seized at the local level by Pentecostal leadership and their congregations, who claim to possess true biblical inspiration and who profess to alone follow the divinely inspired teachings of Jesus Christ. In an effective combination of austere religiosity, critical rhetoric, egalitarian worship practices, open membership policies, and cathartic emotional rituals, these churches have been embraced in seemly every corner of the country, from La Romana to Dajabón.

Central to Pentecostal doctrine is the idea of "Christian perfection" or "sanctification," a belief that it is possible to live free of sin thanks to an act of grace that purifies the soul and makes a convert holy. So sanctified, Pentecostals believe themselves to live spiritual, otherworldly lives apart from or outside of the profane, worldly (and thus sinful) everyday lives of others. This exceptional, in-but-not-of-the-world orientation is cultivated through "rituals of rupture" or "discontinuity" (Robbins 2003b:224–227) such as conversion, baptism, baptism of the Holy Spirit, and other ritualized practices of differentiation like behavioral prohibitions and the waging of spiritual warfare. These practices of differentiation are central to Pentecostalism's characteristic dualism and are important vectors of cultural change wherever Pentecostalism takes root (Robbins 2004a).

Converts learn to experience their transformation in Christ in terms of this dualism, as a marked division between their life before and after conversion represented by distinct moral worlds characterized in the local idiom as "*el mundo*" and "*el evangélio*"—"the profane world" and "the gospel," respectively. Division between *dos mundos*, or "two worlds," is promoted and renewed through a strict ascetic moralism converts are enjoined to follow upon entering the church.

While studies of evangelical Protestantism, Pentecostalism, and conversion in Latin America are bountiful (see Burdick 1993, 1998; Martin 1990; Smilde 2007; Brusco 1995; Willems 1967; Lehmann 1996; d'Epinay 1969; Chesnut 1997; Stoll 1990; Steigenga and Cleary 2007; Corten and Marshall-Fratani 2001; Glazier 1980; Boudewijnse, Droogers, and Kamsteeg 1998; Cleary and Stewart-Gambino 1997), similar studies have been slower to materialize in the Caribbean despite parallel patterns of growth and popularity across the region (a few notable exceptions are cited later).[12]

Today evangelical Christianity is everywhere in popular Dominican culture; even Juan Luis Guerra, perhaps the most internationally renowned merengue artist to date, has converted! From popular movies, to television shows, to popular public events, to radio programs and Christian music stations, to "Jesus Saves" stickers, flyers, and literature—Jesus, it seems, is everywhere you turn these days.

Pentecostalism is by far the fastest-growing religious denomination in the Dominican Republic. It is becoming politically significant at the national and local levels.[13] The following chapters are concerned with the social and cultural effects of this growth at the local level, the meaning of evangelical religion to believers on the ground, and the ways in which Dominicans put their faith to work in their everyday lives. Evangelical Christianity today is not an altogether separate sphere of religious life, a denomination perceived as a foreign import or regarded as an obscure marginal cult; rather, it has become an integral part of Dominican society and culture, dynamically engaged in the social drama, as much a part of everyday life in the republic (especially for barrio residents) as any other cultural, political, or religious reality.

Conclusion

Due largely to the historical legacy of Christian and African-derived religions on the island, Dominicans, for the most part, are Christians of a particular type who share the main tenets of faith in an all-powerful God and the existence of an effectual spiritual world. According to the World Christian Database (WCD), 95 percent of the Dominican population identifies as one type of Christian or another. Catholicism's historical collusion with the Dominican state has meant that public forms of Christianity are celebrated above and contrasted with heterodox forms of popular religion, particularly those inspired by African or Haitian religious forms.

The established framework of Christian hegemony, common throughout the Americas, is exactly the characteristic that makes the entrenchment of Pentecostal and evangelical Christianity in the New World unique when compared with other regions of the world such as Africa or Southeast Asia. For the Dominican Republic, as with many other Latin American countries, Protestantism—and indeed today more than any other group, Pentecostalism—has become an alternative or second Christianity in opposition to the dominant state church of Roman Catholicism. The country's current religious transformation is hardly unique, as similar currents of religious revival have long been taking shape throughout the global South (Jenkins 2002). This development is by no means simple and is no doubt curious in its elaboration. Many analyses have taken the church to be an entirely separate institution, one among many in a field of religious "options," choices to maximize pleasure and diminish pain within a diverse spiritual marketplace, and have attempted to explain the church's popularity based on its difference from Catholicism and other presumably distinct religious traditions. One example of this is attributing the church's success in the developing world to its transnational connections to the United States or elsewhere abroad (e.g., Austin-Broos 2001; Bastian 2001). In the Dominican Republic, I suspect that it is not Pentecostal Christianity's difference from the local or its connections with the transnational so much as its *affinity* to the religion of the state that makes its appeal enduring and, as a matter of course, legitimate in local terms. It will become clearer over the next several chapters that the acceptance of Pentecostalism at the local level is based on its acknowledgment as an exemplar of Christian orthodoxy, its distinction among believers as a more authoritative Christian alternative to Catholicism.

What does it mean to be a Christian and who gets to be one are important and contentious issues. They are eminently important in the New World, where Christianity as a cultural system shapes moral worlds, figures local value systems, and structures relationships of status and privilege for society's members in myriad ways.

Villa Altagracia

El Pueblo Caliente.
El Pueblo Profético

The Town

Villa Altagracia, named after the patron saint of the Dominican Republic, *Nuestra Señora de la Altagracia* ("Our Lady of the Highest Grace"), is one of eight municipalities of the San Cristóbal province and is located roughly 30 kilometers northwest of the capital city of Santo Domingo. "Villa," as it is affectionately referred to by residents, is located along Autopista Duarte, a 270-kilometer stretch of highway connecting Santo Domingo, Santiago (the republic's second largest city), and the northern coastal town of Monte Cristi. The municipality covers 426 square kilometers and is home to around 84,000 residents according to the most recent census data, with a little over half of the inhabitants living in rural districts and the rest in the town itself. Thanks to rainfall about 200 days a year, Villa remains green and lush year-round. Villa has its own website, which, according to the webmaster, was created in 2007 for residents, former residents, and "children of Villa abroad" who want to stay connected with the local community and keep up with local events and happenings.[1]

I visited Villa for the first time in February 2008. Moisés, a man whom I had met through mutual friends in the capital, had learned that I was interested in Pentecostal Christianity and invited me to his church.[2] I did not have a car, so getting to Villa was a matter of public transportation. Anyone who has taken public transportation in the Dominican Republic, or anywhere in the Caribbean for that matter, can appreciate the risks involved when trying to get from here to there. During my first two years in the country I experienced a number of hair-raising moments; however, none of them compared to the multiple trips I would take weekly to Villa in *carro publico*. The trip itself is notoriously treacherous. This particular stretch of highway claims the lives of motorists and their passengers on a seemingly regular basis.[3] It was common to see fellow passengers say a prayer before taking off from *kilometro nueve*, the last transit stop out of the capital, on our express route to Villa. Joined by the driver and no less than five daily commuters, we would pack into a rundown Honda Civic in the late afternoon heat and brave the chaotic congested traffic out of town.

It takes about thirty minutes to reach Villa in *carro publico* from the capital. Just off the exit at the entrance of town is a very large shrine devoted to the Virgin. The statue within is a three-dimensional representation of Altagracia as she is depicted in the allegedly miraculous image housed at the basilica in the town of Higüey. The shrine sits at the entrance to the main road that runs through town and cuts through most of the barrios. Along this road one encounters the central plaza, or *el parque*, the main *colmadones* (large bars) in town, and most major cross-streets. Along Duarte, the main road, are most of the central commercial businesses as well as the main baseball field, and the old *ingenio* (a large state-owned sugar mill). Merenguero Sergio Vargas, perhaps Villa's most famous resident, was responsible for the public works project that saw many of the main roads in Villa paved. Despite this effort, however, much of Villa remains unpaved, while the streets that are paved remain in poor condition.

Villa Altagracia is a place of extremes. From the outer lying *bateyes* (some of the poorest communities in the country) to the *fincas* (countryside estates) of Sergio Vargas and other wealthy residents, a simple drive through town reveals extremes of poverty in addition to several examples of comfortable opulence. But Villa is, on the whole, poor, not only for rural residents who suffer the greatest conditions of poverty but also for most of the municipality's barrio residents; life is indeed a struggle for many. According to a 2002–2004 report by the World Bank, 41.5 percent of the residents of San Cristóbal province live below the national poverty line, compared with 36.5 percent for the country as a whole. According to a local study conducted in 1993 of poverty throughout the country (Pérez 2003), Villa Altagracia ranked fourth among all municipalities with 10,344 homes in poverty, or 78 percent of all homes in the municipality. Of those homes, 4,293, or 32 percent, were considered to be in extreme poverty. According to a national study (*Atlas de la Pobreza en la República Dominicana 2005*) published in 2005 but citing information collected in 2002, 58 percent of homes in Villa were impoverished, and 9 percent were in extreme poverty, down considerably from the decade before. Much of this transformation was due to the success of free trade zones, or "*zonas francas*," and the attending increase in employment opportunities. However, according to a 2008 publication (*República Dominicana en Cifras 2008*) based on studies by the national office of statistics (*Oficina Nacional de Estadisticas*), in the span of just four years, from 2003 to 2007, Villa Altagracia went from having 2,013 jobs generated by the *zona franca* in 2003 to only 228 by 2007. The loss of free trade zone jobs has hurt the local economy as a result.

Before becoming Villa Altagracia, the community in and around today's municipality was once called Sabana de los Muertos (Geron 1980). Sabana de los Muertos was sparsely populated until 1926 when a developer, Ulises Henríquez, built the first permanent hotel in the area, which in no time became an important regional hub for social and commercial exchange. It was not until 1936, when the town was elevated to the category of "municipal district," that the name was changed to Villa Altagracia.

For forty years Villa was an important center for sugar production in the region. Before the *ingenio* was built, Villa was a rural community where most people made a living doing light agriculture, raising livestock (primarily pigs), and engaging in small farming. Most people worked their own small land holdings until the arrival of the United Fruit Company, which bought up large plots of land for banana cultivation. Countless people in the area stopped working their own land in order to work on the plantation as salaried employees of the company. Many people moved to the area during this time, which accelerated the process of urbanization. By the late 1940s the banana plantations were converted by then president Rafael Trujillo to grow sugar, and in 1948 the *ingenio* Central Catarey was built.

As well as playing an important role in the Dominican economy at the time, the existence of the *ingenio* created relative economic prosperity in the region. The sugar mill provided jobs and economic security to many workers and was responsible for the influx of residents and the raising of the town. Villa became a prosperous community. It was also during this time that many Haitians migrated or were brought as laborers (braceros) to work in the cane fields around the *ingenio*. They were housed in small, rudimentary settlements called *bateyes* that remain today. In 1961, a paper factory (*la Industria Nacional del Papel*) opened, which further made Villa an attractive place to find work (the factory has also since closed).

Villa experienced significant changes in the 1980s and 1990s due to the decline of sugar production and the change to garment export processing. The move from agricultural exports to that of manufacturing exports has had a great effect, not just on Villa but on the entire country. Since the original colonization of the islands, economic growth in the Caribbean has depended on the export of various goods. Historically, the island of Hispaniola has relied on the production and export of sugar, primarily, as well as coffee, tobacco, and fruit. Since the 1960s, the Dominican Republic has moved relatively quickly from an agricultural economy based chiefly on sugar exports and import substitution industrialization to a service economy dependent on tourism, export manufacturing, and agribusiness (Safa 2002:14, 1995). With the fall of sugar prices in the early 1980s, emphasis quickly shifted to export manufacturing. The *ingenio*, which sustained Villa's economy for more than forty years, closed in 1986 due to decreased productivity, the fall of sugar prices, and a devastating cut in U.S. sugar quotas to the country. The sugar mill was Villa's principal employer. A free trade zone took over the existing buildings, including a large Korean-owned garment plant that employed about 2,500 workers (mostly women). Helen Safa, a sociologist of women and development in the Caribbean, has noted that Villa represents a microcosm of the changes from sugar production to export manufacturing that have occurred in the Dominican Republic since the 1980s (2002:15).

Today, few stable, well-paying jobs exist in Villa. Many of the traditional sources of employment that residents relied upon in the past, either in the factories or in the fields, no longer exist. Wilfredo, a longtime resident, had moved to Villa in the early 1970s from the *campo* (surrounding rural areas). There were few houses in his neighborhood then, and Villa was still quite small. He began working at the *ingenio* at the age of thirteen and made, as he put it, a very respectable two Dominican pesos an hour. It was also during this time that gold was discovered in a nearby mountain and a mine was built that brought more work opportunities to the area. Wilfredo describes Villa as much more vibrant and in fact more "crazy" twenty years ago when people had jobs and more money to spend. According to another informant, there were six *fabricas* (manufacturing plants) at one point; now there are two. Today, "*el Citrico*," or Consorcio Cítricos Dominicanos, a fruit processing company, along with Agua Santa Clara, a water bottling plant, are the largest employers in town. Companies such as the Korean-owned BJ&B (which has since left and been replaced by an apparel outfitter for universities named "Alta Gracia" operated by Knights Apparel out of South Carolina) and T. K. Dominicana, which produce hats and other garments for companies like GAP and Banana Republic, continue operations in the free trade zone but have drastically reduced their number of employees.

The absence of local jobs has forced many residents to commute to the capital for work. Some work as taxi or bus drivers, some work for the national police or military, some work as caretakers and maids, and others are employed as part-time or contract laborers. A number of my informants made this commute every day. Others work farther away in Higüey, in Bonao, or at the resorts and hotels in places like Boca Chica, Bavaro, and Punta Cana. They leave on Monday morning and do not return to Villa until the weekend to be with their families. Others work more erratic schedules in the *campo*, sometimes seeing their families only once a month. Maria, a mother of ten, looks after her children alone because her husband works in La Vega and returns home once every fifteen days or so. Alternatively, many people have moved or migrated to the United States, Puerto Rico, Argentina, Spain, Providencia, Martinique, or some other country with the hopes of making enough money to send back to their families. At least three of my informants had parents who lived abroad and sent money home to Villa. Juanita, a sixteen-year-old whom I met on my first visit to Villa, lived with her father, stepmother, and two younger brothers because her mother had moved to Argentina to work as a domestic servant. Radames, a young man who lived on his own for the most part, had very little contact with his father, who had moved to New York when Radames was just a child. Remittances to the Dominican Republic from residents abroad are estimated to be $3 billion USD annually, and many Dominicans rely on these funds to cover basic necessities like food, shelter, clothing, health care, and education.

Both Josefina and Maria had worked at the Korean-owned garment facility located at the *zona franca* when the plant was open for operations. Josefina began working there shortly after moving to Villa but was not old enough to work there legally, so she purchased a *cedula* (identification card) with a different birth date so that she could be hired. Her husband, Denny, was twenty-five at the time and made very little money, so it was necessary for her to do what she could. Josefina described her work at the factory as very taxing. She worked from 7 a.m. to 9 p.m. without food and felt hungry and exhausted daily. She endured mainly out of necessity. Josefina and her husband were renting space in a home, and after working for nine months her first daughter, Karla, was born. Josefina's cousin took care of their daughter so that she could continue to work long hours. After their second and third children were born (Mayalin and Junior), Josefina and Denny moved into a vacant house where they live today. She said that she left the facility after Junior was born because it was too difficult to leave her children with someone else.

For the average worker at the garment factory, long hours and a demanding environment were routine. The Koreans were notorious for treating people poorly, and I heard nothing but contempt for them if ever they were mentioned. Factory rules emphasized high productivity, discipline, and obedience (Safa 2002:18). According to both Josefina and Maria, it was a great-paying job where they made a minimum wage close to $50 USD a week. Today a typical week at the *zona franca* will net an average employee about $1,529 DOP, or about $45 USD, a week (*Oficina Nacional de Estadística* 2008, "San Cristóbal en Cifras").[4]

By 2008, when I met most of my informants, few of the women I interviewed worked traditional or wage-paying jobs. Josefina, for instance, did just about anything she could to make money. Her husband, Denny, had lost his job as a taxicab driver because the car that he had owned and operated broke down, and there was not enough money to fix it. As a result, Josefina took a greater role in the family's moneymaking enterprises. She is perhaps one of the most clever, resourceful, and capable people I have ever met. It appeared to me that there was very little that this woman did not or could not do. Most of the time she worked from home engaged in a variety of undertakings. Whether in the morning, afternoon, or evening by candlelight, Josefina was usually at work. She would either be making curtains on her sewing machine, carving intricate designs into wax candles that she had shaped and molded, or literally making furniture sets by hand for people around town on the roof of her house. Ironically, Josefina explained to me that she only worked twice a week: Tuesdays and Thursdays when she gave classes on how to make curtains and bed sheets. She occasionally gave classes on how to make candles as well. About once a month Josefina would make a trip to the capital to buy clothing in order to resell it (for a slight profit) out of her home to neighbors and friends. All of this generated some kind of income either by selling furniture, candles, and drapes; by re-selling marked-up clothing; or through selling a skill or technique to others, like how to make candles. She charged $500 DOP (or about $14 USD) per person for the class.

The informal economy is where most people make ends meet. For the San Cristóbal province, 60 percent of workers are employed in formal-sec-tor jobs, and 35 percent work in the informal sector (*Oficina Nacional de Estadística* 2008, "San Cristóbal en Cifras"). This statistic does not say, how-ever, whether workers employed in formal-sector jobs also make money in the informal sector. Although people also rely on extended family networks to resist poverty and make ends meet, according to my observations, most households earn some income in the informal sector, be that through spo-radic contract labor, looking for houses to clean, buying and selling clothes, or just offering labor and services where they can. Some of my informants have skilled trades like carpentry and masonry but regularly have trouble finding work. A young man by the name of Renato had worked as a cabinet-maker and mechanic at various times but was unemployed for the greater part of the year I got to know him. He worked irregularly, assisting others with temporary jobs as they came up. And Wilfredo, who ran a successful body shop out of his front yard, supplemented much of his income by pur-chasing totaled cars, rebuilding them, and selling the restored vehicles for a profit. Wilfredo's business was successful enough to allow him to employ at least three other people at any given time to assist him.

Lack of reliable employment opportunities in and around town is only one of the everyday challenges faced by Altagracianos. Despite occasional protests by residents, Villa, like the rest of the country, lacks potable run-ning water and experiences regular power outages. Many people have run-ning water no more than a few hours a day, and often residents go without for days on end. There is no relying on the fact of water on any given day, so people collect rainwater, which they store in large containers to drink, to clean their home, and to wash clothes. *Apagones*, or "blackouts," are an ev-eryday nuisance, and few people can afford their own generators. On good days the electricity might function for six hours, usually for a couple hours in the morning, maybe for some time in the late afternoon, and again in the late evening. However, like running water, one can never rely on the electricity. Weeks go by when people only have electricity for several hours a day. Additionally, the sewage system is not maintained, and garbage, if and when it is collected, has no place to go. At one point during my fieldwork the city mayor, or *sindico*, in somewhat of a scandal, started dumping large amounts of refuse along the highway just outside of town. Otherwise waste piles up on street corners or along the river. As in other parts of the country, much of the trash is burned along the highway because there is no collection or place to put it.

Barrio Francisco (pseudonym), where I conducted my fieldwork, is a typical neighborhood. Most homes are small, built by their current or former inhabitants and in various stages of repair, construction, or completion. Wood and/or cinder block homes are the most common, many topped by corrugated metal roofs. Although homes are usually built on a foundation of large concrete slabs, many, particularly in the poorer areas, sit on dirt floors. According to the 2002 census, 43 percent of homes in San Cristóbal have a toilet within the home itself, 50 percent share a latrine with neighbors, and 7 percent have nothing at all (*Oficina Nacional de Estadística* 2008, "San Cristóbal en Cifras"). This appeared to be the norm from what I observed in Villa as well. Bernardo, for example, a twenty-four-year-old who commuted to the capital for work, lived with his pregnant wife and their two little children in a tin-roofed shack made of wooden planks and built on a small concrete foundation. The home had two rooms—the bedroom and the main room. The stove was partitioned from the main room by a half-wall. They shared a latrine a few doors down with their neighbors. They were a young family, and Bernardo did not make much money. His wife did not work at all. Alternatively, some people could afford to build a home out of concrete. These construction materials are more expensive and generally function as status markers for those who can afford them. On top of that, concrete is safer in a tropical storm– and hurricane-prone region, and thus is far more desirable. Juan Pablo and his wife lived in a two-story exposed cinderblock home. They had "finished" the house a few years earlier, but it remained, in my estimation, half-built. They lived happily in what appeared to me to be only the shell of a home. There was no tile, no walls to cover the concrete, no window frames, no doors dividing rooms within the home, and no rugs. Though not as finished as some other homes such as Denny and Josefina's, Juan Pablo's house was an enviable structure for much of the neighborhood.[5]

It is difficult to assess exactly how much money people live off of a month because it often varies with the unpredictability of work and everyday expenses. The prices of food, transportation, gasoline, and propane gas change frequently, and most of the neighborhood feels the effect of these changes immediately. Those who net the peso equivalent of between $150 USD and $200 USD a month get by in barrio Francisco. Those who earn around $475 USD a month do well. Many households make less than this, and few people have a vehicle of their own. For most families, owning a vehicle of any kind is simply out of the question, but a few are able to purchase small motorbikes. Cars are prohibitively expensive for the average resident around the country. New cars can cost anywhere between 30 and 50 percent more than they do in the United States (a new Honda Accord purchased at a dealership in Santo Domingo in 2008 would have cost around $45,000 USD). Motorcycles are the most popular mode of transportation in Villa. They are a prominent feature of the visual and aural landscape. Motorcycles abound in the streets morning, noon, and night. The *motoconcho* (motorcycle-taxi), sometimes pejoratively described as *taxi de los pobres*, or "taxi of the poor," provides the primary means of getting around town for residents. It is in fact the cheapest mode of transportation available, and, outside the capital, one can take a *motoconcho* virtually anywhere. Drivers wait alongside highways at the entrance of towns, at major cross streets, at central plazas, and at bus stops, ready to shuttle passengers wherever they need to go.

Although barrio Francisco is not the poorest neighborhood in town, especially when compared with the neighboring *bateyes*, it is poorer than many other areas. As such, many of the social issues attending poverty have had a profound effect on the community, including high rates of HIV/AIDS, high rates of drug use, street violence and gangs, prostitution, corruption at the level of local government, underage pregnancy, high rates of domestic violence, and chronic malnutrition, just to name a few. Although HIV/AIDS is a problem throughout the country, the most vulnerable areas tend to be the poorest or those places most affected by the sex tourism industry. Outside of sub-Saharan Africa, the Caribbean region has the highest rates of HIV infection in the world. Just a few doors down from Josefina and Denny's house lived a twelve-year-old girl who had contracted HIV at birth from her mother, who had gotten it from her boyfriend, the girl's father, who had died of AIDS after refusing to acknowledge the disease or to get treatment. According to World Vision, more than 66,000 people in the Dominican Republic were living with HIV or AIDS in 2009; around 3,600 of them were under the age of fourteen. Only half of those infected with HIV actually receive antiretroviral drugs (*la Dirección General de Control de Infecciones de Transmisión Sexual y SIDA*). One pastor in barrio Francisco informed me that there were a number of church members in his congregation who were HIV positive, but it was not something that people really talked about. Other diseases like dengue fever also threaten the community, and because of inadequate diets people often live with weak or compromised immune systems, compounding the threat of serious illness. Deplorably, 20 percent of children in Villa between the ages of six and fifty-nine months suffer from chronic malnutrition (*Oficina Nacional de Estadística* 2008, "San Cristóbal en Cifras"). Education, or lack thereof, is also a point of concern for residents and their children. According to a report by the National Office of Statistics in 2008, 68 to 73 percent of the population of Villa does not have any secondary education. Pedro, a twenty-two-year-old completing his second year of high school, did not go to class for over a week because, as he put it to me, he could not afford a notebook. Few can make it to the university, let alone afford it. Technical schools are probably the most likely reality for residents who want to learn a trade, though a couple of my informants did go to the university in the capital (both of whom endured a weekly commute to the city center that would take upward of two hours during the day).

Street violence in Villa is attributed to drugs and gang activity. All manner of gangs exist in Villa, and the town is carved up into turf that belongs to any one of a number of them. The central plaza is divided between *los sangre* (Bloods), *los reyes* (Latin Kings), and *la trinitaria* (Trinitarios). Gang-related assaults are committed with machetes that are regularly carried and brandished by gang members. They use the tools to cut, maim, or sever limbs (or, colloquially, "*dale un machetazo*"). Also commonly employed are homemade guns called *chilenas* and, if they can afford them, shotguns, .22s, and other firearms. But gang members are not the only ones who are armed. Many residents of Villa, along with much of the country, have guns and carry them on their person daily. As I often heard expressed in Villa, "*todo el mundo 'ta armada*" ("everyone [in Villa] is armed"). It is common to see guns around town and on any given day in the Dominican Republic. It is not uncommon to see a pistol tucked into the belt of a man or a woman on the bus, at a bar, or even at a baseball game. Many commercial establishments in the capital employ armed guards, so it would be quite difficult to go an entire day without seeing a firearm of any kind. A woman from Villa told me a story one day that summarizes the general attitude of residents toward guns. A few years ago a man was drinking in a bar near the center of town with his friends when another gentleman at the bar began to bother him. He told the man to leave him alone, but he kept harrassing him. This continued for a while until the man became very irritated and told the pest that if he didn't leave him alone, he would have to shoot him. Despite the warning, the man continued to hassle him, so, true enough to his word, he shot the man dead, right there in the bar. When the police arrived witnesses said that the dead guy had been bothering the other man and that he had clearly indicated that he would shoot him if he did not stop. Because the man did not heed his warning and did not leave him alone, he shot him. The police, so it was said, accepted this explanation and did not arrest the shooter. Although anecdotal, this story nicely sums up a sentiment toward guns that I found to be true in many parts of the country—they mark a certain status, and those wealthy enough to have them tend also to be wealthy enough to use them without regard to the law.

Villa has been described as *caliente*, or "hot," by outsiders and residents alike because of the real or perceived high levels of violence and lawlessness. The characterization has merit if you consider the fact that at least twice at the end of 2008 the city was shut down by violent protests. Control of the city is, on occasion, taken over by street gangs, who virtually lock the city from within and prevent cars from coming in or out. Protests of this nature follow weeks of excessive blackouts and/or water shortages. Protesters block off intersections with burning tires and broken glass and prevent people from leaving or entering the barrios. If people are caught out on the streets, they are sometimes assaulted. Businesses are closed and locked up, and people are instructed to stay in their homes. The effort of protestors rarely has an effect on the electricity or the water, but is an effective demonstration of power (if not, certainly of frustration).

Villa is *caliente* in another sense as well: its lively revelry. Viewed from the outside as a spirited party town, on any given day—but especially on the weekends—the biggest *colmadones* are filled with people drinking and having a good time. The central plaza is surrounded by four large *colmadones*.

On popular nights, crowds at the bars spill out into the neighboring plaza and surrounding streets. People drink, and fights are not infrequent. There is a police station at the center of town too, but there are few patrols, and the police force responsible for the municipality is small.

Barrio Francisco is a small community less than a mile from the central plaza. Residents grow up together and know their neighbors well. For children, most of the day is spent outdoors playing in the streets with other kids. Teenagers visit with neighbors and go to the park or river with friends. When not working, men and women sit outside their homes chatting. Some may go to the bar to drink and play dominoes, while others go to church or visit friends and family in their spare time. There are approximately forty Protestant churches in Villa that compete with a Catholic parish church (Parroquia Nuestra Señora de la Altagracia) at the center of town and a smattering of small incorporated chapels in select neighborhoods. There were at least four Protestant churches in barrio Francisco that I was aware of, three of them Pentecostal, the other Seventh Day Adventist. The Pentecostal churches offer daily activities to residents. Most have *culto* ("worship" or regular services) five nights a week, with doctrine and Bible classes rounding out the rest of the week.[6] They organize regular social activities for members, arrange prayer sessions, take fieldtrips, and plan special events. Additionally, together the churches regularly organize concerts and *cultos* in the street for the public.

Villa is a microcosm of the Dominican Republic: it sits at the intersection of the decline in sugar production, the rise of export manufacturing, economic change, and popular Dominican life. In many ways barrio Francisco is a model of everyday life for many Dominicans on the island. Residents face the same problems, deploy the same solutions, and enjoy the same activities as Dominicans do all over the country. It was this character that drew my attention to Villa upon my first visit and has kept my interests there ever since.

Unlike in the capital where extreme class differences are brought into sharp relief by overt discrimination and a racist division of labor, people in Villa tend to see themselves as all in the same boat, as it were, proclaiming "*somos un pueblo unido*" ("we are a united people"). Few are rich; whether you are dark-skinned or light, you are probably no better off than your neighbor because of it. That is not to say that cultural preferences for lighter skin or negative stereotypes about black or dark-skinned people are not operative—they are—only that they hold less immediate salience locally for those whom I came to know, who rarely if ever spoke explicitly or reflexively about issues of race or discrimination. For most of my informants, class is perceived to be the primary identity of exclusion that they experience; they often note that people with money are treated far better than anyone else.

In contrast to the denotation "*el pueblo caliente*," Christian residents and visitors who choose to focus on the deep religious fervor that characterizes much of the town's community refer to Villa as "*el pueblo profético*," supposedly because of its reputation in evangelical circles for having produced a lot of prophets. While I come to focus here largely on religion, it is important to recognize the intereffective relationship between domains considered spiritual or sacred and those understood as mundane or profane. Religious beliefs and devotional practices are intimately woven into popular culture and everyday life in Villa, just as they are in the country as a whole and indeed social life more generally the world over. As such, it may seem arbitrary or even crude to separate the religious from the so-called nonreligious, especially when there is often no clear division that can be discerned. Life is complex. While religious identities and beliefs about the supernatural can be central to people's lives and even have momentous effects on their thoughts and actions, they are never absolute; people draw from the totality of their experiences in life to create meaning and to act in the world. I think this dynamism is important so I do not want to ignore it. "*El pueblo caliente*" and "*el pueblo profético*" epitomize diverse perspectives on the same complex whole. Both labels refer to a town not unlike any other, but index a different sense of it—in one sense the earthly and in another the numinous, aspects of life that are always intertwined but which are frequently viewed as separate and distinct. A study on worldviews and political monism conducted by Vanderbilt University's "Latin American Public Opinion Project" in 2008 found that 80.4 percent of Dominicans see Dominican politics as a battle between good and evil, the highest percentage among Latin American and Caribbean countries polled (Orces 2009). To view politics as a battle between good and evil is indicative of a propensity to see relations of power as having both righteous and wicked aspects. Among other inferences that can be made, this finding is a striking example of the powerful influence of Christian dualisms on the Dominican Republic. The tendency to divide social life into two opposing values, to perceive reality in terms of good and evil, is indicative of the pervasive Christian worldview permeating Dominican society. This sentiment, like the differing perspectives on the moral identity of Villa itself, represents a profound orientation toward binary models of perception and explanation that figure in everyday life in the country and, for Pentecostal Christians, becomes the conceptual raw material upon which to anchor their dualistic worldview, a Manichaean dualism representing an idée fixe of the church's doctrine.

The Churches

I conducted the bulk of my anthropological fieldwork with individuals from two churches in barrio Francisco—both of them Pentecostal charismatic institutions.[7] The first, Iglesia de Dios (IdD), which was the larger of the two churches with close to eighty registered members, is a Church of God denomination whose international headquarters are in Cleveland, Tennessee. Church of God is the second largest Pentecostal denomination in the country (behind Assemblies of God [Asambleas de Dios]) with around 80,000 total members, 640 churches throughout the country, and over 800 total ministries. The second church, Iglesia Evangélica Pentecostal (IEP), is an independent Dominican Pentecostal charismatic church with around forty registered members.[8] Although there were some apparent differences between the two churches, very few people acknowledged or even recognized dissimilarity between them.

IdD is located a couple blocks off the main road through town and serves the northwest region of the barrio. It is a small, one-room church with a stage, a lectern, a few rows of pews, and a considerable number of plastic chairs that fill out the rest of the space. The pastor, Ramón, lived above the church in a very modest two-room dwelling with his wife and two teenage sons. The church offers some kind of activity seven days a week. Sundays from 8:30 to 11:00 a.m. is a Bible study class (estudio biblico) where neophytes, but sometimes visitors and longtime members, read and study passages of the Bible under the guided instruction of the pastor. On the first Sunday of every month the Bible class is shortened, and they have a retiro, or "spiritual retreat," from 11:30 a.m. to 3:30 p.m. Participants in the retiro typically fast and come to the church during the free time to pray with others.[9] Otherwise a women's prayer group or a Sunday school class for young children follows the Bible study. Every Sunday at 7:00 p.m. they hold a formal culto, which is the best-attended service of the week. Often well over

100 people pack into the small church, requiring chairs to be set up outside to accommodate the extra patrons. On Mondays there is no formal *culto*, and many members take a break from daily church activities while others organize prayer groups around the neighborhood and meet in a member's home. The youth group gets together to socialize in an activity they called *compartir*, a social gathering among the teenagers and young adult members of the church. Tuesdays at 7:30 p.m. they hold regular *culto* at the church, with the women's group leading the services (*culto de las damas*). Wednesdays there is no *culto*; instead, a doctrine class (*doctrina*) is held for newcomers and those wanting to be baptized. Taught by the pastor, the doctrine class focuses on topics like "what we believe," "what it means to be a Christian," and "how we should act," and covers the rules and regulations of the church. On Thursdays at 7:30 p.m. regular *culto* is held but is specially geared toward adolescents. Friday *culto* begins at 7:30 p.m. as well, but is run by the men's group (*culto de los caballeros*). *Cultos* on Saturdays at 7:30 p.m. are led by the church's youth group and typically entail a playful and creative aspect organized by the teenagers and young adults (*culto juvenil*).

IEP offers the same services and activities but with a slightly different schedule. Bible classes are held on Tuesdays instead of Sundays, for example, and because IEP is smaller and is not as well attended, it does not have a group for adolescents. Not including children, who were numerous and varied in ages from newborns to preteens, there were about forty regular members. This small church was founded and run by an elderly woman I refer to here as *la pastora*. She did not live in barrio Francisco but commuted nearly every night to attend the church services from her home in Pantoja, about a twenty-minute drive away. Although the official pastor of the church, *la pastora* delegated much of the everyday business of the church, including preaching and evangelizing, to four deacons and several other elders in the church. IEP was smaller than IdD and in my estimation more conservative on the whole. Men and women were to sit on opposite sides of the church separated by an aisle dividing the small one-room church. Rules for dress and comportment were more strictly observed, and the community itself was more tight-knit.

Methodology and Approach

My research involved qualitative data collection and analysis using participant-observation and ethnographic interviewing methods and procedures.
I conducted the bulk of my anthropological fieldwork over a two-year period (2007–2009), during which I recorded over thirty-five semistructured
interviews (no less than an hour each) with thirty-three church and community members. My interview sample represented a cross section of both
churches and includes laity, leaders, recent converts, and visitors. I also
spoke with and interviewed local residents not affiliated with the church.
I interviewed both men and women ranging in ages from thirteen to sixty-
four years old. I utilized a semistructured interview approach using specific
questions to help guide the data collection process and ensure a level of
uniformity throughout. Interviewees were asked general and often open-
ended questions regarding a range of topics, including the nature and quality of their social relationships, past and present associations with others,
evaluations of self and community identity, demographic information, and
roles and statuses, as well as ideas about acquaintances, friends, and family
members. I also collected narratives of conversion and personal histories,
and asked people to reflect on their own values, goals, and positions in the
community. These questions supplemented my discussion with interviewees about the content of their faith, the role of religion in their everyday
lives, and the rewards and challenges of being a believer.

In order to understand the influence of evangelical Christian identity
on certain forms of daily experience, interviews were conducted concur-
rently with extensive participant-observation and "deep hanging out" (Clifford 1997:90). I attended and observed church services, public and special
events, informal community events, Bible classes, prayer groups, a wed-
ding ceremony, and public and private gatherings. This level of participation was necessary to access the nuances of everyday religious life and to
connect my broader theoretical questions to the lived experiences of my
informants. In order to understand the full range of experience, I observed
the social interaction of church members outside of the church as well and
surveyed relations in the public sphere and in Dominican society at large.
This meant spending a significant amount of time outside the church with
members during the day, at work, in between jobs, and whenever possible.
Fortunately, I was able to cultivate close relationships with many of my in-

formants and was invited into many of their lives. This afforded me the opportunity to discuss informally the issues of culture and identity that are essential to my informants' lives and crucial to the overarching theme of my research presented here. It was primarily through the unstructured day-to-day interactions with my informants over the course of my fieldwork that I learned the most about them. Faithful Christian identity informs their lives outside the church as much as within it, in many ways by complicating it, enriching it, transforming it. Sitting beside my informants at the dinner table, no less tagging along on a quick trip to the corner store or an afternoon lime by the river, was just as enlightening as sitting beside them in church or accompanying them on a spiritual campaign. Their lives and the insights contained herein were shared with me through friendship so much more than they ever could have been through interviews alone.

All interviews and conversations were conducted in Spanish, and all of the translations here and throughout are my own. The process of translation is not an easy one, as anyone who has been tasked to do so knows (and as the professionalization of translators attests to). It was my practice to balance as exact a translation as possible with communicating what I understood to be the general intention of the speaker at the time of our communication. At times, this has meant choosing clarity over exactness and at other times sacrificing coherence for honest reproduction. Block quotes and those within quotation marks are direct quotations, most of which were taken from transcriptions of audio recordings of informal discussions or interviews.

Almost all of the interviews that I conducted, along with a number of recorded conversations, were transcribed in the Dominican Republic. It took over a year and more than three different transcribers to complete the transcriptions that I wanted to use and analyze here. I would have liked to have been consistent and to have used only one transcriber, but unfortunately time, resources, and other exigencies prevented this from happening. While all of the transcribers did, in my estimation, a phenomenal job, they did so in their own way and under the constraints of their own level of expertise. None of them were professional transcribers, and thus there were unavoidable differences and inconsistencies across transcriptions. For example, while one transcriber chose not to transcribe words that were repeated by a speaker, another did. While one transcriber may have transcribed the exact locution used by a speaker—*pa'* instead of *para, montao* instead of *montado, señol* instead of *señor*—another chose not to. This varied with experience and oftentimes was not consistent even within a given transcription. Additionally, there was frequent and varied use of slang during some of the interviews, and in some cases it was not transcribed to my satisfaction. Because of these inconsistencies, I have chosen not to include the original Spanish alongside (above or below) my English translations.

There are, of course, some words and phrases that simply do not translate well into English from Spanish—so much so that at times I was left with no good options. In the event that I simply could not find a justifiable way of translating a thought or idea, I have chosen to leave it alone. Sometimes, however, a particular translation of a word or phrase is crucial to my analysis even while an "exact" translation simply does not exist. In these cases I have chosen to include and discuss the idea in relation both to the original Spanish and my English translation.

I took seriously the words, thoughts, and feelings of my informants and have chosen here to build my analysis principally upon their words. This means that we hear a lot from my informants in the following pages. An important goal in putting together this book was to render the voices of my informants audible and intelligible. In some cases I have deferred to their own interpretations to enrich my own. This has, in my mind, always been the great contribution of anthropology: that is, to give an analysis of local experience, to take the "natives'" point of view, to record *their* story, and to represent meaning in context. It is what separates anthropology from philosophy (which too often, in my estimation, have been all too willing bedfellows). Anthropology is the quintessential humanistic social science, and its strength lies in its methodology no less than in its modes of self-reflection. As such, I hope this book shows as much as it tells about the experience of Dominican Pentecostals.

Conducting Interviews

I found people to be very candid and honest in their interviews. Only very seldom did I encounter any reluctance or hesitation in answering my questions, and only in rare cases did I ever receive dodgy answers. Anthony, a captivating evangelist from Pantoja who had at one time been jailed for drug trafficking before his conversion, comes to mind as an exception. Today a seriously reformed individual, I could see the uneasiness with which he approached questions about his past. He would never answer them directly, usually brushing them aside by responding dismissively. Whether we were having a friendly conversation at his home or at the weekly farmers market on an occasional Sunday morning, no less than when I pressed him during an interview, he seemed always reluctant to answer questions about his past. But this was understandable I suppose. He feared reversion back to his old self and fought hard to relive the past through his testimony with any detail.

I wondered, before conducting fieldwork, if people were going to be honest with me. At that time I understood honesty to mean being entirely candid and utterly self-reflexive. I found that people were honest, but not in the sense that I had initially thought. Importantly, they told me what they wanted to tell me and what they wanted me to know about themselves. This self-reflexivity (and not the critical reflexivity I had naively expected) played an important role in the details and ways in which my informants discussed Christianity with me. The Christian ideas and practices that they discussed at times portrayed an infallible belief system and utopian future. I regularly asked informants to describe themselves—not to record an objective description of identity but rather to understand how certain individuals came to see themselves over time, shaped by particular discourses of faith, gender, fidelity, and community. There were others, however, who were amazingly self-reflexive and who offered me a picture of themselves in the world that was ripe with contradiction and fallibility. Through our regular day-to-day exchanges and through our structured interactions in the form of interviews, I learned a lot about my informants, not just from what they told to me but also from *how* they told me, and what they chose to highlight.

For converts, Pentecostal Christianity in the barrios is largely about distinction and credibly representing oneself as a faithful born-again child of God. Whether people are trustworthy or not is quite frankly beside the point; rather, it is how they go about convincing others of their trustworthiness that I find interesting here. This negotiation with me as an ethnographer was no different from the everyday negotiations over identity that Pentecostals partake in routinely with others in the neighborhood. In nearly all cases they drew from a familiar cultural script, made reference to difference and distinction, and tried to convince me of their enlightened, ameliorated alterity in terms of the church, conversion, and the Christian message of repentance and salvation that they had learned.

From day one of my fieldwork I explained to everyone the nature of my research and my reasons for being in Villa with them. I was candid from the beginning with my informants, and they were told that I was not a Pentecostal and that I was not there as a believer or with the intention to convert. My main informants, along with the congregations of both churches, respected this fact, and I was never asked to join the church and never asked to participate in any activity in any capacity other than as an observer. Having been met with such respect and hospitality, first as a stranger and then later as a friend, I cannot help but be a sympathetic observer and analyst in the last instance.

Pluralism, Heterodoxy, and Christian Hegemony

In this chapter I trace the dimensions of popular religion as manifest in Dominican barrios. I advance the argument that the predominant religious institutions in barrio Francisco (a microcosm of the country's religious diversity) share basic cosmological assumptions and precepts that underlie religious meaning locally and establish the terms of cooperation and conflict—agreement and discord—across the religious continuum. It is within this implicit sharing that believers constitute themselves as effectual religious actors, prosecute their religious identities, and negotiate spiritual authority. In Villa Altagracia, meaning (or meaningful interaction) in the realm of the sacred is dependent upon the articulated practical and symbolic relations of agreement obtaining between local religions (primarily popular Catholicism, so-called Dominican *vodú*, and evangelical Protestant, namely Pentecostal, churches) within the context of Christian domination.

Efficacy across the religious spectrum in Villa is achieved as a result of the cosmological assumptions that religious institutions share at the local level. For example, conversion to Jesus Christ represents an effective means of removing initiates from compulsory service to the saints/spirits of Dominican *vodú*, just as the existence of these spirit entities is an acknowledged fact of the known universe for believers of all types locally, even for converts. This is possible only within a context where diverse institutions agree on the rules of the game and in fact share in much more than they differ. Even while disparate religious actors may disagree on the relative merits of each other's beliefs, and despite fostering open hostilities at times, they abide by the same conceptual rules and acknowledge the same basic contours of a shared spiritual universe wherein a range of perspectives is accommodated. This implicit agreement (or sharing) structures the religious conflict and cooperation that proceeds from living in plural religious contexts dominated by Christian hegemony and provides the bedrock upon which Pentecostals and others stake claims to religious authority.

In order to flesh out the nuances of this accord, I utilize a case study of a woman named Mariela Consuelo, whose religious career has traversed all three major local religious horizons. As a representative example, her story illustrates the exceptional role of Pentecostalism in the everyday social drama and highlights the reciprocal relations of meaning that obtain between ostensibly disparate religious traditions, revealing the remarkable ways in which individuals and their communities navigate diverse religious environments and derive meaning, efficacy, and identity in plural, heterodox contexts.

Mariela Consuelo

People in Villa widely believe themselves to be vulnerable to mystical forces, among them witchcraft, sorcery, and demonic possession, along with related misfortune and sickness resulting from such procedures. As in other parts of the world, witchcraft and the acts of malevolent spirits are frequently blamed for illness, misfortune, and death. Supposedly, beliefs such as these tend to be more widespread in rural areas of the country, but in Villa, and commonly elsewhere, people are just as anxious or quick to suggest that an unexplainable illness, an untimely death, or a suspicious accident is not the result of chance or natural causes, but instead the consequence of supernatural maleficence.

Mariela's account of sickness and of health, of sin and redemption, begins at the intersections of jealousy, witchcraft, illness, and sorcery. Her trajectory through the religious continuum is a common one and tells us a story about religious pluralism and the aesthetics of religious life in Villa while illustrating the intimate links connecting belief, morality, and religious identity across Dominican society. Beginning with possession illness through witchcraft, she was baptized into the service of spirit beings, worked as a diviner and spirit medium, then converted to Pentecostal Christianity. Her spiritual biography reveals interesting limitations and possibilities prompted by her religious career by highlighting the fluid logic of Dominican religiosity as it unfolds in time and space and is given expression in everyday life.

Mariela grew up a practicing Catholic. She went to church regularly with her family until the age of thirteen, when she "separated from it" because, according to her, she was young and had "lost hope in God." This separation from the church, however, was only partial. She retained her "Christian beliefs" and, in her mind, continued to have a sound "fear of God" that she claims never wavered, but she stopped attending Mass with any regularity, and the parish church ceased to figure prominently in her day-to-day affairs.[1] Her story of spirit possession begins some years later when she was overtaken with illness:

> I remember perfectly, it began as a physical sickness. They brought me to various different doctors, but they couldn't find anything wrong with me. The analysis [of medical tests] revealed nothing and there appeared to be nothing wrong, but I was always tired and everyday I would go to bed without eating or bathing or drinking water. It could be a week like that, laying down, feeling bad physically.

Mariela's husband became concerned about her health because she was sick for weeks and showed no signs of recuperating. She grew weaker by the day and began to neglect her family and friends. Not long after falling ill she began to have bewildering dreams: "Sometimes strange things would happen and I would dream of people who I would later recognize as 'seres' but who, after converting to the Lord, we call demons."[2] Until this point in her life, her visions had no precedent; she was unfamiliar with the figures who appeared to her sporadically, and she did not understand their sudden presence in her dreams. Her husband recognized the signs soon enough and quickly sought the help of a diviner—a local sorcerer, in Mariela's terms a "brujo"—who could uncover the cause of her illness and perhaps determine the source of her visions:

> My husband was very much a believer in [the power of diviners] and he saw that I was always sick and that the doctors were unable to find anything [wrong with me]. So he brought me to a brujo or hechicero

[sorcerer]. There the *brujo* determined the cause of the sickness and told me that someone had sent something upon me. They say it like that here, *"que me habían enviado algo"* ["that I had been sent something"].

The diviner determined that witchcraft was to blame for Mariela's affliction and that a magical consignment had been sent to do her harm.[3] He also divined the origins of the witchcraft that was making her sick and concluded that the magical attacks were coming from her husband's mistress:

My husband had another woman, a lover besides me, and she envied me. Everything began because she had a daughter with him and the little girl died and this woman said that it was I who had killed her. This woman was a spirit medium too and demons would possess her and when the little girl got sick a demon possessed her and said to the people who were there in attendance that it was I who was killing the little girl. But it was she in fact who was killing the little girl. The little girl died of a sudden illness. She had been sick with bronchopneumonia, a sickness that infects the lungs, and when the demons possessed this woman she grabbed the little girl and put her in a wash bin full of cold water. Imagine doing that to a sick little girl! When the girl died she said that it was I who had done it.

Due to the girl's sudden illness and subsequent death, the mistress believed that her daughter had been the victim of witchcraft and that Mariela was to blame. A spirit who possessed or "mounted" the woman accused Mariela of the crime, which in turn led the distressed woman to seek revenge. Mariela professed to have had nothing to do with the child's illness or death and tried to absolve herself by proposing that the child had died of natural causes (pneumonia) brought about, in her mind, by the irresponsible, in fact, wicked acts of a woman driven mad by demonic spirits. Nonetheless, the mistress blamed Mariela for her loss and allegedly conspired with evil forces to cause her harm:

The *brujo* I was brought to said that someone was doing witchcraft to me. He told my husband where it was and where the *brujería* had been put in her house. So my husband took me home and he went to the woman's house and began to look for the witchcraft where the *brujo* had told him it would be. There in her house he found it: a lit candle, along with my name. This was a scandal [*un rebú*] with the police and everything because he was armed and began to hit her. It was something ugly! But I continued feeling sick because everything that she got was obtained in order to do [bad] things to me.

After learning that the witchcraft was coming from a woman with whom he had a relationship, Mariela's husband went to the woman's house and discovered an oil-wick lamp that had been lighted along with Mariela's name on the floor of the bedroom—provisions typical of household sorcery—exactly where the diviner had instructed him to look. He was furious and supposedly assailed the woman for it. But Mariela continued to feel unwell and believed that her husband's mistress continued to perform spells and to send magical attacks against her:

Later they brought me to someone else [another *brujo*] who said that I had "*seres*" and that I would have to be baptized in order to cure myself. Initially I refused because I had my beliefs. I knew that it was bad, to do certain things was bad, to visit *brujos* was bad before God. But my husband fought with me about it, about me always being sick, and eventually I accepted it.

Mariela had dreamed of these beings shortly after falling ill. The witchcraft that had been sent against her had apparently exposed her to malign spirits. This diviner, instead of trying to counter the magic presumably doing her harm, informed her that the only way to get better was for her to be baptized and to serve the spirit beings who were making her ill, a proposition about which Mariela was not a little bit ambivalent, but she went along with it in the hopes of satisfying her husband and finding an effective and lasting cure for her chronic malaise.

She was brought from Villa to the great basilica of *La Altagracia* in Higüey, a town in the east of the island, and was initiated there by a woman whom she considers today to have been "a powerful and terrible *bruja*," and with this, was baptized into service of the saints (or *santos*, local spirit beings variously referred to as *seres*, *luases*, or *misterios* ["mysteries"]). After her initiation, the sickness vanished, and she no longer felt ill. She became a spirit medium (also called a *caballo*, "horse," or *espiritista*) and started to hold consultations for paying clients in her home.[4] Clients began to seek her services and the advice and wisdom of the spirit beings who spoke through her.

> I began to consult in my house and people would come by asking for me. . . . People would come and say to me, for example, "call so-and-so demon for me"—a saint that they wanted to call who have their different names and certain rites of how to invoke them. The demon would come and they would tell it what they wanted. I had a great big altar with all the images [of the saints]. Eventually I had many clients and I made a lot of money because, you know, people will fight over any little thing but not to give their money to a *brujo*. Women would come looking to "bind" [*amarrar*] their husbands [magically, to prevent them from cheating]. In fact the majority of women came so that their husbands would stop cheating on them with other women. People would also come to my house for lottery numbers and people would play the numbers that the demons would give them. . . . The demons gave the numbers through me. When the demons arrived and possessed me, they gave numbers to the people who were there [for a consultation]. They gave many lottery numbers to me as well. If this demon appeared to me and gave me a number I would play it because I was sure that it would be the winning number. One would appear to me and would say to me "look, tomorrow this number will be the winning number." Sometimes the number would appear to me on a wall and I would play all the money that I had and sit and wait for the winning number to come.

This kind of divination can be a profitable enterprise for those who are capable and respected specialists, and Mariela made a modest living for herself by providing magical formulas and winning lottery numbers to her paying clients. However, with time she was inclined to wager her own money on the lottery but soon became dissatisfied because her clients would get the winning numbers and she would lose out. That, combined with the ritual demands of serving the spirits over time, led to her disillusionment; she realized that her relationship to the *seres* was taking more than it was giving (this is not an uncommon thread in testimonies about working with the *lwa* in Haiti as well; see Métraux 1972). She had few options. She had considered abandoning her duties and ritual obligations to the saints, but this would have its consequences, and she was afraid of becoming sick again: "I had the pressure from my husband who said that if I left it that I would go back to being sick again and go crazy."

The *seres* themselves are fastidious, jealous, and moody. They share the tastes and habits of their human followers, and, like their earthly servants, they can be envious, lascivious, sensitive, vengeful, and given quickly over to rage (Métraux 1972:94). Moreover, if they are not propitiated to their satisfaction, they may turn on their servants through involuntary possession and/or sickness (Deive 1992:249; Schaffler 2004:8). Anyone who dares leave their side runs the risk of violent repercussions and spiteful retribution. Bad luck, illness, or even death may be visited upon believers who choose to forsake the spirits they once served and revered (Métraux 1972:352–356). Work with the *seres* or saints is not always based on love and voluntary devotion; sometimes it may also be based on fear or obligation (Lemus and Marty 2010:42). Mariela insists that she was ambivalent about her ordeal, even from the beginning:

> I was never okay with it, maybe at first, had I not known God, it would have been different, but I had my Christian beliefs and I knew that the things I was doing were not good. To visit *brujos* was bad before God. . . . Even though I practiced sorcery [*hechicería*] I never did it to hurt anyone because I feared God. . . . Even though I did all of these things, I never clung to it because I didn't like it. . . . At the beginning I would always dream that I was falling from a cliff and I would ask God that he not lose me. . . . But I was sick and I fought with my husband about it but he eventually convinced me. He was a believer in the power of witchcraft.

Her professed ambivalence reveals at least two important points. First, she never thought of herself as anything but Christian; she insists that she maintained her Christian beliefs even while she worked as a medium performing divinatory acts for clients. In the most plain sense this suggests that she sees her evangelical conversion as effecting a new investment in the Christian faith as a Pentecostal, viewed emically as a renewed commitment to traditional orthodox values, nevertheless having always considered herself more or less Christian (Catholic), even as she "served the saints" of Dominican *vodú*. Second, her willingness to serve the saints, in the end, was based on an evaluation of its effectiveness and not its relative truth or falsity with regard to her Christian beliefs. Today she sees her former behavior not in terms of true or false but rather of right or wrong—moral evaluations that crystallized upon conversion. In any case we need not believe her professed reluctance to take heed of the fact that ambivalence was the cornerstone of her decision to serve the spirits just as it would be in her decision to leave them: she did not choose to do so on a whim one day, much less following an exhaustive evaluation of her secular and spiritual options. She came to it as a result of an incurable sickness that followed from a malicious enchantment, which led her to serve the beings that possessed her (rather than exorcise them), presumably out of necessity—not exactly by free choice, but immediate need. In this way, committing her life to spiritual work with the saints and *vodú* spirits was not unlike joining a church or becoming a member of any other religious institution. There are many push and pull factors, not the least of which is trying to find solutions to difficult questions of health and happiness. Ultimately, she used a similar evaluative process to leave the *seres* and join the Pentecostal church.

Perhaps separation from her husband provided just the impetus to leave her practice and the *seres* behind (on this point, however, she was silent). She had made a living off of her consultations, and she also knew that to renounce the *seres* was to incur their wrath. Few options exist for those who wish to disavow them. One cannot just give up on the saints, especially those people who have taken vows to serve them. Remarkably, one of the more viable solutions available to the reluctant or despondent adept is conversion to Protestant Christianity, and this is precisely the route that Mariela took.

Conversion is generally accepted as a long-lasting or permanent way out of this lifestyle—the only viable remedy or solution to the binding obligations of serving the saints. Joining the Protestant churches requires converts to renounce the spirits in favor of allegiance to Jesus Christ alone. But conversion does not assure that believers will be entirely clear of the beings they once vowed to serve. The spirits themselves neither become less important nor vanish entirely from a convert's life after joining the church. Rather, through an inverted transfiguration of sorts, they become demonic beings (e.g., Meyer 1999), evil spirits who torment and seduce but can no longer possess (or "mount") their former devotees:

> For a time after I converted the demons continued to torment me, but they couldn't possess me because I had the seal of the Holy Spirit in

my life. They couldn't touch me, but they made war with me. I could see them and I could hear their voices where they told me ugly things. It was a battle, *muy fuerte*, where I fought body to body with them.

I have never been afraid. I get tired sometimes. I felt tired the other day and everything but I have never been scared. I hear voices, they appear to me and they say to me things like "kill yourself!" or "die!" I had many battles with them. They attacked me with sickness too. I had many experiences with them after I converted. I had more experiences with demons after converting than I did before.

Listen, that's how life is. I had more encounters with them making war with me after I converted. On one occasion, [one of the demons] gave me something that made me sick and I was dying. [My family] took me to the clinic and I confessed to the doctor that I was dying because I had this terrible spiritual battle [with the demons]. . . .

They still attack me [today]. It has been ten years since I reconciled with the Lord and yet the battle is never won because after one becomes independent of them they continue attacking. That is why I have had these experiences. You must stay united [with God] because if one separates from him just a little, Satan will try to destroy you.

The spirits may take revenge on converts who turn their backs on them. This is how misfortune after conversion is often understood (see Métraux 1972:355 for a number of examples in the Haitian context). Mariela was confronted by the *seres* who attacked her with illness but who could no longer possess her, their ire likely a manifestation of ambivalence she experienced as a result of turning her back on them.[5] She is still, occasionally, harassed by the spirits that she once served, but they no longer "mount" or possess her, nor may they cause her any great harm as long as she stays faithful to Jesus Christ. Today she uses these experiences to frame her new identity as a triumphant Christian victor and as a moral exemplar of the Christian faith. For Mariela, as long as she stays connected to God she is protected from the malign spirits she once served. But if she turns away from God, perhaps like she did when she was younger, she opens a door again to demonic influences.

There is, of course, a lot here to unpack, so I will refrain from commenting on each and every significant detail of Mariela's story. I would, however, like to consider several general questions: What are we to make of Mariela's apparent sickness by witchcraft and her subsequent initiation into mediumship and recourse to magic and sorcery? After serving the spirits profitably for years, how and why does she come to leave them, and, perhaps more astonishingly, why is conversion her most practical way out? And what are we to make of her professed ambivalence throughout this ordeal and the continued although transformed relevance of the spirit beings in her life today? Finally, how does she make sense of her journey with hindsight, and what does her experience tell us about religious pluralism and shared cosmologies in the Dominican context?

Sorcery, Illness, and Spirit-Mediumship

In Villa Altagracia, witchcraft and sorcery are frequently blamed for unfortunate and otherwise unexplainable events (cf. Evans-Prichard 1976:18–33). Yet if an otherwise "reasonable" (culturally appropriate) explanation can be found for an accident or illness, it is not necessarily judged to be witchcraft. Take Mariela's initial affliction, for example. If the doctor had been able to identify a biomedical basis for her ailments from the start, presumably she would not have sought the services of a diviner and later attributed her illness to spiteful magic. Predictably, she and her husband reasoned that because the physician could not make her better, the origin of her sudden poor health could not have been medical—undoubtedly, it must have been spiritual.[6]

By making this determination, Mariela located herself and her illness within the context of a particular worldview characterized by a shared set of expectations, assumptions, and rules regarding the spirit world, illness causation, its character or expression, and its likely remedy. This precise constellation of culturally organized ideas about the sacred and its relationship to health governs interpretive possibilities along the religious continuum by delineating a hierarchy of values chiefly responsible for configuring relations of cause and effect between the human and spirit worlds. The idea that the hidden or unseen—the spiritual or supernatural realm—acts on the physical, observable human world and does so in a particular and predictable manner is a product of this worldview and is among a number of key assumptions that are shared among nearly all believers in the neighborhood, regardless of their religious affiliation.[7] What is understood here is that if magic makes you sick, then it is magic, not biomedicine, that can make you better. An antibiotic works wonders on any number of intestinal bacteria or parasitic amoebas that cause diarrhea and indigestion but would do little to deter a stomach malady caused by a *guangá* (a magical consignment) or an improperly prepared or ill-fated *resguardo* (an enchanted amulet or charm of protection that is sometimes swallowed). For these portentous woes, only an appeal to the powers of the supernatural and resort to the interpretive logics of the otherworld will do, and this with little hesitation is the recourse to which Mariela turned.

It should be noted that Mariela had the option to consult any of several opinions regarding her illness—namely, any expert within the pastor-priest-diviner triumvirate, any one of whom would have been able to recommend an appropriate remedy according to their preferred methodology and approach to the divine. Mariela was pressed to see a *brujo* on the insistence of her husband, but had she been so inclined at the time, she could just as easily have consulted a pastor at a nearby church. Were she to have gone to a Pentecostal church, for example, her experience would not have been altogether different. The pastor too would have "divined" a reason for her illness and gone about the business of treating her through prayer, exorcism, or some other institutionalized solution available to him. The illness itself, whether the result of witchcraft, spirit possession, sorcery, jealousy, or some combination of these, would be jointly acknowledged as having resulted from a mystical force and thus a force against which only spiritual means are effectively deployed. No matter where one falls on the religious continuum, here magic and sorcery are held to be powerful and potentially dangerous modes of action, indeed, mystical operations that require supernatural intervention to combat.

That all popular religious institutions in the neighborhood acknowledge the power of mystical forces like magic and sorcery and mobilize human and spiritual resources either to utilize or to resist them demonstrates an important quality of shared religious life in Villa. The local debate over magic is not over whether it works, but rather for whom does it work and at what cost? While many employ magic for practical material ends, either unmoved or perhaps inspired by the powers at work, others, like the Pentecostal Christians, invest considerable time and energy into combating magic (which they define as witchcraft or sorcery) through prayer and spiritual campaigns (*campañas*) aimed at snuffing out such influences in the wider community. For local Pentecostals, "*brujos* heal, but with consequences," believing that while the power of the Devil is great and can bring about temporary health and riches, such ill-gotten rewards also come with conditions, the consequences of which inevitably outweigh the immediate and fleeting returns of any appeal to evil forces. In any case, magic constitutes a non-trivial ritual form, an important spiritual agency either to be harnessed or suppressed. Part of the simultaneous popularity of the Pentecostal church and the client-based magic and divination associated with Dominican *vodú*, particularly in poor urban contexts like Villa, can be attributed to their joint success in offering practical solutions to the threat of malign spirits, demonic (or "negative," unwanted) possession, and the persistent menace of witchcraft assaults (for a similar rendering of Pentecostal popularity in Haiti, see Métraux 1972; Brodwin 1996). Even while disturbances like these are not always central to day-to-day life, they readily appear to flirt at the margins of the seen and unseen, lurking in the shadows of routine anxieties that plague impoverished communities, and ever threatening the boundary between the real and unreal. Seemingly everyone has a story about the occult dealings of their neighbors. At the same time, witchcraft, although out of sight and rarely owned up to, is never quite entirely out of mind and seems always there to provide an answer for the unfortunate and unexplainable, giving meaning to the everyday trials of human life in the barrio undeterred by the promise of modernity's disenchanting encroachment.

Vodú, Magic, and Ambivalence

In the Dominican Republic, any form of magic, whether used for good or for bad, might be deemed witchcraft. The term itself has a long history in anthropology that I do not wish to recite at length here (see, for example, Evans-Pritchard 1976; Crick 1979), but suffice it to say that the term carries no small amount of analytic baggage. One issue is the difficulty in defining witchcraft so that it functions as a useful analytic tool cross-culturally. Evans-Pritchard's famous distinction between witchcraft and sorcery, for example, is difficult to reconcile in the Dominican context because the terms "*brujería*" and "*hechicería*" ("witchcraft" and "sorcery," respectively) are indiscriminately applied to the same phenomena—that is, a complex of mystical rituals (whether described as good or bad, helpful or harmful, white or black) that include, but are not limited to, variants of magic, divination, spirit possession and conjure, miraculous healing, or often any other practice employing ritual means for magical ends. Forces of psychic ill will—the classic definition of witchcraft—may also fall under the general rubric of *brujería* depending on the situation and one's perspective. To complicate things further, the terms "witchcraft" and "sorcery" are also employed to denote the instrumental source of spontaneous fortune or misfortune under certain conditions. For instance, people who appear to enjoy auspicious economic favors relative to or despite the widespread struggles of their neighbors are sometimes suspected of using witchcraft or being witches themselves, just as witchcraft or sorcery is often blamed for the sudden or unexpected death of a child regardless of the apparent cause. It is not an uncommon belief that children who suffer from anemia and rickets are the victims of witches (Deive 1992:261), and, to be sure, it was the premature death of her young daughter that led Mariela's husband's mistress to accuse Mariela of the offending witchcraft (someone of whom she was no doubt envious).

Muddying the waters even more, spirit mediums along with experts in magic and divination are regularly referred to as witches or sorcerers—*brujos* or *hechiceros*—regardless of whether they practice helpful or harmful magic or are viewed sympathetically or with scorn. While most *brujos* (sometimes also called *bokors/bocós* [priests] or *mambos/mambosas* [priestesses]) deny using magic for the purposes of inflicting harm, they profit from the common belief that they are capable of "working" or "serving with both hands"—that is, using their powers for ill to call *petroses* or *espíritus malignos* (evil spirits) or to use their mystical knowledge to prepare and dispatch a deadly *guangá* (Deive 1992:245). Even though most sorcerers make use of their powers for curing and protection, depending on the needs of their clients they may use harmful magic if the situation warrants. Their role, according to Deive, "consists as much in protecting clients from the dangers and evils that come to them as it is in offering formulas and enchantments with which to bend the will of enemies and reluctant lovers" (1992:245, my translation). Sorcerers like these are therefore liminal, ambiguous figures (much like the shaman of traditional anthropological imagination) simultaneously feared and respected for their esoteric knowledge and revered access to divine power.

Sorcerers (or *brujos*), therefore, occupy an ambiguous place in Dominican society. Many people rely on them for medical cures and solutions to a variety of problems and malaises through their knowledge of magic and herbal medicine; at the same time, they fear their potential power to do harm and to perform wicked acts. While the majority of *misterios* and/or saints are considered benevolent, some people can and do put them to work for evil ends (Deive 1992:163). For skeptics, these workers of magic are merely charlatans out to take advantage of the poor and desperate; for others, they are sincere powerful agents of the supernatural with expert knowledge of the otherworld and its mysteries; for the faithful, *brujos* are a necessary fixture in any neighborhood community. It would be wrong, of course, to see all Dominicans as feeling one way or another about them. It is true that many do not pay such characters any mind and dismiss them as panderers of superstition and old wives' tales, while others dare not make an important decision without first consulting the saints. However one may regard *vodú* sorcerers, with disdain or approval, they no less play an important role in the micropolitics of everyday spiritual and quotidian life as major brokers of privileged access to the supernatural within the local religious economy.

The point I want to make here is simple (and, in my mind, relatively uncontroversial): because a sorcerer's spiritual work may be used for helpful or harmful purposes, it is essentially morally ambiguous. As the social context dictates, then, under certain moral constraints magic will become witchcraft (or wicked) in the eye of the beholder. The predominance of Christian ethical values in Dominican society means that any form of magic, no less spirit possession or divination, could be construed in negative terms and disparaged as witchcraft or otherwise illicit behavior; this in part explains Mariela's ambivalence when first deciding to see a *brujo* and the hesitation she expressed in becoming a spirit medium herself. This is not to suggest that every client, medium, or sorcerer is shackled with the same uncertainty that Mariela recounts, but it does help explain how Mariela herself was able to justify her willingness to serve the saints in a way that, at least at some level, contradicted her Catholic beliefs and the orthodox Christian ideal she was raised to favor. Furthermore, her claim that she never practiced sorcery to hurt anyone is consistent with the public stance of most so-called *vodú* practitioners—that they operate on behalf of the Christian God to heal and perform acts of good (see Deive 1992:211; Brodwin 1996:142).

As is sometimes the case, the normal exigencies of life occasionally require human action that can be construed (if not normatively defined) as evil, particularly in social environments that feature cultural oppositions or conflicting value systems, here evidenced by the antagonisms between orthodoxy and heterodoxy, but generally reflected in and typical of the tensions obtaining in the New World between the inherited cultural traditions of Europe and Africa (see Herskovits 1964; Smith 1965; Manning 1973; Wilson 1995; Mintz 1989; Abrahams 1983). Caught between the ideals of her Christian faith and the immediate necessities of her worsening condition, Mariela appealed not to the hegemony of Christian orthodoxy but to the efficacy of an Afro-Creole heterodoxy and the attending logic that defines wicked acts, not by essence—as fundamentally good or evil—but by intent. Tellingly, she is careful to note that although she *did* practice sorcery, she "never did it to hurt anyone," effectively declaring the moral innocence of her actions. This sentiment is suggestive of the customary approach to morality frequently encountered in the African American world (see Whitten 1973:414) and indeed parallels traditional African thought and philosophy, which holds no spiritual agent to be entirely good or entirely bad, but that evil inheres in intent and is realized in practice, not in some essential quality or essence as implied in Christianity (Herskovits 1970:242; Raboteau 1978:287; Simpson 1978:217; Mintz and Trouillot 1995:131).

Of course, I am taking seriously here Mariela's claim that she believed, even before converting, that what she was doing was unacceptable to God and that she never quite felt right about practicing sorcery. She insists that because she had her "Christian beliefs," she knew that going to see a *brujo* was wrong and that practicing sorcery was wicked before God. Although her ambivalence in this regard may not be universal (it is also, of course, impossible for us to be certain of her convictions before her evangelical awakening), it is quite likely where an uncertain compromise between Christian and African-inspired traditions and their respective value complexes prevail. Even while believers seemingly cross the threshold of orthodox Christianity into the heterodox practices of Dominican *vodú* and back again with little overt conflict, they do so undoubtedly with some ambivalence. By accounting for Mariela's ambivalence, we can better understand how it is that she was able to take up practices maligned by so many of her neighbors and country folk but that are just as often relied upon to meet their diverse spiritual needs. I propose that her ambivalence, once considered within its proper cultural context—that of a religious pluralism dominated by Christian hegemony—is hardly surprising and, to the contrary, might well be expected in the Dominican Republic given the widespread respect for Christian ethical values alongside equally common forms of heterodoxy that challenge and oppose them.

I suspect that Herskovits's notion of "socialized ambivalence" is resonant here. In describing the psychological conflict facing Haitian peasants as a result of antipathies and contradictions between African and European ancestral traditions and their historical elaboration in Haitian society, he outlined, though did not elaborate much upon (Bourguignon 2000), a kind of psychological adjustment or response adopted by Haitians to deal with the irreconcilability of competing values, or what Bourguignon (1952:319) summarizes as the "simultaneous attraction and hostility toward the same object" characterizing individuals who are attracted to opposite ways of life, most notably apparent with respect to *vodou* (Bourguignon 2000:109; Bastide, Morin, and Raveau 1974). Indeed, there are aspects of Christianity and the *vodú* complex that are in anything but accord. For Herskovits (1964:299), the concept of socialized ambivalence:

> describes the tendency to manifest those rapid shifts in attitude toward people and situations that characterize the responses of the Haitian peasant to such a marked degree that the same man will hold in high regard a person, an institution, an experience, or even an object that has personal significance to him and simultaneously manifest great disdain and even hatred for it. As outwardly observable, this takes the form of recurring and often rapid changes in behavior toward the object of attention. In attitude, there is vacillation from one emotional tone to another. In its broader implications, as a matter of fact, it is entirely possible that this socialized ambivalence underlies much of the political and economic instability of Haiti, so that, arising from a fundamental clash of custom within the culture, it is responsible for the many shifts in allegiance that continually take place, as it is for the change in attitudes in everyday association.

He goes on to propose in reference to an observation he describes earlier in the text (Herskovits 1964:299–300):

> This type of approach cannot but give insight into such occurrences as that of the man whose unwilling possession by the gods of his ancestors was, as described, brought about through the fascination of their forbidden rites for him, despite his strict Catholic upbringing. His

vacillation between the desire to understand and worship the gods of his ancestors and his utter remorse after he had done this illustrates one way in which conflicts in a cultural setting can affect the outward responses and unsettle the inner adjustment of the individual who is exposed to such a situation. From a broader point of view, such an analysis of Haitian psychology suggests a more realistic understanding of the individuals in other cultures who have likewise fallen heir to conflicting traditions.

In Mariela's story, we see this same complex clash of customs play out in the Dominican Republic between Christian orthodoxy and its antagonistic relationship with popular heterodox forms. It is apparent that Mariela was both compelled by the cult of the *seres* and yet uncertain of her role in serving them when weighing her professed Christian beliefs. Although she was able to move seamlessly from lay Catholic to spirit medium to Pentecostal congregant without any major logical conflicts or paralyzing cognitive dissonance, she did so with some uncertainty, something Herskovits's observations advise might be characteristic of similar cultural settings that pit Christian domination against subaltern heterodox alternatives. The spread of Protestantism may have made the prospect of this ambivalence even greater for barrio residents as Pentecostal churches propagate even stricter moral divisions between traditional orthodox Christianity (coded as good) and heterodox or non-Christian, nonascetic religious forms (coded as bad or evil). Mariela's evangelical conversion partly resolved her ambivalence by channeling her experience into definitive orders of good and evil, before and after, right and wrong, solving for her the conflict of transgressing her orthodox values in favor of morally conflicting alternatives. Bourguignon (1952:318–319) understands this resolution in terms of "compartmentalization," a process by which it is possible to accept simultaneously contradictory patterns of belief and behavior without requiring a reorganization of the total patterns of experience and therefore of ultimate meaning. Based on observations she made in Haiti, she argues that individuals exposed to conflicting cultural patterns relegate opposing beliefs to different spheres of life, so that such beliefs are walled off from one another, enabling them to coexist seamlessly without a total upheaval or complete restructuring of an individual's conceptual world. In this case, by rendering her former beliefs as evil rather than "false," Mariela is able to embrace her renewed orthodox convictions and the critical perspective that attends Pentecostal moral asceticism even as she comes to reconcile her ostensibly paradoxical adoption of Dominican *vodú* prior to conversion, all while maintaining an essentially integrated view of the world by consigning her former patrons to the realm of the demonic.[8]

Given the social pressure to conform to normative models of Christian morality and comportment, then, it is far more common to encounter ambivalence than confident certainty apropos of magical acts and the subject of spirit entities, much less the calling of saints and other mysterious powers. This is the case for several reasons. First, the idea that magic and sorcery are entirely negative and antisocial is a view propagated widely by the Catholic Church, not to mention Protestant churches throughout the island. Disdain for sorcery and any cultural heritage attributed to Haiti or Africa is disseminated widely by the popular media. In light of this appraisal, most people, even those who practice sorcery or who frequent these heterodox institutions, are not eager to discuss or to advertise their patronage much less their use of magic or divination largely out of fear that such affiliation carries with it considerable social stigma. This is particularly so among the upper classes, for whom respectability and social distinction are dominant values. For those farther removed from the centers of economic and political privilege, however, the stigma of such beliefs becomes less acute, and the advantages of sorcery may outweigh the demerits of its questionable morality (in relation to Christian orthodoxy, that is). Second, many of the magical practices in the country are imputed negative social value based on their association in the popular imagination with Africa and Haitian religion, which, as we have seen, in Dominican society is opposed to and contrasted with the Dominican national myth of Christian origin, orthodoxy, and fidelity (see chapter 1).[9] In fact, the stigma attached to Dominican *vodú* is so pervasive and insidious that there is no clear broad-reaching benefit to claiming an association with its participants or membership within its ranks. The consistent denial that *bokors* and *mambos* work for anything less than the good or on behalf of the all-powerful Christian God is indicative of this social pressure; this also goes for patrons of these specialists as well as academic commentators concerned with the defense and legitimation of stigmatized religions. According to Deive (1992:211), some *brujos* take offense to the accusation that they practice witchcraft and "vehemently affirm that their gifts have been granted by God and that they heal in his name" (my translation; see also Brodwin 1996:142). The necessity to make assertions like these and to downplay the primacy of sorcery and the summoning and worship of spirit beings reveals the consequences attributable to the dominance of Christian morality in Dominican society and the strides taken to legitimate stigmatized religious practices by insisting on their Christian provenance and publicly declaring their benign intent.

It seems reasonable to assume that the predominance of Catholic identities over Haitian, African, or creole identities in the pantheon of Dominican *vodú* (Deive 1992; Davis 1987; and see Herskovits 1937; Bastide 1971, 1978, on the syncretism of neo-African and creole gods with Catholic saints) is the historical result of Roman Catholic supremacy in the eastern two-thirds of the island and the active derision of all things Haitian while simultaneously fetishizing the purported purity and incontrovertible orthodoxy associated with the Christian tradition. After all, the essential virtuousness of Catholic saints is rarely questioned in popular discourse (putting aside the evangelical critique for the moment) while the provenance, either good or bad, of Barón del Cementerio, Papá Legbá, or Belié Belcán is constantly up for public debate.

Although it seems obvious to me, I want to be clear that while there exists at the level of popular discourse a general condemnation of sorcery and magical practices, particularly those associated with Haitian *vodou* and its Dominican variant, this does not mean that such practices are intrinsically evil or wrong, or that they are in some ways lesser than any other. This also does not mean that there are not people who openly and proudly defend the morality of such practices or benefit greatly from their observance. I only want to point out that under certain constraints that develop within the scope of specific forms of dominancy and historical relations of power, these practices are interpreted in terms of a particular order of values unique to Dominican society and are determined to be good or bad depending on one's investment in that order and relative position within it. The standards of respectability in the Dominican Republic, for example, require that admirable or "serious" Dominican men and women embody Christian ideals and distance themselves from heterodoxy and the much-maligned beliefs and practices associated with the lower classes and neighboring Haiti. This is not to say that wealthy, "respectable" Dominicans do not invest in sorcery or solicit the advice or assistance of *brujos*, only that when they do, it is rarely of public record. Mariela's election to serve the spirits and become a medium herself, while personally empowering and liberating at multiple levels, was also experienced as an undeniable internal conflict because it represented a betrayal of her professed Christian beliefs and an adoption of a perspective she knew to be outside of respectable (or "acceptable") behavior, but regardless, offered the only logical approach available under the circumstances of her situation.

Despite its widespread (if covert) employ and uneasy coexistence alongside Catholicism, the practice of magic, as well as other practices typically associated with Dominican *vodú*, is very much taken to be incongruent with dominant definitions of "proper" Christianity—that which is acknowledged as licit spirituality—in the country. In many ways such practices (including divination and spirit possession) are antithetical to the Christian project as conceived by believers and very much posed in opposition to cultural images associated with the "good Christian" or *"cristiano verdad."* Nonetheless, in spite of its generalized social disdain, the institutions of magic and sorcery within the purview of Dominican *vodú* typically serve the pressing concerns of a largely poor and disenfranchised community, offering accessible solutions to immediate problems of barrio life. Mariela's ambivalence might be understood as a socialized product of the conflict between the demands of her environment and the larger structures of value that disparage magical acts but make them the most likely and accessible means to problem solving available to the poor.

This dynamic recalls the spiritual and cosmological compromises made by enslaved Africans in the New World and the creative strategies employed by blacks and their descendants to adapt their ancestral beliefs to the necessities of life on the plantation by incorporating Christianity, the religion of colonial whites, in imaginative ways to serve their own pressing needs. It has long been noted that practitioners of *vodou* and other African-derived religions are unlikely to see a conflict between their magical beliefs and Christianity (see Powdermaker 1968:286; Genovese 1976:232; Simpson 1978:218; Raboteau 1978:287–288; Chireau 2003:12). This compatibility is a feature that owes its distribution to the uneven exposure of enslaved blacks to Christianity and the irregular adaptation of ancestral beliefs from Africa recuperated in the New World. It seems reasonable to suppose that today beliefs in magic and possession persist alongside Christianity because they serve ends that Christianity cannot, and Christianity closes the void that magic leaves ajar (Raboteau 1978:288). In the Dominican Republic, Christianity, spirit possession, divination, and magic together constitute a complex but interrelated whole within which believers barter spiritual goods and services with the divine and negotiate shared meanings across divides of orthodoxy and heterodoxy in fluid, reciprocal ways.

In acknowledging the efficacy of magic as well as the reality of spirit possession, along with a multitude of other supernatural phenomena, local religions join in their understanding of the basic contours of their shared mystical universe, even if they disagree about the relative virtues of various elements or actors operating within it. Indeed, this is a world of spirits, demons, saints, Jesus Christ, and God Almighty. By subscribing to this reality, residents of Villa consent to being subjects of the same conceptual universe no matter where they may locate themselves within it. Mariela's experience is illustrative of this assent and is a demonstrative case in point: the object of the competitive ire of her husband's lover, she was drawn into a familiar drama that she (although initially resistant) was always already a part of and sought decisive relief in the form of established channels of mystical aid, first as a diviner's client, then as a spirit medium, and finally as a Christian convert. In so doing, she moved with relative ease between three religious traditions often perceived by believers and observers alike to be profoundly dissimilar and irreconcilably opposed. What I hope to show here is that what makes her story coherent, her initiation and subsequent conversion without contradiction (even if characterized by ambivalence), is in fact an agreement of sorts, a shared understanding that joins local religions to one another and facilitates their communion whether in the service of conflict or consensus.

The communication or exchange between religious institutions, each accommodating to one degree or another the presuppositions of the next, makes it possible to be harmed or healed by magic, to be possessed or "mounted" by spirits, or to resist possession through conversion no matter where one is positioned along the religious continuum. This consensus guaranteed that Mariela could be victimized by witchcraft, possessed by spirit beings, cured though spirit-mediumship, and eventually freed by conversion whether she called herself a Catholic, a Pentecostal, or a *bruja*. We ought to ask why any of this should have been possible if she did not believe in these spirit beings to begin with, if she did not wish to become that which she allegedly despised (a *bruja*), and, after becoming a faithful servant of the saints, why conversion would be her only feasible way out. There is nothing obvious or necessary about these outcomes, but what this consensus reveals is a common denominator—a shared grammar of belief—that enables effective communication across diverse religious perspectives, specifically with regard to supernatural cause and effect but also relating diverse cultural forms to one another in a coherent universe whereby each is intereffective and mutually intelligible.

Below I discuss in more detail the conversion exception, an example that elaborates these linkages, and why the hegemony of Christian values in the Dominican setting augments the meaning of evangelical conversion. For the moment, the point I would like to stress might profitably be summarized as follows: because there is consensus, meaningful exchanges occur across divides of religious difference that shape experience in ways that call into question the presumed discreteness and irreconcilability of religious pluralism locally. Their mutual intelligibility enables both conflict and compromise because the terms of their engagement are, essentially, agreed upon from the beginning and follow from shared premises. Ambivalence results from differing moral perspectives within these shared worlds, even while the rules or underlying grammatical principles appear to remain the same for everyone, allowing Christianity and Dominican *vodú* to coexist in relative harmony and for believers who go back and forth across divides of religious difference.

Entangled Institutions: San Miguel Archángel

Mariela's changing conceptions of her ordeal, her shifting ideas about the true nature of the spirit beings in her life, from benign apparitions to powerful saints and spirits, to deceptive and harmful demons, illustrates an important feature of the local religious continuum. No matter what her religious convictions or where she found herself along the continuum, some baseline postulates remained unchanged. While accepting the putative involvement of spirit beings in her life, her perception of their true purpose—not their true existence—changed over time. That is, even after conversion, the spirits she once served, far from disappearing from the scene, continued to be important symbols even as their imputed role and indicative meaning in her life transformed considerably. As a Catholic, the saints were accessible holy intercessors to whom she could address prayers and other special requests. Her initiation into spirit-mediumship meant that many of these same saints, along with other spirit beings, became entities that could be summoned for the purpose of spiritual work and propitiated for gifts and favors. Her conversion to Protestant Christianity represented yet another shift in perspective when the beings she once served were cast anew as Satan's minions, demonic forces sent to lead humankind from salvation. The continuity of her perspective is underscored by her insistence that the demons she confronts today are the very same entities that had once made her sick and the same beings that at one time she dutifully served. Mariela insists that it is she herself who has changed, not the essential reality of the spirit entities, a change that today she credits to conversion and the transformative role of the Holy Spirit in her life.

Mariela's spiritual transformations followed from her changing attitude with regard to spirit beings in her life and her evolving relationship with them. While her immediate needs, circumstances, and desires changed over time, the spirit figures themselves remained a constant instrumental feature and continue to be useful cultural symbols upon which to record and express her evolving religious ideas today.

To better clarify this dynamic of diversity and coherency representative of religious pluralism in the neighborhood and in order to better grasp Mariela's religious career and her shifting perspective with regard to the supernatural, particularly as one very much coordinated by Christian hegemony, consider the varying local perspectives on the popular spirit figure San Miguel Archángel.

San Miguel is at once venerated and served by devotees, solicited and propitiated by Catholics, and opposed, feared, and exorcised by Pentecostals. His symbolism and mythology are both shared and contested across the local religious spectrum. Who is San Miguel really, and who gets to decide are contentious issues that are played out in everyday negotiations between believers invested in one or another interpretation: San Miguel as saint, *misterio*, or demon. Who is San Miguel is a question whose answer depends, of course, on whom you ask. For Catholics, he is a charitable benevolent saint representative of spiritual strength who may be petitioned to intercede on behalf of parishioners for assistance or auspicious blessings. For others, he is a powerful saint or *misterio* frequently coupled or associated with Belié Belcán, his alter ego, who may be called into the head of a medium or manifest himself in the flesh of a devotee. Summoned to solve any manner of concern, San Miguel is an important spiritual figure in the pantheon of Dominican *vodú*. For Pentecostals and other evangelical Protestant groups, he is regarded as a "terrible demon" who "likes to fight." Perceived as disingenuous and unambiguously evil, he is thought to wear the mask of saintly virtue but not to embody it—to be sure, a deceptive move said to conceal his truly wicked intentions and unscrupulous ways. The demons, it is said, take biblical names in order to mislead the people; San Miguel has come to represent for local Pentecostals the sinfulness of the profane world and the trickery of demonic forces that conspire to lead them astray.

The local debate over San Miguel, like the apparent disagreement between religions in the neighborhood, is not over his power or influence, over his existence, or even over many of his personal attributes; rather, the dispute coalesces around his moral identity and whether he represents good, evil, or something in between. For Catholics, he is the epitome of goodness. As a saint he represents exceptional virtue and the highest degree of holiness. He is the object of appeals because of his achievement of righteousness and proximity to God the Father. As already discussed, for Protestants in the neighborhood, and in particular Pentecostals, he is the personification of evil, a demonic spirit to be exorcised and resisted. When he manifests in the Pentecostal church, he does so in a demonic trance performance not unlike any other malefic unsolicited spirit possession, except in this case the personality of the intruding spirit claims to be a saint. Somewhere in the middle are those who consider San Miguel to be morally ambiguous or mostly good but certainly capable of causing harm should the situation warrant. For those who summon San Miguel, he is a special kind of saint, sometimes represented by Belié Belcán, but he is certainly not identified as a demon.[10] His good works far outweigh his temperament or volatility. It must be acknowledged, however, that even for his devotees he is not unambiguously virtuous. San Miguel, in this setting, wields a machete and enjoys smoking cigars and drinking rum (the principal accouterment given to his "horse" upon his bidden arrival to the ceremonial stage), and if angered he may exact punitive reprisals against his very own servants. It is possible too that he might be called for wicked ends depending on the temperament of the summoner or the work needed to be done. In light of this, San Miguel, despite how much love and devotion he receives from his devotees, is likely neither the picture of sanctity, as he is for Catholics, nor the paragon of evil he represents for Pentecostal Christians, but instead a being basically good but capable of both harming and healing depending on the situation. Thus, in this sense he is considered "amoral" (Lemus and Marty 2010:53), modeling not the sharp dualities characteristic of Christianity but rather the fluid African-derived perceptions of the spirit world as neither essentially good nor essentially evil.

These three different perspectives on San Miguel are not only indicative of three predominant religious orientations in Villa but also show the shared symbolic but contested moral aspects of the principal cosmology organizing religious conviction in the barrios. In each instance San Miguel, a readily accessible symbol, is an important icon taken under revision by religious actors attempting to harness spiritual power and legitimacy. The fact that San Miguel is originally a Catholic symbol is not insignificant and hints further at the sometimes strident attempts to claim, control, and define the scope of Christian authority across Dominican religious communities. In taking him to represent Christian perfection, Catholics employ San Miguel as a model of holiness and spiritual strength. His inversion in Pentecostal Christianity might be interpreted as a native critique of Catholicism: relegating his worship to that of idols and graven images, the rejection of saintly authority is simultaneously a refutation of Catholic spiritual hierarchies and the legitimacy claims of an entrenched priesthood. And, for their part, his creolized appropriation in Dominican *vodú* can be understood as a subaltern attempt to bring Christian authority under unregulated popular control. Putting the divine to work for the marginal and less powerful is an age-old story; by appropriating symbols of spiritual power, the Dominican poor take possession, so to speak, of religious authority and put it to work for their own goals and religious projects.

San Miguel is an important figure in the Dominican Republic because he is reckoned across the religious spectrum as a diverse idiom of good, evil, danger, and protection, and serves as an important moral signpost in a diverse religious cosmos. He is, after all, a Christian symbol, Catholic in origin, and in his varied expressions locally, represents the diverse challenges and concessions to Christian domination engineered by creative believers in search of spiritual power despite their structural subordination. As a local manifestation of religious enthusiasm rousing both positive and negative responses, San Miguel offers a unique vantage from which to read the local politics of religious difference and the remarkable dynamic of a shared but contested spiritual terrain.

Spiritual Differentiation and Religious Identity

Largely what differentiates individual believers in the neighborhood then is not a rigid division between religious identities or conflicting worldviews but rather a difference in moral perspective on the enchanted environment in which they live. With this understood, it is easier to see how relatively effortless it was for Mariela to move across the religious spectrum—from Catholicism, to Dominican *vodú*, and then to Pentecostalism—with no significant disequilibrium; at the same time, it begins to clarify her ambivalence, which follows from a moral conflict—not a logical one—regarding her religious decisions. As her opinion regarding beings like San Miguel changed, and with it her religious commitments, in her mind her fundamental Christian beliefs remained intact; indeed, in her mind she was always a Christian, just a better or worse one at different times. As we learn in chapter 4, conversion in the barrio does not necessarily mean "believing" something new—it means "being" or "acting different." Instead of adopting an entirely new identity, belief system, or theology, Mariela might better be understood as having adapted her perspective at different times within a relatively well defined cosmology inclusive of local religion and characterized by Christian domination. Herein we see the relationship of unity-in-plurality evident in the supernatural universe of the barrio: San Miguel is a demonstrative example of this as he is an intelligible and adaptable symbol to all believers in the neighborhood, even while his moral identity is rendered differentially, but we could just as easily have explored the Bible or some other important shared element of the religious field and come to similar conclusions.[11]

Despite her experience within three apparently distinct religious traditions, Mariela remained, in her estimation, a Christian throughout, just in her mind a better or worse one over time. Her insistence that she continued to be a Christian the whole time is consistent with identifications with the Christian church at all levels of popular religion in the neighborhood. Whether believers attend Mass, summon *seres*, or join a Protestant congregation, they often do not cease to see themselves as faithful Christians of one kind or another. This is not to say that her Christian beliefs had not changed over time; they certainly did. Rather, the issue is that no matter what she believed, her convictions were profoundly shaped by a dominant

Christian ethic she felt compelled to obey in conjunction with a consistent self-identification as a "Christian believer."

Mariela's experience and the nuances of her account can challenge our assumptions about religious difference locally, particularly as it relates to the experience of complementary and conflicting perspectives on the spirit world, and may help cast an interpretive light on the sometimes curious shades of religious accommodation and minutiae of religious identity, especially in this part of the world where, at least since the modern era, religious life has followed from an intimate bricolage of traditions and putative clash of cultures (see Mintz 1989; Smith 1960, 1965). Mariela does not, for one, consider these perspectives as if they were separate, discrete modules of belief. She sees them as more or less better or worse ways of being Christian. Very few others believe differently, which is why so few terms exist locally to refer to Dominican *vodú* and its heterodox practitioners.[12] Instead, believers approach the religious continuum as if it were a single integrated whole characterized by a plethora of differing moral positions within a largely Christian universe. The logical paradox of having to "choose to believe" is, at least in Mariela's case, rendered immaterial by the simple fact that her religious "choices" were hardly choices (in a strict sense) at all: the dynamic relations of exchange propelled her from one end of the spectrum to the other thanks to forces compelled not by economic rationale (or "rational choice" for that matter) but by the logic of everyday practice in the context of culture, power, and history that determined the shape and possible range of her religious elections as well as their frequency and duration. The differences between Catholicism, Pentecostalism, and Dominican *vodú* were not the impetus for her movement between them, nor was a "rational" evaluation of their comparative costs and benefits; rather, it appears more likely that it was their common links and correspondences, their entwined cultural logics that drove and ordered her evolving religious identity as a different kind of Christian subject across a familiar and intimate spectrum of belief and identity.

Consider the simple ethnographic fact that Catholicism proper or "being Catholic" is not what distinguishes a *vodou* priest from a lay parishioner; it is largely, rather, their diverse views regarding, and alternative ritual orientation toward, the saints and other spirit actors. People involved in propitiating or calling the saints in Dominican *vodú* do so as Catholics; many are in fact fiercely Catholic and carry out all of the sacraments and adhere to even the most minor and routine observances. As it was explained to me, because the saints come from the Catholic Church, in order to serve them properly one must be a Catholic and worship in the Catholic Church. Catholic liturgy, symbolism, and iconography complement ritual work within Dominican *vodú* and sustain its spiritual efficacy.[13] Examples of this include Catholic prayers (*oraciónes, promesas,* psalms from the Bible, and so forth) used to invoke spirits, cast spells, make special requests, et cetera, and certain Catholic rituals like the *novena,* which are done in order to obtain special favors from the *misterios* (Deive 1992). With little doubt, Catholicism is an integral feature of any *vodú* ritual. In Haiti, Métraux recorded a similar sentiment expressed by a peasant farmer who stated frankly: "To serve the *lwa* you have to be a Catholic" (Métraux 1972:323). And, in practice, even de Heusch (1989) concedes that believers are baptized and participate in Catholic masses without any paradox or contradiction. The same, more or less, is true for the Dominican Republic: in order to serve the saints or *misterios,* one must be a Catholic (Deive 1992:211; Miniño 1985:38). This basic native truism is underscored by the fact that in order to be baptized into her role as spirit medium and prepared to serve the saints, Mariela had to be initiated at the basilica in Higüey—arguably the most important Catholic pilgrimage site in the entire country.[14]

The degree to which Dominican *vodú* represents a distinct religious institution is a question of definition and depends upon somewhat arbitrary boundary formation, categorization, and reification. We could, of course, imagine a closed system of beliefs, a unique institution defined by specific tenets and practices and call it Dominican *vodú*; several observers have done just that. While attempting to legitimize widely disparaged practices by insisting on their qualification as a "religion" and not a "cult" or simply an amalgam of magical beliefs or superstitions, many well-meaning commentators have assigned system and structure (fixed practices, rules, identifications, and so forth) where little have ever truly existed. Owing to its regional variation and popular participation, no set rules, centralized authority, or static doctrine obtains in the practice of Dominican *vodú*, in some cases making it difficult to determine, for example, exactly where the practice of popular Catholicism ends and where that of *vodú* begins.[15] Given this uncertainty, Mariela's story seems to take on even more interpretive utility as we see that she was never asked to assimilate an entirely new worldview or theology, but rather she took up practices already very much a part of her religious and cultural horizon, only appearing to change her perspective within it at different points in time.

Another important point that must be made is that unlike Christian orthodoxy, Dominican *vodú* is not antisyncretic. Because the complex is flexible, inclusive, and highly adaptive—qualities characteristic of creole religions—many practitioners view their participation in *vodú* rites as merely a practical extension of their Catholic beliefs—in a sense, nothing more than ancillary spiritual activities that supplement their formal religious commitments.[16] In this way, believers do not see how their magical practices contradict their Catholic identity. In the church, believers of all kinds ally themselves with an institution providing them a moral community beside a shared identity with an authorized religion.

While Catholicism is an inextricable component of *vodú* practice, especially in the Dominican Republic where saints rather than their creole counterparts predominate, Protestantism is conspicuously set apart from it. While being a Catholic is a prerequisite to serving the *misterios*, being a Protestant is a fundamental disqualification. This rule is observed internally, of course, by Pentecostals (they are prohibited from calling spirits, building altars, or performing magical rites); even so, perhaps more unexpectedly, it is also observed by the *vodú* priests and priestesses, who for the most part ignore or otherwise avoid going to Protestant churches and who concede the incompatibility of their convictions with the gospel as it is preached by local pastors. In practice, this means that spirit mediums do not pay Protestants much mind at all, and, for the most part, both groups keep a safe distance from each other. One is repeatedly assured in evangelical circles that *"los brujos no van a la iglesia"* ("witches/sorcerers don't go to the [Protestant] church"). So taken for granted is this axiom that conversion in the community has become institutionalized such that it represents an effective escape from unwanted spirit possession and compulsory service to the saints of Dominican *vodú*.

Leaving the Spirits Behind

In Pentecostal and other evangelical churches, men and women have found refuge from malicious or taxing spirits and demons (Métraux 1972; Meyer 1999). People convert for a variety of reasons, but illness, dissatisfaction, and misfortune figure heavily in cases involving conversion due to witch-craft or spirit possession. In Mariela's case, it was her only viable option to break free of her ritual obligations and the oath she swore to serve the saints. Indeed, across the island conversion to Protestantism is viewed as a highly effective (often cited as the *only* effective) way out of this relation-ship, an exception providing what Métraux has described in Haiti as a "shel-ter" or "magic circle, where people cannot be got at by *lwa* and demons" (1972:352). The saying among *vodou* practitioners of Haiti is: "If you want the *lwa* to leave you in peace—become a Protestant" (Métraux 1972:352).[17] Métraux proposed long ago that many *vodou* practitioners converted to Protestant churches, not because *vodou* failed to meet their needs of a more "legitimate" or "loftier" religion but rather because Protestantism offered sanctuary from angry or spiteful spirits (1972:351–352). Very much paral-leling Mariela's reasons for converting, Métraux tells the story of a *vodou* priest who converted because he could no longer satisfy the demands of his *lwa*, who demanded offerings and sacrifices that depleted his resources and extended him well beyond his means (1972:354). Interesting still, Mé-traux (1972:352) reports that sometimes it is even the *vodou* priest himself, faced with the ineffectiveness of his treatment and unable to solve his pa-tient's problem, who advises his client to abandon the spirits and to "try Protestantism."

Yielding to evangelical exceptionalism leads to my final question: why does conversion represent an acceptable, indeed, conventional way out? To be certain, several exit strategies exist, but few are considered to be as ef-fective or as permanent a solution as Protestant conversion, here exempli-fied by the Pentecostal church because of its reputation for being the most austere of the Christian denominations.[18] Intriguingly, conversion here is an authorized exemption consented to by *vodou* priests themselves and some-times even prescribed to clients! In the context of Pentecostal conversion, the exception makes perfect sense: it is an act of denying or rejecting the profane world and of accepting a new life in Jesus Christ, a resolution to live a life apart from one's previous affairs "in the world." But there is no obvious reason why conversion should be respected by *mambos* and *bokors* or even acquiesced to by the saints and spirits themselves, who are left behind in the wake of a convert's sometimes abrupt and apparently always antagonizing retreat.

Protestant conversion angers the spirits. According to Mariela, even though joining the church meant that they could no longer possess her, no longer "mount" her, they turned against her, fought with her constantly; they even torment her today. In this way, conversion is not a total or complete immunity or stepping out. In fact, there are two important ways in which in practice it is the opposite: the spirits remain influential figures in the life of a convert as prominent agents in the spiritual war for salvation; and converts must accept the conditions of conversion such that if they fail to meet the expectations of the faithful, they are rendered vulnerable to satanic powers and the threat of returning to a life of sin. This means that if they do not effect a "true" conversion—if they do not complete a sincere transformation by committing themselves wholly to the service of Jesus Christ and Jesus Christ alone—they run the risk of falling victim to the spirit beings they formerly betrayed.

The spirits are a jealous lot and are angered by affronts such as conversion. They are known for taking brutal retribution against those who have offended them, and their anger is blamed for bad luck, illness, and even the death of family members as a result of leaving their side (see Métraux 1972:355 for a number of examples in the Haitian context). In Mariela's case, desirous of her downfall, the spirits are held responsible for "making war" with her. While today the seres-cum-demons can no longer possess her, they continue to play a pivotal role as demonic adversaries in her new life as a Pentecostal convert. Now as demonic beings, they function as symbols of her evolving faith and constant struggle to remain true to God and to her reformed Christian identity. Recall that Mariela claims to have had more experiences with the beings *after* her conversion than she did before, stressing the reciprocal relations of meaning uniting Pentecostals with their surrounding cultural environment despite their otherwise oppositional, competitive orientation. Just as Pentecostals look to step out of el *mundo* to renounce the secular world in favor of a spiritual path with God, in many ways they are drawn deeper into it, locked in a spiritual battle for the souls of the living against the forces of evil embodied by local spirits and those who revere them.

In this way, Pentecostals do their part to reinforce and enliven indigenous cosmologies even as they work to malign them. This idea was smartly explored by both Conway (1980) in Haiti and Meyer (1999) in Ghana; Conway goes as far as to suggest that "no one in Haitian communities proclaims more publicly the existence and power of the *loua* and of other Vodoun forces than do the Protestants" (1980:12–13). The reinvigoration of local spirits through the process of demonization is a noted feature of Pentecostalism globally. Robbins (2004a) observes that a distinct characteristic of Pentecostal cultural change is that it preserves that which it breaks from through continued ritual engagement with the native spirit world. Thus, Pentecostal culture is preservative inasmuch as it is transformative—although it insists on new moral orientations, Pentecostalism adopts local culture in such a flexible manner as to maintain, and in some cases even empower, traditional spirits and indigenous cosmologies.

Synergy in a Plural Religious Field

The threat of demonic influence and the power of local spirits require that evangelical converts live ascetic spiritual lives apart. Mariela's fidelity to Jesus Christ and promise of salvation depend upon her ability to remain vigilant in her quest to stay faithful. She is constantly at risk of being thwarted if she is not careful and by chance separates herself again from God and returns to the fold of the profane world of *el mundo*. She is obliged to abide without exception by the rules and expectations of the church that provide her only refuge. Should she backslide or be remiss in her observance of the church's prohibitions, she concedes that her conditional sanctuary will be compromised and her immunity from the spirits rendered void. This goes to show that her perception of her ordeal is incorporative and holistic, a fact that underscores the principle of unity synchronizing religious pluralism in Villa. Despite proclamations to live lives spiritually apart, Pentecostal daily life very much conditions and is conditioned by the surrounding environment and the spiritual worlds within and alongside which they operate, influencing as much as influenced by the nation's ancestral religious traditions, Catholicism and Dominican *vodú*.

For some time observers have acknowledged the shared cosmological aspects of popular religion: in the Dominican Republic (Davis 1987:57), in Haiti and its diaspora (Mintz 1989:269; Brodwin 1996; Rey and Stepick 2013), and in America's other African American religious domains (Chireau 2003:44–45). Dominican popular religion is inclusive, having incorporated African-derived beliefs, Catholicism, and Haitian *vodou* as well as elements of indigenous and other religions (including Espiritismo [Patín Veloz 1975:142]), and, of course, Protestantism. The assumption for a long time has been that the ancestral religions of the island were the only relevant mixing parties, but it is clear today that Protestantism has become a prominent feature of Dominican popular religion in undeniably meaningful ways above and beyond the sizable number of its participants nationally. Despite Pentecostal Christianity's oppositional discourse and ritualization of difference (see chapter 4), its relationship to local culture is entangled and complex, demonstrating processes of continuity no less than discontinuity with the traditional such that its relationship with Catholicism and *vodú* is better characterized by a positive and negative synergy of sorts, mutual influence and multiple intersections more than any state of temporalizing difference (see Lindhardt 2009 for how he relates this idea to African popular religion). Far from upsetting the cosmic order of things, conversion in fact confirms it through a synergistic incorporation of traditional Dominican cosmologies.

Religions, of course, are rarely if ever homogeneous bounded wholes, hermetically sealed off from external stimuli and the inevitable possibility of change. It is clear that what amounts to religion in Dominican barrios is a complex plural amalgam that cannot be viewed as simply a mix of Catholicism and African-derived religion without erasing one of the most relevant Christian identities available to believers in the country—Protestantism and its popular evangelical forms. To describe Dominican popular religion without reference to evangelical Protestantism ignores the basic reality of religious life on ground and the empirical relations of dependent meaning across faiths as they are experienced, practiced, and negotiated by regular believers.

Conclusion

I propose that the conversion exception here should be understood within the context of a shared spiritual universe where the Protestant gospel, particularly as it is realized in the Pentecostal church, has come to represent, based on its emphasis on a world-rejecting theology and promotion of discontinuity and symbolic rupture with the past (Robbins 2003b, 2004a), a domain of spiritual immunity acknowledged to be as important for Christian converts as it is for the broader religious community where such exceptions are legitimated through passive or frank acceptance. It is equally important that Pentecostals and other Protestant denominations have drawn on the authority of Christian orthodoxy to realize this exception in practice and insist that conversion be recognized as an exceptional spiritual calling offering protection from spiteful spirits and the formal ritual obligations to serve them.

The exceptionalism granted to Protestant conversion is based on the perception that individuals who commit their lives to Jesus Christ—and Jesus Christ alone—are protected from the compelling reach of the local spirit world so long as they live a reformed ascetic life committed to a born-again lifestyle. This concession occurs on Pentecostals' own terms, including the demanding requirement that converts dedicate themselves fully to this austere form of penitent Christianity. Capitalizing on dominant cultural values that privilege religious purity and a conservative form of Christian orthodoxy, Protestant groups, with Pentecostals taking the lead, have assumed a role as flag-bearers of Christian authority based on their strict interpretation of the Bible and unwavering performance of its moral directives. The sometimes vague relationship between Catholicism and Dominican *vodú* is seized upon by the evangelical community as "proof" of the national church's dubious claim to Christian authority. The very fact that many Catholics participate in *vodú* ceremonies, consult diviners, and cultivate relationships with *misterios* is exactly that which is turned against them by their Protestant critics, who treat this ambiguity as evidence of spiritual poverty and moral decadence. The Pentecostal church, along with other Protestant denominations, has proffered its own teachings as examples of true Christianity in opposition to Catholicism, which it portrays as tainted illicit beliefs marred by magical practices and idol worship.

Pentecostal conversion is a regular feature of religious life in the barrio today and demonstrates a unique connection with indigenous cosmologies and local forms of religious practice. The conversion exception illustrates a compelling compromise between apparently divergent, opposing institutions and the integration of Protestant cultural logics within traditional Dominican culture. Indeed, the exception would not exist without the acknowledgment of outsiders, those against whom Pentecostals look to compare themselves.

Furthermore, the conversion exception follows from the local acknowledgment of Christianity broadly as an institution of definitive moral and spiritual authority. To state this is not to claim the essential illegitimacy of Dominican *vodú* or other heterodox religious forms but to acknowledge their situation within a set of power relations that have a profound effect on how religious actors view, call upon, relate to, and receive their co-constructed spiritual world. The idea that local spirits become powerless to possess a true Christian convert indicates, at least in theory, a cultural logic that defers to Christian hegemony. The exception is spurred by a hierarchy of Christian values that places the ultimate service to God, among the most admirable of spiritual goals, squarely within notions of Christian orthodoxy championed not, curiously, by the Catholic church, but instead by the Protestant evangelical "sects" represented by the local Pentecostal church.

Of course with hegemony there is always counterhegemony; resistance to Christian domination and alternatives to orthodox morality abound despite the churches' sizable reach. Christian supremacy is not totalizing here, but for reasons discussed above, has unquestionably made its mark on the tenor of the religious environment. "Hidden transcripts" (Scott 1990) embedded in the ritual performance, magic, and folklore of Dominican *vodú* empower the dispossessed to critique hegemony off stage behind the backs of power-holders even while Christian authority is almost always conceded openly and publicly. Burton (1997) has proposed that creole cultures, by dint of their very "creoleness," cannot get entirely outside of the dominant system in order to effectively resist it. Dominican *vodú*'s imbrication with Catholicism reinforces the underlying structure of Christian domination even as it visibly looks to challenge it. Believers cannot get completely outside of the hegemony of Christian values that to this point have so effectively been asserted as *the* moral exemplar at the expense of other alternatives.

Consider one final example of how Protestant conversion has become that exemplar, even for many Catholics. Another remarkable node of correspondence between these ostensibly distinct traditions, and a point that further highlights the apparent spiritual authority of local evangelical religion, are the commonplace Catholic vows called *promesas*, which are sometimes fulfilled by converting to Protestant Christianity. A *promesa* is a Catholic vow made to God or a saint to carry out an act of devotion if and when a request, made along with the vow, is fulfilled. The vow enters the believer into a contractual agreement with the divine. If a person makes a *promesa* and the request is not fulfilled, the vow is annulled, and the pledged act need not be completed. A believer may enter into a *promesa* in order to secure a job, to cure a sick family member, or maybe just to see a long-lost relative; one can do a *promesa* for just about anything. Common *promesas* are pledges to make a pilgrimage to a holy site, to fast for a given period of time, or to pray for the duration of a promised number of days. Most interesting, however, it is also common for people to take an oath to convert to Protestantism as payment for a favor or request that was fulfilled by the divine patron. At least several members of Iglesia Evangélica Pentecostal and Iglesia de Dios converted under exactly these circumstances. A *promesa* made with a vow to convert communicates the intention of a votary to commit himself or herself to a dedicated spiritual calling, itself fulfilled only by membership in a Protestant church. This curious intersection of Protestant and Catholic faiths is a concrete example of reciprocity across religious boundaries and another good indicator of how Pentecostalism has been able to establish itself as a premier Christian church for believers in the barrios as an exceptional act of Christian devotion. Added to that, recognition of the authority of genuine conversion is a powerful reinforcement of Christian cultural hegemony.

Even in recognizing this authority, however, it is not a complete submission to it, as the saints and *misterios* continue to influence converts and to impose their divine will. To be sure, in any context of domination there is resistance to be found. In accepting the conversion escape, *bokors* and *mambos* are not endorsing Protestantism, nor are they conceding that their beliefs and ritual practices are inferior; instead, what it demonstrates is a compromise of sorts, evidence of a shared religious experience within which everyone agrees at least implicitly to participate and to be subject to the same rules, under the condition that evangelicals live up to their side of the bargain—that is, that they step out of the world completely and live spiritual lives apart from the rest of society. They accept, just as Pentecostals recognize the power of the *seres* to threaten their salvation, that the church wields a kind of meaningful Christian authority that must be respected, at times acquiesced to no matter the vagaries of one's faith.

An apt metaphor for this situation might be that of a soccer match where two teams that have very different styles of play and competitive objectives agree to conduct themselves, at the very least, in accordance with a basic set of rules in order to ensure that a coherent and fair "contest" will take place. Within the rules of the game, anything goes, and each team is permitted to play or compete as it wishes granted that such play follows within the permissible limits of the contest and the established conditions of competition. The social and cultural expression of spirit possession and witchcraft constitute such rules, as does the conversion exception discussed above. Without this implicit agreement, magic and possession would have no significant power or effect and would cease to be relevant after conversion, and evangelical identity would carry with it little significance to nonbelievers. Conversion would be fruitless if it could not fulfill its most basic promise; conversion is transformative renewal, or it is nothing. It is precisely because of this consensus that Pentecostal identity can truly become what it purports to be and sorcerers can affect the world through magic rituals, and saints and spirits alike can influence the living. Just as *bokors* and *mambos* empower evangelical Christianity every time they acknowledge its exceptional status in the barrio, Pentecostal Christians enliven creole magic while empowering local spirit entities every time they attribute illness, bad luck, or demonic possession to the saints and *misterios* of the local pantheons.

We cannot assume that such a condition exists everywhere or even elsewhere. I think about the religious panoply in the United States and imagine that similar concord does not—in fact, cannot—exist across the religious spectrum. The predominance of Christian cultural values in the Dominican barrio has provided a language of unity, a standard about which people agree to aspire but which they vary greatly on how to achieve. Mariela's story is one that bears out this tension, foregrounding the logic of religious affiliation, conflict, and agreement in the Dominican Republic.

I have set out to show that while these diverse religious institutions are at times hostile toward one another and divided along complex moral axes, they thrive in symbiotic relation to one another with permeable, indefinite boundaries. As Dominican *vodú* was forged with and against Catholicism, and the popular expression of Catholicism was forged in the pestle and mortar of Dominican culture, politics, and history, so too Protestantism has grown alongside Dominican religious diversity such that an incorporated religious world both made and was made by religious actors moving back and forth and between affiliations rendered mutually intelligible by their intersecting commonalities.

There is a surprising amount of synergy in the religious field, and it would be hasty to suggest that the popularity of Pentecostal Christianity in the barrios is based on its exceptional status alone. Chapter 7 considers in detail what is given up by converts, so much in fact that in some cases it is difficult to find a satisfactory compensatory explanation for conversion. As Mariela is careful to point out, the exceptional status she enjoys is conditional upon her continued fidelity to Jesus Christ and sincere commitment to the gospel, stipulations that require constant effort. Her conversion is a vow like any other, an agreement with God that she will commit herself wholly in exchange for salvation, but if she slips up or backslides, she will give up her immunity and lose her exceptional status.

There is another lesson here as well: for individuals to have meaningful conflict over spiritual matters, they have to share, to one degree or another, basic assumptions in order to translate certain ideas so that they become meaningful to one another. San Miguel is an example of this as he plays a role for every believer in the neighborhood; whether that role is defined as good or evil depends on one's perspective, but in any case his influence is taken for granted. He cannot be approached in a vacuum, but always as part of a totality. To borrow an example from Crick (1976:116, quoted in Stewart 1991:15):

> The identity "witch" is only one on a [chess]board which contains other persons with differently specified characteristics. Moreover, this one system intersects with others—with concepts of human actions, evaluatory ideas, and other systems of beliefs. We could say that to tackle "witchcraft" as if it were an isolable problem would be like someone unfamiliar with the game of chess, observing a series of movements and writing a book on "bishops." The point is that the "bishop" cannot be understood apart from—indeed exists only by virtue of—the whole system of definitions and rules which constitutes chess. In Saussurian terms, the value of the bishop (or witch) derives from all the other pieces which the bishop (or witch) is not. Neither has any significance in isolation.

I consider this insight to be crucial in comprehending form and function in the religious realm along with the patterns of signification that animate religious identities. It is especially relevant for grasping the place of Pentecostals in the plural religious context of the barrio discussed here. For example, the Pentecostal pastor and the *brujo*, while distinguishable cultural figures in their own right, operate in relation to one another and other religious experts within a cultural field informed by myriad spiritual practices, values, and convictions. The same goes for other religious identities whose meaning in the local spiritual economy can only be read in relation to other religious subjectivities. Catholicism "means" something in Villa only insofar as it is understood in relation to Protestantism, Dominican *vodú*, and so forth. Correspondence between distinct faiths enables a kind of religious conversation that amounts to something of a linguistic metaphor: while cultural forms vary across the continuum at the "sentence level," an underlying structure or "grammar" ensures intelligibility and shared meanings throughout. Disagreement and conflict may occur at the surface or sentence level; however, it never truly threatens the grammatical structure or meaning of religious conversation because the underlying rules remain the same for all believers.

By considering the religious field as a whole, rather than training the analytic lens solely on a particular tradition with potentially arbitrary religious boundaries, we can better conceptualize the spiritual in Villa as believers do—as a total universe, a coherent whole within which believers are differentially motivated but similarly governed by a shared vision of the supernatural and its assumptions.

Christians Apart

Being and Becoming Pentecostal

This chapter is about the process of being and becoming Pentecostal and the specific ways in which converts negotiate evangelical identity on the ground. Over the following pages I explore the folk construction of *cristiano* as a public category of personhood and consider the practical strategies Pentecostals use to claim an orthodox or "true" Christian status. By looking specifically at the meanings that people attach to being Christian converts and by locating exactly how those meanings are mobilized for the validation (or rejection) of others, I outline a politics of Christian identity crucial to the practice of Dominican Pentecostalism in the urban barrio.

Fundamental to the politics of Christian identity for Dominican Pentecostals is the importance of conversion (and adult baptism), testimony, and the satisfaction of behavioral norms or prohibitions—what we might consider pivotal expressive genres indexing the key notions of transformation and discontinuity at the core of Pentecostal cultural frameworks (see Martin 1990:163; Robbins 2004a:127–130). Popular evangelical identity is defined locally by commitment to strict moral precepts that distinguish between those Christians who have converted and those who have not (for more on Pentecostalism's emphasis on ascetic moralism, see Austin-Broos 1997; Brodwin 2003; Robbins 2004a). Failure to uphold the strict moral requirements of the faith and to fully satisfy the behavioral standards expected of "serious" *cristianos* will jeopardize the fragile legitimacy converts work so hard to establish within their local communities. Pentecostals must continuously reaffirm their piety by substantiating their claims to sanctity as part of realizing an exceptional status. It is not enough to make a profession of faith on its own; Pentecostals are required to "act as Christians should" so that others might confirm the sincerity of their convictions and certify their spiritual transformation as genuine.

As such, Pentecostalism in Villa is social and public in ways that show conversion here has more to do with the public performance of piety than with private conviction. On the one hand, Pentecostalism emphasizes inward, personal transformation alongside individual commitment to faith through conversion, ascetic self-discipline, and prayer; on the other hand, in order to confirm the sincerity of their conviction, in order to be recognized as true men and women of God, converts in Villa must successfully convince others of the genuineness of their spiritual transformation through physical enactments of piety (before their congregations in order to be baptized as well as before their neighbors in order to be acknowledged as spiritual leaders and respected as Christian authorities). In this chapter I advance the argument that the core of Dominican Pentecostalism in urban barrios is the *performance* of piety, not personal conviction or belief per se. Converts ultimately constitute themselves as exceptional Christians, or Christians apart, through public rituals of personal affirmation—namely, the interrelated conventions of conversion (and adult baptism), testimony, and the observance of behavioral prohibitions.[1] Because being Christian in the context of the barrio is a continual process that is mediated publicly, and because it renders the rewards of fidelity based on a tenuous achieved status that must be renewed regularly, the role of personal belief or conviction becomes subordinate to the proper performance of piety and the successful courting of public approval. This chapter theorizes Pentecostal ritual practice as projects of identity formation that precede conviction and make belief possible but not necessary.

Who Are the *Cristianos*?

If you go to any barrio in the country and ask about the *cristianos*, you will be understood as inquiring about the *evangélicos*, or Protestant Christians, in the neighborhood.[2] In the Dominican Republic, the term "*cristiano*," or "Christian," is reserved in popular speech for Protestants, most of whom are evangelical and, as is common in most barrios, more often than not members of the Pentecostal community. This convention is hardly unique to Villa or the country as a whole; similar colloquialisms are applied to Protestant groups throughout the Americas, including parts of the United States. To be clear, the term for "Christian" is infrequently used in the Dominican Republic to describe Catholics. In fact, the term "*cristiano*" is by and large set in opposition to that of "*católico*," which in this context refers just as often to a cultural identity as it does to any specific religious membership or conviction.[3] For many in the country, being Catholic has little to do with actually practicing Catholicism (attending Mass or partaking in Roman Catholic sacraments). It is common, for instance, for people to consider themselves Catholic without having stepped foot in a church or to have demonstrated any fidelity to Catholic customs or devotional practices. The successful appropriation of the term "Christian" by so-called upstart Protestant *sectas* looking to reform (or to "save" in emic terms) the population from the ground up is noteworthy for what it says about how Pentecostals have claimed legitimacy in historically Catholic countries, and in particular in the Dominican Republic, where evangelical forms of Christianity are considered by many to be the favored route to spiritual redemption.

To be sure, a *cristiano*, in the main, is a certain type of Christian. Reserved for those who act a particular way, the term has come to denote Christians who have set themselves apart from the rest through conversion, a "good testimony," and the satisfaction of behavioral prohibitions. *Cristianos* are recognized for how they carry themselves in public—for how they act—not necessarily because they are known to proselytize in the streets or are known to be members of a congregation. Insofar as Pentecostals are distinguished by the performative demands of their faith and their attempts to achieve sanctity, they are known more for what they do (testify, preach, and so forth) and for what they are prohibited from doing (drink, gamble, and so forth) than for any specific tenets of faith or, more frankly, for what they believe.

There is a general sense in Villa, and perhaps nationally even a consensus, that Christians of all kinds, ideally, believe in the same sorts of things—after all, they share the same book and pray to the same God. Doctrinal differences between denominations become salient to followers and the local community only to the degree that they are lived by believers. This is evident in the fact that few converts record significant differences between themselves and members of other Protestant churches.[4] Differences in Christian faith are underscored by differences in ritual observances and the alternative application of biblical teachings to the practice of everyday life. If belief in the divinity of Jesus Christ along with other basic tenets of the church is ubiquitous among Christians everywhere, then differentiation between them occurs not on the plane of theology or personal conviction so much as on the field of embodied practices and the performative execution of diverse religious perspectives. This is especially the case for Christians in the barrio, where believers vary greatly in their understanding of the theological tenets of their chosen faith. Pragmatically, then, Christians in Villa are distinguished day to day not by *what* they believe but by *how* they believe. *What* they believe is a more or less standard account of the Christian Gospels, but *how* they practice or embody those beliefs differs greatly between them. In fact, these are crucial matters day to day: if believers light candles to *la Virgen* (like Catholics) or shout prayers to Jesus at the top of their lungs (like Pentecostals); if they wear a rosary around their neck or carry a Bible by their side; if they partake in Holy Communion or invite possession of the Holy Spirit, belief is understood here as that which is carried out for all to see.[5] These distinctions are important markers of religious difference in the barrio and form the basis of spiritual differentiation among believers. The public debate here is not over the value or primacy of Christianity per se, but over the meaning of those diverse practices and how best to *be* Christian where churches abound.

Looking to separate themselves from Catholics and to redefine for the community what "being Christian" means, Protestant groups like the Pentecostals have insisted on a practice-based definition of Christian identity— maintaining that in order to be a Christian, an individual must make an active public commitment to God (conversion), be initiated into the faith through formal institutional channels (adult baptism), act in accordance with behavioral mandates that create empirical differences between oneself as a Christian and one's neighbors as non-Christians (behavioral prohibitions), and concretize one's born-again status and fidelity to Jesus Christ through vivid narratives of transformation and redemption (testimony). By way of these procedural methods, Pentecostals distinguish themselves as exemplary Christian followers—fashion themselves "true Christians"—and claim their place among the faithful as privileged subjects of God. Due to the fact that popular Catholic identity in the country is not necessarily tied to the actual practice of Christian orthodoxy, Pentecostals deliberately call attention to their own objective, practical observance of piety in order to establish a discernible difference between themselves and other Christian believers. Strategic emphasis here is put on substantiating religious claims through purposive action because Christian orthodoxy—and its associated spiritual and moral capital—is itself an object of contentious interpretation, reinterpretation, revision, and ceaseless contestation.

"In the World but Not of the World": *Dos Mundos*

An important aspect of Pentecostal symbolic worlds is the rigid superimposition of a Manichaean dualism on everyday life. The tendency to organize experience into binary oppositions such as good and evil, right and wrong, sacred and profane, provides the basic conceptual framework for Pentecostals to interpret the world around them (for more on world-dividing dualisms characteristic of Pentecostal Christianity globally, see Robbins 2004a:127–130).

For Pentecostals in Villa, there are *dos mundos*, or "two worlds." One world to which they aspire to belong is the spiritual realm—*el evangelio* (the gospel)—ruled by righteousness and the divine word of God. It is opposed in kind to the mundane, earthly world—*el mundo*—governed by human lust, greed, and sin (so-called desires of the flesh or earthly pursuits of humankind). Converts profess to be "of the spirit" while maintaining that others are "of the flesh." To be an *evangélico* means to live a spiritual life categorically set apart from the profane world. Pentecostals in Villa often declare "*estamos en el mundo pero no somos del mundo*" ("we are in the world but we are not of the world"), repeating a well-worn Christian maxim by which they mean to say there is something that makes them different or sets them apart from others in their community. The idea originates from the four canonical Gospels of the New Testament, in this case, particularly that of John 17:13–18: "13. But now I come to thee; and these things I speak in the world, that they may have my joy made full in themselves. 14. I have given them thy word; and the world hated them, because they are not of the world, even as I am not of the world. 15. I pray not that thou shouldest take them from the world, but that thou shouldest keep them from the evil one. 16. They are not of the world, even as I am not of the world. 17. Sanctify them in the truth: thy word is truth. 18. As thou didst send me into the world, even so sent I them into the world."

Conventionally, when Pentecostals refer to *el mundo*, they are referring to the bad or evil things that exist in the world, the sins of humankind and the behaviors that are against or not pleasing to God. A person is considered to have left "the world" for higher, spiritual pursuits when he or she converts and accepts the path of Jesus Christ; thus *el mundo* often stands for "that which is *not* Christian"—the profane irreligious world. For Pentecostals in Villa, it signifies the practices of nonbelievers and, among other things, means to live in sin, to not follow Christ, to not obey the Bible, to do as one wishes as if one has no fear of God, to live a disorganized or undisciplined life. The tendency to divide the world into opposing halves finds traction among believers and scriptural support in 1 John 2:15–17: "15. Love not the world, neither the things that are in the world. If any man love the world, the love of the Father is not in him. 16. For all that is in the world, the lust of the flesh and the lust of the eyes and the vainglory of life, is not of the Father, but is of the world. 17. And the world passeth away, and the lust thereof: but he that doeth the will of God abideth for ever."

The dualisms characteristic of Christianity broadly such as spiritual/ earthly, sanctity/sin, heaven/hell, good/evil are elaborated in a variety of ways locally. Some examples of common oppositions emphasized by Pentecostals in Villa include: *las iglesias* and *los colmadones* (churches and bars); *la iglesia* and *la calle* (the church and the street); *los cristianos* and *los tígueres* (Christians and "macho men"); *las congregaciones* and *las naciones* (congregations and street gangs); *el gozo* and *el vicio* (joy and vice); *el espíritu* and *la carne* (spirit and flesh); *la oración* and *la brujería* (prayer and witchcraft); *la santidad* and *el pecado* (sanctity and sin); *el santo* and *el picador* (saint and sinner); *el creyente* and *el impío* (believer and nonbeliever); *adentro* (*la iglesia*) and *afuera* (*la calle*) (inside [the church] and outside [the street]); *arriba* (*el cielo*) and *abajo* (*la tierra*) (above [heaven] and below [earth]).

Significantly, these divisions are composed often, applied liberally, and observed by the faithful to reveal fundamental divisions of good and evil in their day-to-day lives. Believed to adhere firmly to a greater truth, the *dos mundos* framework guides right and wrong behavior for churchgoers, allowing for neither ambiguity nor transgression. An individual should best be on one side of the fence or on the other, so to speak, inside (the church) or outside (in the world)—a Christian or heathen, a saint or a sinner. Preferably there should be no in-between. In policing this boundary, no less in exploiting it, believers define the meaningful limits of the moral order they wish to effect and position themselves within it as Christian exemplars, ideally as moral authorities set apart from the mundane ("sinful") everyday world, necessarily transformed and fundamentally different from others.

Transformations: Being Christian Means Being Different

When man serves the Lord he must mark the difference.
He must be something different.

Domingo

The difference is that I don't do what they do.

Yamilca

Conversion, for the faithful, means accepting Jesus Christ as one's savior. This usually entails a public profession of faith followed by a commitment to practices that signal and confirm one's new identity as Christian convert. Conversion requires a significant lifestyle change, especially for men who must forsake the conflicting values of male-dominated street culture for the prerogatives of church and family. Emically, this means a rejection of the profane world, *el mundo* and its associated trappings, in favor of *el evangelio*, the idealized spiritual life, a morally disciplined approach to one's personal and social affairs. Characteristically this involves observing a series of behavioral prohibitions or rules (*reglas* or *normas*) that function to mark converts as outwardly transformed, expressed by the faithful as "being different."[6] As such, a profession of faith and acceptance of Jesus Christ as one's savior are only a subset of a number of procedures required of converts to manifest their new identities as *cristianos*—where being Christian means being different and necessarily transformed.

Much of the work of differentiation is accomplished through compliance with a series of behavioral prohibitions outlined by the church that believers refer to as the law of the gospel. Obedience to what they interpret as unalterable biblical rules for sanctified living constitutes one of the more obvious public symbols of Pentecostal cultural difference. Contrary to scholars of the religion who tend to define Pentecostalism in terms of its emphasis on charismatic gifts and the theological importance placed on speaking in tongues, for believers in Villa it is first and foremost God's word and the attending rules that they dutifully endeavor to obey through compliance with a set of prohibitions that makes them unique among Christian groups. In José Luis's estimation (a young man we will learn more about in the next chapter), abiding by the rules of the gospel is the very essence of being an *evangélico*:

> [The rules and prohibitions] are necessary because if it wasn't like that it would be like the popular church, what we know as the Catholic Church, where thieves, *tígueres*, and delinquents go. They leave the church and they go to the *colmado* [to drink]. That is to say that if it weren't like that, if there weren't rules, it would not have the essence that one has of being called Christian, which the Bible says is to be saintly; I am a saint. So were it not for the laws and statutes within the church that prohibit us from doing certain things it would not have been called the Evangelical Church and it would not have been called the Pentecostal Church. There are certain churches that do not prohibit anything—you do whatever you want. But here in the church, in this church, in the evangelical Pentecostal church, one is prohibited from having [for example] romance with women who are not your wife. People who do not know God see it differently.

Through the practice of self-discipline, by adhering to various limits on earthly pleasures, Pentecostal converts distinguish themselves as moral exemplars and come to understand themselves as a special kind of Christian, indeed so righteous as to be considered or to consider themselves "saints."[7]

In order to be a Christian apart, Pentecostal conversion requires an empirical transformation from the way a person used to be—a sinner—to something ostensibly new and different—a saint. This is confirmed by a specific notion of difference expressed in both literal (objective/physical) and metaphorical (subjective/symbolic) terms. I asked José Luis one afternoon what it meant to be a *cristiano*, and he, like others, cited "difference" as the most salient and conspicuous feature. Here he employs metaphors of transformation and rebirth: "I understand that to be Christian is to be something different; to be a new man; to be a new creature; to be something ... at least to be a mirror for other youths who can't reach what I could not reach at one time." Sonia, a widow and longtime member of Iglesia de Dios (IdD), drawing on the *dos mundos* metaphor echoed the same sentiment when she explained that "when one looks for God he or she has to be a new creature. Those that are in the world continue in the world, but we have to separate ourselves from all worldly things." For Sonia and others, it is precisely this transformation, this rebirth as something new as it were, that makes her different from her neighbors: "Because I am a new creature in Christ, they see me differently."

It is the mark of difference that *la pastora* and members from the congregation of Iglesia Evangélica Pentecostal (IEP) insist distinguishes Christians like themselves from others: "[To be Christian] is to belong to the family of Christ because the family of Christ is different in all senses of the word and different from those that have not accepted him. That is why we have to be different," she explained one day. Likewise, Karla (Josefina and Denny's fifteen-year-old daughter, an enthusiastic young believer who was baptized shortly after her eleventh birthday) too had learned that being a *cristiana* meant being different in several new ways: "There is no comparison [to being Christian]. [To be Christian] is to walk a different path, a different life. It is a new life, to be born anew. The way one acts is different. One's way of speaking, of walking, of expressing oneself is different in all ways." The emphasis on difference and on transformation is exemplified by the moment when an individual decides to convert at the end of a *campaña* or following a special service at the church. Visitors are invited to the front to the foot of the stage and asked not if they want to convert, exactly, but if they wish to make a change, whether they want to accept Jesus Christ and transform their lives for the better. Accepting Jesus Christ as Lord and savior is rarely accompanied by an abrupt cognitive upheaval or an instantaneous ideological revolution, but is usually, at least at first, merely a public profession to transform one's life, to do things differently from here on out. The change people wish to make upon conversion is seldom realized overnight. A so-called true conversion occurs with time as individuals learn what it means to be born again and are incorporated into a community of believers where they learn the proper rules, tenets, and culture of the faith. People elect to convert one day and often return to their previous lives the next. Those who do not effect a permanent or sustained transformation (after the *campaña*, the next day or the next week) are the individuals who renege on their vows and who do not remain in the church. Of the committed devotees, the dedicated transformists are the ones who ultimately endure.

Conversion implies more than just adopting a new set of beliefs and a new perspective on life; a convert must ultimately realize a change in his or her functional character—his or her corporeal disposition—in order to be saved. Put differently, in order to be a saint one must cease to be a sinner in the eyes of the church. Conviction on its own is thought to be insufficient for realizing a true Christian identity if not accompanied by an appreciable change in outward appearance or public demeanor. Difference here is not just about changes in how one thinks about or approaches life, or salvation, but necessarily about the active steps involved in pursuing a personal trans-formation and realizing, through practice, one's new or renewed faith. This exact understanding of difference is not difference for difference's sake, but an idea of alterity constructed both with and against dominant notions of Christian orthodoxy in accordance with popular articulations of respect-ability in Dominican culture. Converts attempt to live admirable lives in strict accordance with the Bible by emulating the example of Jesus Christ. Through this concept of difference Pentecostals aim to externalize religious ideals that, while unattainable in themselves, are through their pursuit con-stitutive of the differentiation they wish to foster between themselves and other Christians. An instance of this can be as simple as never cursing or as complex as perfecting saintly virtues like patience, chastity, temperance, kindness, and humility. By refraining from sex until marriage and by ab-staining from alcohol, for example, converts sanctify themselves through strict probity and the sanitizing impression of steadfast asceticism. The per-fection of physical transformation through self-sacrifice and other modes of behavior modification are primary examples of how Pentecostal converts enact their Christian difference.

According to a young woman from IdD's youth group: "In order to be Christian you have to try to differentiate yourself and *demonstrate* that you are Christian." Another member from her youth group explains, "the differ-ence between a Christian and a non-Christian is that a Christian, wherever they go, must *demonstrate* that they are Christian." To be different, one must mark oneself as dissimilar in nature by showing through demonstrative acts that he or she is unlike the next person. José Luis put it this way:

I don't think like [people of the world] anymore. It's one of the things that makes me different from them. I don't have the mentality that they have. They only have thoughts of *tigueraje* and *el coro*. I have a developed mentality. I want to walk on another level. I want to see from another level. That is to say that what makes me different from everyone else is the way that I talk, the way that I walk, and my way of seeing.

This distinction is frequently emphasized by Pentecostals and is often the contrast that converts make between their former lives as so-called sinners and their newly adopted lives as redeemed servants of Christ—I am no longer the person that I used to be, today I am something different. For Domingo, a deacon at IEP, the phenomenal distinction between those who "serve the Lord" and those who do not is a vital component of being a member of the Christian community: "Because a difference must be made between people who serve the Lord and those who do not serve him. There must be a change. . . . So this is where the difference is marked. As the saying goes here, 'Between the Christian and the non-Christian, the difference must be marked.'" That marked social difference is inextricably linked to Pentecostal Christian practice suggests that an important function of Pentecostal faith in the barrio is primarily relational and dependent upon distinctions with one's neighbors; after all, difference can only be rendered by comparison and constituted through a contrast of similarity and dissimilarity with others. Dominican Pentecostals strive to define their spiritual identity in contrast to that of Catholics, for example, by comparing the relative merits of drinking or not drinking, cursing or not cursing, soliciting or not soliciting the saints, et cetera. Virtually everywhere *cristianos* are embroiled in a dialogue of claims and counterclaims with neighbors over the parameters of Christianhood and the definitive boundaries of legitimate Christian practice, arguing that only the Pentecostal church transforms lives, sanctifies believers, and ensures salvation of the soul, declaring the proof to be in the way they act, speak, and carry themselves publicly.

For Dominican Pentecostals, the image, at least as much as the Word, *is* the message. Perception is the name of the game. The emphasis here being that an onlooker should be able to *see* a difference. The privileged focus on the observer and that which is observed—visual confirmation or "proof" that a change has occurred—is further echoed by the familiar term for the open profession of faith: "to witness" to Jesus Christ.

According to Anthony (the evangelist from Pantoja): "Here, in order for someone to become Christian, he or she must present to society a life of great moral quality." Such a project requires active steps by believers to portray themselves in a particular way publicly, even if that way is not entirely authentic: "The difference" says Moisés, from IdD, "is the behavior, not the joy, but the action, how [Christians] act when faced with whatever problem." And Domingo insists that Pentecostals must pretend to be happy, even if they are not, in order to present a life that is, at least in appearance, superior in Jesus Christ in the hopes that others will be drawn to the faith: "The Christian life is the color of roses on the outside and that of thorns on the inside. As a *cristiano* I am not going to convey to you all of the difficulties that I am going through if what I want is to bring you to the feet of Jesus Christ. I am going to show to you the best, right? So that you see my beaming face, 'look, this man is always joyful,' but only God knows what I am thinking." Both Moisés's and Domingo's views here point to the heart of the issue: they insist that converts must represent the best—happiness and joy, "*el gozo*"—regardless of what may be going on in their minds or behind the scenes in their private lives. Despite how they might be feeling at any given time, Dominican Pentecostals are instructed to express their best publicly in order to demonstrate to others the goodness of God, or, put another way, to show why a "new life in Christ" is better than an old one without him. It is not just other *cristianos* who are watching to make sure a fellow congregant is representing a felicitous life, it is also the public at large. According to Radames, a recent convert to IEP, "God sends us to be saints inside and outside the church—more outside than inside, because outside the church they watch you, they are watching what you do." And Sonia, not unlike the others, seemed to attribute the reason behind much of what she and other *cristianos* do to their relations with the public: "A Christian must walk decently and dress decently so that [others] treat you with great respect."[8]

The idea that believers must behave a particular way in public is discussed often in sermons and impressed upon new converts in doctrine classes (*doctrina*) as well as private consultations (*consejos*). As *la pastora* explained to me, the primary reason for requiring that all new members attend doctrine classes is so that they learn how to behave correctly in accordance with Jesus's teachings. It may be the case that more effort is put into instructing new members on how to behave than is actually put into any other religious instruction. According to Domingo and Juan Pablo, the most important lessons that are taught to the congregation regard how members must conduct themselves in public. In response to my query as to the most pressing lessons both deacons try to teach their congregation, they replied:

> For me, all [topics] are important. In general we focus on how to manage ourselves, Amen! Our behavior [*la conducta*]. We teach what are sins and what is not agreeable to God—things that God rejects. We insist on teaching individuals to have good behavior before society, first, so that they may maintain their testimony before society, their family, and before the church. Because through this, what we call sanctity and purification of our life, our soul before the Lord, is conveyed. [Domingo]
>
> We try to educate the people when they enter the congregation with respect to their pasts. [Some have worse pasts than others.] Some come from prostitution, witchcraft, drug addiction, etc. We teach the word of God, how people must behave, what people must do, what they shouldn't do in order to leave, to get out of those things. If a person converts to Christ and doesn't make an effort to change or to leave whatever custom, to separate from those things, I would say that [their conversion] was in vain because one has to make an effort. [Juan Pablo]

Because of this primary emphasis on behavior and exteriority over conviction and interiority, especially the emphasis on how that conduct is perceived by the public, Pentecostalism in Villa would seem less private, less inwardly focused, and more characteristically public and social than is usually attributed to evangelical faiths elsewhere (cf. Luhrmann 2004, 2012). Even while Pentecostalism emphasizes individual reform (through conversion) and developing a personal relationship with God (through prayer), one cannot fully embrace the faith or be counted among its ranks without securing the approval of others. Converts are acknowledged to be spiritual agents of God, *cristianos* in their own right, only insofar as they are acknowledged to be so by their community. If converts are not recognized as significantly different by those around them, the church will not baptize them, and friends, no less neighbors, will not respect them as admirable authorities of the Spirit.[9]

It is important to recognize that one may not simply join a church and be respected as a *cristiano*; he or she must fulfill the role by following prohibitions and behaving like a convert should. The focus on teaching members the right and wrong ways to act points to a key concern of the church for the discipline and regulation, not just of the religious lives of believers but of all aspects of their public and private existence. Through moral discipline converts demonstrate their sincere devotion, marking themselves spiritually distinct in concrete, observable ways.

I discuss later how this demonstrative aspect is figured within an economy of prestige that shapes the ways in which evangelical Christian identity is received locally (see chapter 7). Suffice it to say for now that the status of reputable Christian identity in the barrios is negotiated with one's neighbors, and it is never a completed process. That is, one does not complete with any finality the transformation to Pentecostal Christian saint after conversion. Converts must prove repeatedly through public acts of devotion that they deserve to be respected as pious servants of Christ. In order to do this they must continuously remake themselves as exceptional believers through daily interactions with the public and their congregations. Converts must constantly reaffirm their beliefs, not through a simple proclamation but through demonstrative rituals that render them identifiable members of a spiritual brotherhood, discernibly holy and presumably saved.

Official membership in a church is not, for example, conferred upon conversion but instead upon baptism, which only follows a convincing and certifiable demonstration of fidelity. While there are baptized and unbaptized members of the church, all converts are expected to work toward the goal of baptism: first baptism in water (by immersion), the means by which a genuine conversion is confirmed institutionally, then later baptism in the Holy Spirit, divine confirmation of a convert's spiritual transformation. In order to be baptized a convert must show a true conversion by offering a testimony demonstrating to others that he or she is truly different—a transformed being, a "new creature" in Christ. At IdD and IEP, a convert is only baptized when senior members of the church decide that the convert has shown that he or she is ready. There is no specific time frame—for some it is a matter of months, and for others it may be a matter of years. It is not enough to want to be baptized, show up to church every day, and pray; both IdD and IEP require that converts attend doctrine classes where they learn how to act like a Christian and to demonstrate that they have experienced a fundamental change that has made them reformed spiritual persons.

Pentecostalism in Villa is therefore an important achieved status for barrio residents, one that is organized around a set of cultural ideas defining the ideal Christian man and woman and negotiated publicly with the wider community. The more different one becomes, the more difficult it is to revert back to one's old self; the emphasis on transformation creates formidable bonds of obligation not easily broken. The following sections explore the various ways in which Dominican Pentecostals perform Christian identity, differentiate themselves—literally make themselves appear distinct and transformed—and fulfill esteemed cultural ideals rooted in Christian orthodoxy. This differentiation is accomplished through signifying practices like the clothes converts wear, the manipulation of language and speech, the places converts go or do not go, and the activities in which they choose to participate. These observances serve to reform the individual from the outside in and signal to others a convert's claim to live a righteous and enviable life in Christ.

Changes in Speech

> It doesn't matter what social class they are from, they can be illiterate, but they will not speak a single obscenity.
>
> Moisés

There is a kind of Christian talk, a folk speech tied to evangelical identity that is unmistakable from the forms of verbal expression otherwise popular in the country. Being a *cristiano* means "speaking well" and regularly discussing Christian themes like salvation, repentance, and the deeds of Jesus Christ, all while assiduously interspersing Bible passages into casual conversation by quoting scripture whenever possible. Preferably converts become crafty raconteurs, entertaining preachers, and persuasive evangelists. By the way they speak Pentecostal Christians look to differentiate themselves from the rest of society and establish their commitment to the faith through everyday talk.

This transformation of speech practices is as important as any other change converts attempt to make when joining the church. *Cristianos* in Villa pride themselves on speaking well—a decisive sign of respectability. Consider one young man named Flaco's evaluation here:

> I've earned respect from my friends by being myself and acting like a Christian. [Specifically] my way of speaking. Because I can't talk as everyone else does. I have to speak coherent things, things that make

sense, things that help. So that when people see you are different and that you speak in a suitable way, that all the things that you speak are positive, then people begin to see you in another way. They can respect you because you don't say everything, because you don't say every little thing that comes to mind. You speak of important things.

It is by speaking differently that Flaco differentiates himself from non-Christians. His way of speaking is, in his estimation, the primary means by which he asserts his evangelical identity and earns respect from others. His way of speaking is his way of "acting like a Christian." In speaking well, Flaco and the Pentecostal faithful align themselves with time-honored cultural values associated with respectability. Bad talk, conversely, is associated with the street and social values antithetical to the church. To speak poorly—to curse, to discuss vulgarities, to lie—is to exhibit poor manners or upbringing; to speak badly is tantamount to dressing poorly and implies a lack of refinement and schooling.[10]

Speaking well is a virtue esteemed in the church as well as the local community, and verbal acumen is a highly regarded, richly rewarded talent. De Moya (2002:120) points out that the expression *hombre de palabra* (man of words) functions as an honorific bestowed upon dominant, respected Dominican men. The venerable *cristiano* has a way with words. Able to proselytize without offending those they court, they speak truth to power with confidence. The effective evangelist is a compelling credible spokesperson, a talented orator. Along with the stirring preacher, these biblical wordsmiths rely on their linguistic talents to lead the congregation, to incite conversion, and to save the lost and fallen. The Bible—or perhaps more rightly here "the Word"—is itself considered a privileged conduit of spiritual knowledge and sacred authority, its mastery in prayer, preaching, and testimony very much linked with renown in the church community.

Talk, maybe even more than any other attribute, is a crucial vector of Pentecostal identity politics, the significance of which can be observed in simple one-on-one consults (*consejos*) along with the centrality of the spoken word in testimony, in prayer, and perhaps above all, in preaching (for more on the place of "orality" in Latin American Pentecostalism, see Schultze 1994).

Language, because of its power to represent, is seized upon as a powerful tool in the Christian converts' repertoire. Many of the most important ritual

Changing Clothes

Upon conversion, a physical acting out of the transformative metaphor shores up an individual's symbolic transformation into a new and different person. Nicol's story of evolving attire illustrates this vital point. Her sartorial choices in the past came to signify her previous life and her former identity, just as her new clothes would come to signify her new identity in Christ. In both IdD and IEP women are expected to wear dresses and are prohibited from wearing slacks, revealing blouses or halter tops, jewelry, or short dresses (relatedly, women are also discouraged from wearing makeup or having overly styled hair or manicured nails). When Nicol converted she did away with her old clothes (her short dresses, her pants) and bought new ones to reflect the new person she had become. When she was *descarriado*, when she backslid and left the church for a time, she gave away the dresses she had purchased and returned to wearing jeans:

> The minute I converted, the first thing I did was I changed all my pants and bought dresses.... The very next day I took all my pants and gave them away, all the sleeveless blouses I threw out, the earrings I gave away to my nieces, the dresses that were too short I gave away.... Yep, that week I did all that. I also bought lots of dresses. I had many long dresses.
>
> When I left the church, I gave all the dresses to other Christians.... I didn't think that I was going to return to the congregation. I only kept two that I wanted, but I didn't wear them when I left. I went back to wearing them when I converted again and returned to the church.

Clothes for Nicol were personal symbols of her spiritual transformation. When she left the church she felt compelled to give away the dresses she bought to wear after conversion, not because the clothes ceased to have a function but because she did not think she would convert again; to continue wearing the dresses would feel inauthentic, perhaps even shameful after failing to follow through on her commitment to a Christian life. When she converted a second time she bought new clothes and in no time returned to wearing long dresses yet again.

Nicol's modest garments like denim dresses and unassuming blouses make her easily recognizable as a *cristiana*. Her plain, shoulder-length hair pulled back in a simple ponytail makes her appearance unpretentious. Pentecostals in Villa are encouraged to dress modestly. This usually means that women wear blouses and dresses (not pants) while men are entreated to sport clean, pressed, button-up shirts; slacks; and leather shoes. Neither men nor women at IEP or IdD are supposed to wear jewelry, but this is less strictly enforced.

One young man from IdD suggested to me one day that, in his estimation, about 90 percent of *cristianos* were recognized because of their clothing and the other 10 percent by their behavior. It is something that Pentecostals take pride in, he proposed. I was told by more than a few Pentecostal men that the reason why women are attracted to Christian converts is because of their look, their clean clothes, and the way that they take care of themselves physically. Whether this is actually the case is uncertain; however, it does suggest that Christian men, not unlike Christian women, take special care in their day-to-day sartorial presentations in a minimal effort to reflect the refinement of their new constitution in Jesus Christ and to project the respectability thought to be achieved with a genuine conversion.[12]

Clothing signals an outward transformation of identity and represents an attempt to demonstrate a sensibility in line with dominant articulations of social distinction. Brodwin (2003:91) has suggested that Haitian Pentecostal men in Guadeloupe take care to have shined shoes, sport coats, and ties in order to project the "bourgeois norms of stability and civility" that Haitians by reputation are thought to lack as stereotyped migrant laborers to the island. Likewise, in the Dominican Republic, dress shirts, ties, and leather shoes project an air of respectability for those stigmatized by poverty or plagued by ethnic and racial stereotypes.

In a similar way it is also common for Pentecostals to carry Bibles with them everywhere they go as a public symbol of their professed Christian identity. It signals to others their claim to be both knowledgeable about the Book and beholden to its message. Having the Scriptures at their fingertips for easy reference permits *cristianos* to share the Word at a moment's notice. The sudden presence of a Bible in a convert's hand, like the change in a convert's clothing, no less the new ways in which he or she speaks, is an externalization of a believer's inner transformation in Jesus Christ and gestures to the world that he or she is to be regarded as a *cristiano* and, by extension, with respect.

Physical Transformations

> Every time I look at myself in the mirror I say "Wow!
> This man is not the Juan Carlos of yesterday."
>
> Juan Carlos

Pentecostals at IdD and IEP do not just claim to do different things—go different places, speak in different ways, dress differently—but they also claim to *be* different people. A personal transformation should be so profound that a convert no longer looks like the same person he or she once was. The goal is to be so different that people no longer recognize you as the person you were before. According to Héctor, a thirty-five-year-old member of IEP who had three years in the church when I met him, people who have not seen him in years encounter him today and are in disbelief at how much his appearance has changed since converting. Domingo and others claim that with conversion, people change physically, and that this transformation is visible in their countenance and physical appearance:

> That is why, when a person comes to Jesus Christ, he or she changes. When the Lord comes into the life of a person it must change, that is why, I don't know if you have noticed that when a person, can be any type of person, comes to the feet of Jesus Christ, they change: they become more beautiful, they change in all aspects, they look very different. Because we are ambassadors of Jesus Christ, Jesus Christ is the light of the world, if we are representatives of the light of Jesus Christ it must shine on our faces. That is why one sees a change. There is always a change in the person. [Domingo]

The change that Pentecostals claim attends conversion to Jesus Christ is thought to be a visible, physical transformation. According to Héctor: "People say to me, 'Look at you, physically! I didn't want to say anything, but I noticed a change in your face.'" And José Luis's transformation was often mentioned when such discussions of looking different arose with members of IEP. So stark was his transformation that his friends insist that I would not have recognized him as the same person had I met him years earlier. His hair, clothes, and demeanor were different; supposedly everything about him was different. No one that I knew regarded José Luis's conversion as anything other than profound. As such, José Luis embodied the Pentecostal ideal of transformation from sinner to saint; an appreciably changed soul unrecognizable from his former self, he was applauded for being a living testimony, a reflection of the grace of God and a sign attesting to the power of conversion.

Emically, this notion of appearing different is sometimes rendered as an analogy to batteries in a flashlight. Popular with evangelicals elsewhere, the analogy draws on the importance of the indwelling Holy Spirit in the lives of believers and goes something like this: a person without salvation is like a flashlight without batteries; when converts invite Jesus Christ into their lives, God fills them with the Holy Spirit, and like the batteries in a flashlight, gives believers the power to fulfill God's plan and to reflect the light of the Lord out onto the world. Converts endeavor to be "the light of the world" and to have the light of the Lord shine through them. Like the batteries in a flashlight, the Holy Spirit is understood to be the power that God puts inside believers to inspire change and to transform their lives. The light, according to the faithful, is seemingly undeniable—"that is why one sees a change," according to Domingo, and why Juan Carlos claims to see a different person today when he looks in the mirror.

Naming Difference

Frequently a convert's transformation is represented by a change in moniker. Residents of Villa, like Dominicans all over the country, commonly employ nicknames to refer to friends and family; in some cases individuals may go by as many as three or four different names. It is not uncommon for people to go by a name other than their given name. Few if any of my informants were known by their given names, and most went by a nickname or some other appellation given to them by family or friends. Such was the case with José Luis. Suggestively, however, it was not until after he converted that he began to use his given name, José Luis, and his family name, Abreu. Before converting, he was known by his friends as Quico. After converting, he started to go by José Luis:

Those that know me they have a name for me, some call me "*aleluyasa*," others call me "*la gloria son de Dios*," others call me José Luis, and some call me "Abreu." That is to say that they know me by different names. I have friends that are both believers and nonbelievers that know me as such.

Today José Luis is proud of being referred to as *varón de dios*, or "man of God." His experience suggests that because people know him by different names, by proxy, they know him by different personas. His various different names correspond to distinct selves, alternative identities cultivated before and after converting. José Luis no longer sees himself as Quico; that name represented an identity of the past, a street persona he no longer embraces. As his conversion represented a renunciation of that lifestyle, so too it meant adopting a new self-identity. People today no longer call him by the names of his former identity (Quico the gang leader; Quico the *tíguere*), but acknowledge his transformation formally by referring to him in a new way, further articulating a marked break from his sinful past by underlining his rebirth as a new person in Jesus Christ.

Likewise, Juan Carlos, before converting, was called *Matica* in the streets as well as *el verdugo* by his enemies. He was proud of those names at the time but regrets them today, as he finds them shamefully repugnant. Undeniably they evoke images of a particularly violent and thuggish character who reveled in sin. Juan Carlos today compares his former identity as *el verdugo* with his current identity as pious reformed sinner and celebrated evangelist known simply by his given name, drawing attention to the inspired transformation his conversion occasioned and the new birth in Christ that his given name (or Christian name) denotes. Testimonies of men in the church frequently cite nicknames that characterized their former lives in the streets: "Before converting they called me . . ." "Before I became a Christian I was known as . . ." are common formulations. These details accentuate the fundamental transformation converts wish to convey to the world and the clear division they want to make with their former lives in the streets and their new lives in the church.

In a somewhat different but no less related sense, it is widely known that Pentecostals refer to each other as *hermano/hermana* (brother/sister), *varón/varona* (terms of respect for a man/woman), and *siervo/sierva* (servant of God). Such terms acknowledge a shared Christian identity and indicate mutual respect for one another's beliefs. The public may also use these same terms to refer to *cristianos*, typically as a form of respect. Use of the term *"varón," "hermano,"* or even *"evangélico"* to refer to Pentecostals is a common way for non-Christians to show respect and express their approval. Followers themselves apply the terms to build solidarity with one another, to create community across congregations, reaffirming their shared spiritual kinship with other like Christians.

Just as Pentecostals have naming practices for themselves, they also use special terms to refer to non-Christians, such as *impios* (people who are "ungodly" or "unfaithful"), *mundanos* (people of the world), *inconversos* (the unconverted), and *no creyentes* (nonbelievers). Labels like these help realize the Manichaean dualism converts want to lay bare while, once again, underscoring the important division Pentecostals make between themselves (believers) and others (nonbelievers). In naming differences between spiritual and nonspiritual persons, *cristianos* further mark themselves as distinct from their neighbors.

Differentiating Aspects of the Spirit

Charismatic gifts, or *charisms/charismata*—also variously referred to as "spiritual gifts," "Holy Gifts," or "gifts of the Holy Spirit"—are central to Pentecostal theology and serve important functions in the church and for the faith community.[13] In its original Christian formulation, *charismata* referred specifically to gifts of grace conferred by the Holy Spirit, while "charisma" refers to a divinely conferred power, grace, or favor from God.[14] Outlined in 1 Corinthians 12:7–11, these spiritual gifts are considered by many today to be extraordinary graces bestowed on the faithful for the benefit of all and include miraculous talents such as the gift of healing, wisdom, prophecy, the working of miracles, and speaking in tongues. According to many observers and believers alike, reception of the Holy Gifts—in particular glossolalia, or speaking in tongues—is the property that distinguishes the Pentecostal church from other Protestant, evangelical, and/or mainline denominations.[15] Their very appellation comes from the biblical Pentecost, when the Spirit of God descended upon the Apostles "and they were filled with the Holy Spirit, and began to speak with other tongues, as the Spirit gave them utterance" (Acts 2:4). This same experience is said to have been repeated in 1906 with the "out pouring of the Spirit" in Los Angeles at the Azusa Street revival, the original birthplace of the worldwide Pentecostal movement (Hollenweger 1972:26n.1, 21–28; Synan 1997:84–106;

Cox 1995:45–65; Wacker 2001:35–57). From its early beginnings, speaking in tongues appears to have been what defined Pentecostals' religious identity more than any other belief or practice (Wacker 2001:42). According to Wacker (2001:35), "when early Pentecostals wanted to explain themselves to the outside world—indeed when they wanted to explain themselves to each other—they usually started with the experience of the Holy [Spirit] baptism signified by speaking in tongues." "*Los dones*," locally, these charismatic gifts continue to inspire Pentecostal enthusiasm and play a role in the church's current popularity while clearly marking its ritual distinctiveness in relation to Catholicism and other Protestant denominations in Villa.

Reception of the Holy Gifts serves a double distinguishing function by marking those exceptional or "true" believers with spiritual faculties corresponding to talents like the ability to prophesy or to heal. In addition to empowering individual believers in ways that make them stand out from Catholics and other Christian groups according to their privileged access to the Spirit, reception of the Holy Gifts, which is initiated by Holy Spirit baptism, differentiates those converts who have "truly made it" and those who have yet to effect a definitive spiritual transformation despite their conversion.[16] In other words, Holy Spirit baptism legitimates a convert's transformation in Christ by confirming the sincerity of his or her conversion experience through an unmistakable sign of divine endorsement (see Harrison 1974:405). According to her observation of American Pentecostals, Hine (1970:63) submits that the subjective experience after which converts feel themselves to be most different is the baptism of the Holy Spirit attending or subsequent to baptism by immersion. With it, converts receive what they perceive to be divine confirmation of their spiritual transformation, a change in status otherwise marked institutionally by their baptism in water as initiated by the church. This subsequent baptism is viewed as even more authoritative since it comes from God and not from the pastor or congregation leaders who otherwise decide when a convert is ready to be baptized.

The act of baptism by immersion itself functions as a ritual of differentiation by marking the spiritually learned and "truly faithful" from those still finding their way. Church leaders determine when a convert is ready for baptism when he or she has demonstrated genuine faith and has a strong or "good" testimony. Only then does the community acknowledge, in ritual form, a convert's born-again status.[17]

Speaking in tongues is considered evidence of spirit baptism, a transformative religious experience understood in the Pentecostal tradition to be a distinct "work of grace" that confirms one's salvation in Christ (the first work of grace) and initiates the faithful into use of the Holy Gifts.[18] According to several major Pentecostal denominations (Church of God in Christ, Church of God [Cleveland, Tennessee]), there are three distinct works of grace: conversion (salvation), sanctification, and spirit baptism. These churches believe that sanctification or "holiness" is necessary for believers to receive the Holy Spirit baptism. Other significant Pentecostal denominations like the Assemblies of God refer to two primary works of grace: conversion (salvation and sanctification) and spirit baptism, thereby collapsing sanctification into the first work of grace attending the moment of conversion. In both cases, baptism in the Holy Spirit follows baptism by immersion, a public symbol of a conversion that has already occurred, understood in symbolic terms as a rebirth in Jesus Christ subsequent to a sincere or "true" conversion.

While individuals may choose to convert, and church leaders may decide to proceed with a formal baptism by immersion, supernatural verification of an individual's spiritual transformation is best demonstrated by reception of these gifts, and, at least initially, by speaking in tongues. In order to be chosen as a vessel to receive the divine power of the Holy Spirit, to receive the spirit baptism and subsequent gifts of the Spirit a believer must above all be faithful, pious, penitent, compliant, sincere, and exclusively dedicated to the Lord. Having fulfilled this requirement, converts look forward to the heavenly sign of their new life in Christ. Although it is believed that no one can know for sure when they will receive the spirit baptism, as *the* definitive confirmation of one's genuine conversion new converts to the church long for this divine acknowledgment, eagerly awaiting this important sign from God—divine evidence of their sincere spiritual commitment, "proof of their right standing with God" (Wacker 2001:40), a mystical portent that a sinner's conversion is complete.

This special second baptism usually follows from considerable experience in the gospel along with familiarity with church teachings; thus it also tends to mark differences in the maturity of faith between believers. It is not chosen but earned; a convert requests the baptism but does not initiate it; it is entirely a prerogative of the divine and based solely on the grace and favor of God. It follows that within the church itself there are significant distinctions made between believers such as those between baptized and unbaptized members and between those who have received the spirit baptism and those who have not. A sort of hierarchy of holiness obtains within the church that distinguishes recent converts with little spiritual capital from those with years in the gospel who as deacons, pastors, and evangelists wield considerable spiritual authority.

Apartarnos del Mundo: Testimony, Sanctity, and Prohibition

The Pentecostal church is a place where one encounters what is called a testimony: a sign or recount of one's conversion and subsequent transformation in Jesus Christ, a profession or demonstrative example of Christian deeds and identity. To give testimony is to bear witness to the greatness of God, to demonstrate to others the power of Jesus Christ to transform individual lives for good thereupon revealing to others the true providence of God. It is necessary "to maintain" or regularly give testimony in order to establish one's born-again status so that others can be convinced of the transformative power of God. In this way, testimonies do the work of evangelism just as they confirm for the individual his or her new identity as saved repentant sinner. *Cristianos* give oral testimonies affirming their relationship with God and, preferably, give "living testimonies," or embodied examples of God's transformative power of grace as realized in the lives of converts themselves. Above and beyond the stories they recount, living testimonies are phenomenal illustrations of faith and salvation. A testimony is "lived" by following the prohibitions, living a spiritual life in accordance with the law of the Gospels, being a representative example of right living in Jesus Christ. As a requirement of the church, all members must maintain a testimony. It is central to being Christian. According to Juan Pablo, being a *cristiano* means giving a testimony: "It means to give a new testimony, a good testimony so that with time people can convince themselves of the certainty that you are different." At least from the perspective of those outside of the church, though perhaps equally for those within it, the testimony is the single most important confirmation of one's true conversion. One's testimony is verification that he or she has truly changed and become a new person. People who give a bad testimony—a *mal testimonio*, those *cristianos* and others who do not live righteous lives—are viewed as a menace because they give the church a bad name and threaten its relationship with the public. A bad testimony leads people to think poorly of *evangélicos*, calling into question whether the person really changed as he or she claims. It is not until converts maintain a "good" testimony that they are acknowledged to be different and to walk a higher spiritual path, that others are convinced of their professed conversion.

For followers in Villa, the idea of sanctity or "holiness" is essential to maintaining distance from debasing influences. It is thought necessary to confirm one's fundamental transformation before society. Sanctity means to separate oneself from the polluting influences of the profane world, the corrupting desires of the flesh. For Domingo, sanctity means purity or purification:

> We try to teach the congregation that we should look for a way to guarantee the salvation of our soul. That's why we insist on what is called sanctification, purification of our soul. . . . Sanctity means not being impure, [to be free] from impurities or filth. Sanctity means purification. When we speak of sanctity, we are talking about removing something. Before [I was a Christian], I drank liquor regularly, but finally I looked for a way to sanctify myself, my body. I left drinking, because [the Bible] says that drunks do not enter [the kingdom of heaven]. So it's a way of sanctifying. Sanctity is to separate oneself from filth, from contamination, from that which can contaminate my soul. I try to remove it from within me.

This metaphor of contamination is often used to relate ideas about the dangers of witchcraft, possession, and moral corrosion associated with going to certain places like bars and nightclubs or forbidden religious ceremonies. In order to sanctify one's body, in order to live a sanctified life, to live as a saint, one must not contaminate or soil the body with worldly things. Alcohol, because it is ingested and its effects are uninhibiting, is emblematic of polluting substances considered off limits to the faithful. This particular orientation reinforces the symbolic divide between holy and unholy and the other divisions of *dos mundos* that separate the Pentecostal convert from his or her profane existence. The maintenance of holiness is the official key to salvation, according to *la pastora*: "Since I was little I liked the gospel because I liked 'the spiritual cleansing' [*la limpieza espiritual*], recognizing since I was young that God is holy and he says in his word that without sanctity nobody will see him and I want to see him!"

As sanctity is seen as either a condition of salvation or its reward, Sonia reasoned that when she was Catholic, she could not obtain sanctity because she was allowed to sin; in her words, "they did not prohibit anything." She reasoned that ultimately she could not obtain salvation as a Catholic because the church itself was corrupt. She likens her time frequenting the Catholic Church to living in sin. Today she preserves her sanctity by closely observing the prohibitions of the faith.

In order to maintain sanctity, to ensure salvation, to distance oneself from the corrupting elements that presumably abound in Dominican society, Pentecostal Christians maintain a strict regimen of prohibitions. What are also called the norms or rules (*normas* or *reglas*) of the church, prohibitions are a feature of membership in Pentecostal congregations just as they are in many other institutions—at least this is how Renato, a young man from IdD, understood his subjection to the rules of the church:

> It is difficult [to follow the demands of the church], but one tries, because one has to try. . . . Let me give you an example: when you are in school, in an institution there are rules that one must follow, if you do not follow these rules you can't be there. In this case, the gospel is a rule that you have to try to comply with because if you want to get to where you want to go, to the final stage, you have to try to do it. There are rules that you will realize are good and bad.

Renato, for example, liked gold chains but did not wear one because the church frowns upon it. However, sometimes he wears "sporty, comfortable clothes" because he does not like to wear ties, and he does not think that God will condemn him for it. This is in contrast to *la pastora*'s reasons for disallowing women to wear pants in her congregation, saying that she did not want to risk salvation over such a trivial detail: "There are churches that don't have *doctrina* and they accept whatever clothing and any haircut. We do not accept any of that because we do not want to lose ourselves for a 'silly' or 'stupid' thing [*tontería*] we would say." Nevertheless, for Renato and others distinction comes from observing the prohibitions, from "inhibiting" himself. It is precisely this restraint that makes him a *cristiano*: "In the end they come to know that I am Christian because I inhibit myself many things that I know are bad; I restrict myself."

One particularly important prohibition among several is the proscription of where one may go to spend one's time as a convert. Bars and nightclubs are expressly forbidden, but so are popular holiday festivals (*fiestas patronales, carnaval,* and so forth) and places of ill repute. In Villa, the politics of place is effectively a formidable politics of identity. Where one goes and with what areas of town one is associated are directly connected to the way in which the public receives a person. The denotations *gente de la calle* and *en la calle* (in the streets) as personal descriptors of moral character are exemplary of this idea.

These perspectives suggest that prohibitions are instrumental for Pentecostal Christian faith in the barrios. Not only do they facilitate alternative modes of conduct that function to separate *cristianos* from others in both time and space, but they also create symbolic differences between individuals based on actions that are then used to justify spiritual or religious differences. As a result, respected *cristianos* are considered *personas serias* (serious people) and *gente disciplinada* (disciplined people) because they try to live ascetic lifestyles, denying themselves things that most others find enjoyable. Furthermore, the prohibitions support the conceptual division of reality into *dos mundos,* good and evil: they establish a phenomenal difference between discipline and freedom, law and lawlessness, sanctity and sin, chaste and flashy. The flesh they say is weak, and, according to the faithful, "we must govern the flesh."

Physical Metaphors of Transformation

The internal, spiritual change in Christ is reflected externally in physical metaphors of transformation. We have considered strategic behavioral, linguistic, and other symbolic changes, but these are not reflected in or on the body alone; they may also find expression out in the world, for example, in the form and physical structure of one's home.

As discussed earlier, modifications to clothing and behavior are important physical changes that Pentecostals make to reflect their internal transformation (or to inspire it), but we can also consider a person's home—the architecture, facade, and interior design—to see what it says about Pentecostal concepts of faith and spiritual transformation.

Many homes in Villa are relatively crude dwellings made of wood and roofed over with corrugated, galvanized metal, and, as is common in barrio Francisco, are small and constructed by their current or former owners. Other homes are made from concrete or cinder blocks. Few public displays of success and wealth are more visible than the home that a family or an individual maintains. Concrete structures are the most desirable and prestigious, owing to their greater endurance in inclement weather as well as the higher cost of materials used to build and maintain them. Homeownership, as opposed to tenancy, is highly valued as well, making one's physical residence or property a key symbol of status and prosperity in the barrio.

Following conversion Pentecostals are encouraged to maintain, if not construct, a home of their own. This is the ideal (if not always a reality), and homeownership is one of the more diffuse goals of adulthood in Dominican society and for many the clearest indicator of independence and good fortune.

In the context of the church, a convert's home becomes a reflection of his or her spiritual transformation and a physical symbol of his or her testimony. The order of one's home is representative of the order of one's life. Converts frequently make comparisons between their homes before and after conversion. When people describe themselves before and after accepting Jesus Christ, they may refer to how their housing situation has changed; how today they own their own lot and no longer rent; how they have a place of their own; how they built a good home with the help of members from the church. Additionally, the state or quality of a person's home is regularly used as a measure of his or her prosperity since converting.

Building a home out of resilient materials is frequently coupled with the fortifying metaphors used to refer to Jesus Christ's influence on individual lives. The verbs "*edificar*" (to edify, to build, to construct, to raise) and "*fortalecer*" (to uplift spiritually, to fortify, to strengthen, to build, to reinforce) are repeatedly invoked to describe reasons for attending *cultos* and congregating at the church (and for conversion more generally). Just as one's spirit and constitution are said to be strengthened in Jesus Christ, so too is the literal construction and maintenance of a new home as converts mature in the gospel.

A respectable, stable home ultimately functions as a testament to one's fidelity to the church. If a person's living quarters are out of order, it is seen as a reflection of one's shaky or uncertain relationship with God, perhaps indicative of an individual's struggling or fledgling faith. Thus, building or improving one's home is a popular metaphor for working on and strengthening one's relationship with Jesus Christ. The house functions as a concrete symbol of spiritual development and submits to neighbors that perhaps their lives might be better off if they join the church. Life without

Jesus Christ is described by the faithful as disorganized—indeed, an apt metaphor that lends itself effortlessly to the improving condition and strict orderliness of hearth and home upon conversion.

The house itself functions as both a public and private symbol of conversion. The interior of the home is the private symbol of the personal and familial, and the exterior of the home is the public, external symbol. The condition of Juan Pablo's home is exemplary here. That the floors, fixtures, and windows were unfinished and the inside walls were barren (it felt to me much like a cave) was relatively inconsequential; rather, it was the facade of the home that signaled to others his success. Much like the expectation that Christians be seen smiling and happy in public (despite what might be going on inside), that the light of Jesus Christ shine on their faces, it is important for the Pentecostal community to demonstrate to the world that they are better off than their neighbors (who may be irreligious or Catholic), and the house is an important physical example of their relative prosperity and spiritual success.

If it is not clear enough who lives in such a house, evangelicals sometimes advertise their faith with slogans like *"que dios bendiga este hogar"* ("God bless this home") or *"cristo viene arrepientete!"* ("Christ is coming, repent!") painted alongside a Bible, dove, or other symbol directly on the house itself. Perhaps even more familiar are the bumper stickers and vinyl windshield decals of Jesus and various Bible verses that are nearly obligatory adornments on the vehicles of Protestants everywhere in the country. A car, of course, if one can afford a vehicle, like the home, is an important physical testimony of one's prosperity in Christ and functions as a mobile testimony or advertisement for the faith, possibly suggesting that one is quite literally "going places" with Jesus.

The success of the church itself is sometimes conceived of in terms of the same metaphor of construction. *La pastora* relayed to me the history of her church, IEP, by first explaining that at the beginning, when she was sent by her church in Pantoja to raise a place of worship in Villa, she first gave *cultos* out of a member's home; then, as they began to "convert souls" they bought a vacant lot (where IEP is today) and "built a small house of wood" where they held services for several years. Later they decided that "the house of God should be prettier," so they "worked harder" and "by the grace of God" and the help of the growing congregation, it became "a proper temple," a concrete structure with electricity and a generator, "with some small details here and there still to be finished." The longevity of the church and the growth of the congregation are reflected in the building itself, and it has become for the Pentecostal community in barrio Francisco a physical testimony to the success of IEP and the restorative fortifying blessings of God.

In the construction and maintenance of one's home we see reflections of being and becoming a Christian. What a convert's home says about his or her transformation in Christ, ultimately, is as important as how he or she behaves. Moreover, the focus on the home, *la casa*, is indicative of the church's association with and investment in the private, familial sphere of life, particularly as it is opposed to the worldly sphere of public life, otherwise reckoned as *la calle*, or "the street."

Pentecostals in Villa go out of their way to set themselves apart from others and to demonstrate that they are not like their neighbors. For these believers, being Christian is to differentiate oneself. To be a Christian convert requires a fundamental transformation of the self, a reordering of who one is in relation to one's former self and to others, to be acknowledged as different, unrecognizable to former friends and family; it is to be a stranger to one's own mirror image. From the perspective of the church, no less outside observers, it is not sufficient to have made a personal change if it cannot be seen or confirmed by others. Thus, the most important aspect of being a *cristiano* in Villa is not simply personal conviction or a deep knowledge of the theological tenets of the church, but significantly how one represents his or her faith in public, whether neighbors and the local community view him or her with respect or disdain. Ultimately, the social role one plays as a *cristiano*, along with public accountability, is far more important in the context of barrio life than the quality or strength of personal belief, especially if that conviction cannot be demonstrated convincingly. Because the rewards of membership (of conversion, of spiritual transformation, of forgiveness) are directly tied to one's acceptance as a Christian in the public sphere, followers must continue to reaffirm their evangelical identity through acts of distinction—the performance of piety—and public rituals of personal affirmation.

Conclusion

Pentecostal faith in the barrios of Villa is rooted in disciplined behaviors aimed at establishing empirical differentiation between *dos mundos*, the concerns of the so-called earthly and spiritual realms. These evangelical techniques of the body, realized in the logic of Pentecostal practice, function to transform the individual from sinner to saint and emphasize discontinuity with former lives. For these reasons and more, observers like Burdick (1993:224) have described Pentecostalism as a "cult of transformation" or "discontinuity." Conversion, baptism, and Holy Spirit baptism, along with perceptible changes in behavioral patterns and other routinized practices of differentiation, promote a radical break or "rupture" with past selves (Burdick 1993:224; see also Meyer 1998). These "rituals of rupture" perform a kind of ritualized social disjuncture characteristic of Pentecostalism globally (Robbins 2003b, 2004a) while giving the faith a unique property among Christian groups locally. Acting different leads to being different, and being different leads to changes in one's relationship to family, friends, and neighbors—and indeed to one's own self. I draw attention here to the performative and expressive emphasis of the faith in order to locate the principal stimulus behind Pentecostalism's rapid and effective cultural transformation of Dominican barrios. These exemplary performance-based, practice-first features alter the cultural landscape by drawing both public and private responses to the everyday posturing of converts and weaving meaningful new symbolic threads into local webs of significance through conventional ritual practices. Justifying private convictions publicly through demonstrative testimonies of faith and fidelity transmutes the personal into the communal—the private into public—by staging open contests over meaning. The very impetus for Pentecostal cultural change in contexts like Villa and around the Dominican Republic may be the expressive properties of evangelical faith and its dramatic public registers that combine to support the everyday ritual manufacture of cultural transformation.

Much of the focus on demonstration comes as a result of how Pentecostals are viewed by outsiders (see Wacker 2001:40). Because Catholics and others are wont to dismiss evangelical claims to moral and spiritual authority (sometimes with contempt), the response by Pentecostals has been to be more determined in their displays of holiness. For every performance there is an audience. Even though Holy Spirit possession enhances the relevance of the faith for individual believers at a profound personal level (furnishing highly charged, deeply emotional ecstatic experiences), it is always a public occasion with onlookers who are every bit as much a part of the performance as any participant. Wacker (2001:40) concludes from his historical research of Pentecostalism in the United States that while the experience of Holy Spirit baptism might be personal, it is rarely private.

To suggest that belief or private conviction is secondary to ritual practice and the public performance of Pentecostal religion in the barrio is in my mind neither an exaggeration nor a particularly novel claim (the idea is at least as old as Durkheim); however, to pose it this way—as a comparison—is to do something that believers themselves would never do. Nonetheless, I have shown here that believers explicitly privilege practice over theory—"doing" over "knowing"—through doctrine classes that stress behavioral modifications over understanding theological concepts and by favoring appearances over private sentiments. In this case I am not suggesting anything that my informants themselves have not emphasized time and again. To paraphrase: it does not matter what is going on in converts' heads (that is, from time to time everyone struggles with sinful thoughts and the temptations of the Devil); what is important is that converts transform their thinking through daily prayer, rigorous ethical discipline, and faithful obedience to God in order to prove their conviction to others and confirm for themselves sincere renewal in Christ. True conviction is thought to follow once converts commit themselves to living or executing a transformed existence. Understandably, apparent changes in behavior are sometimes mistaken to reflect a definitive transformation of beliefs. However, changes in behavior are not always the result of a genuine internal conversion; many newcomers convert and attempt to follow the prohibitions without entirely understanding their deeper meaning or purpose within the faith. Neophytes change their behavior in order that they *come to believe*. Converts to the faith, especially initially, do not always fully understand its teachings, but all of them are expected to adapt their behavior to conform to a congregation's standards. Complying with the prohibitions is necessary to sanctify the body; compliance entitles converts to call themselves Christians and begin the process toward full conversion. In much the same sense as Geertz (1973:112–113) implied when he remarked, "It is out of the context of concrete acts of religious observance that religious conviction emerges on the human plane," believers insist that a good testimony will follow behavioral changes and that belief in the saving power of Jesus Christ will be realized by a genuine transformation of the self. The conventional rituals of Pentecostal belief frame and focus converts' attention on new modes of self, not only to realize difference from others, as Christian authorities, but also to bring forth new possibilities of character and thought within themselves, furnishing new potentialities of identity and self-worth that were only narrowly possible before.

Belief on its own is not irrelevant, of course, in fact quite the contrary. The Holy Spirit, with whose help they fend off the Devil, resist temptation, and avoid sin, assists converts in their struggle for self-control. It is arguably here where belief is most relevant. In order to sustain the sometimes challenging ascetic demands of the church, converts rely on the belief that God will support them in their time of need and give them the strength to overcome temptation. Faith or "belief" in Jesus Christ is considered to be the necessary support to conquer sin and to live a successfully reformed life. It is upon this assured conviction that believers rely, trusting that their fidelity to the church will secure their salvation.

Other observers too have noted the secondary importance accorded formal doctrine, especially in favor of practical procedures aimed at ends with traceable rewards (e.g., Roberts 1968:767, who connects the popularity of Protestant groups in Guatemala City to the social and economic advantages that they offer). The primacy of method over theory appears to resonate with traditional Pentecostal theology and its appropriation in the global South (Hollenweger 2004:130), contrasting, of course, with "Northern" Protestantism's tendency to emphasize ideas ("belief") over deeds. Schultze (1994:78) has proposed that one reason Pentecostalism has been so successful in Latin America is its privileging of performance and experiential "fun" over textual study. He notes that spiritual inspiration and the ability to "move a congregation emotionally" always seem to take precedent over education and academic study as qualifications for Pentecostal ministry (Schultze 1994:78). Robbins (2010:164), along with a growing chorus of other observers, points out that despite relatively little anthropological theorizing dedicated to ritual among Pentecostals, Pentecostal life is in fact "saturated with ritual to an unusual extent" (see also Lindhardt 2011). Citing impromptu prayer, spontaneous praising, frequent church services, and regular healing sessions, Robbins (2010:164) notes that Pentecostals devote a good deal of their time to ritual practice such that it permeates their everyday life (see also Csordas 1997, 2011; Albrecht 1999). Csordas (2011:129) insists that Pentecostal ritual performance "has the potential, for individuals and communities, to bring about the transformation of everyday life" and "to generate a new habitus." Although conscious acknowledgment of ritual practice within Pentecostal communities is somewhat rare, with Pentecostals themselves tending to reject the term "ritual" as something "unscriptural," "unspiritual," and even perhaps "dead" (Albrecht 1999:21), authors like Albrecht argue that ritual functions as a vital component of Pentecostal spirituality despite its negative framing within the faith itself. Scholars for many years have noted the experiential appeal of the faith to converts, attributing its popularity to its manner of worship (Robbins 2004a:125–127). Today, commentators are now taking note of the regular and significant role of ritual in the practice of Pentecostal Christianity, helping to highlight the material and embodied ways in which converts *do* their religion.

The criterion of evangelical Christian belonging is based on more than just *what* one believes but importantly also on *how* one believes. I have proposed here that the function of belief as a category of religious identity in Dominican Pentecostalism is subordinate to the function of performance and the *doing* of evangelical Christianity. Active participation prevails over idle spectatorship in any Pentecostal service. To be a *cristiano* requires that one not just elects a Christian identity but necessarily *performs* one.

For most, conviction is a matter of process, of *being* and *becoming* rather than of absolute achievement or final completion (besides, followers fear a confident state of mind could arouse dangerous complacency). Local Pentecostals view Christian identities as projects continually at work, constantly made and remade anew through social interaction. It is therefore envisioned as an achieved status, a personal accomplishment, one not ascribed at birth or finally realized upon conversion, but earned and continually renewed by demonstrative acts of fidelity. For the Pentecostal community in Villa it is not enough to simply proclaim one's Christianness; a convert must substantiate it. It follows that a believer's spiritual development in the gospel is rewarded institutionally through adult baptism and compensated mystically through "spirit baptism" or speaking in tongues. Spiritual transformation of the individual is sanctioned at different stages through such rites that also serve to mark a convert as saved, sanctified, and therefore "different" from his or her neighbors.

Being Christian becomes the status that converts claim most important in their lives—indeed, the most significant personal and public identity that they maintain. Being a *cristiano* structures how converts act, talk, dress, and think. So profound is conversion to Jesus Christ in Pentecostal churches that "being different," rather than, say, salvation or spiritual redemption, is for members the most salient feature of Pentecostal theology even if, in the last instance, they proclaim redemption to be their ultimate goal. However accessible the intellectual benefits of salvation theology may be, personal change and the idea of sanctity are always more present and tangible to believers, especially in places like Villa where they provide immediate satisfaction in the form of respect.

People join the Pentecostal church for a variety of reasons, but belief is not a necessary condition to join or even to start attending a church—in fact, one may become a *cristiano* before one truly "believes." The reasons that I encountered for why people join the church ranged from "I wanted to go out with a girl at the church but I couldn't because I wasn't Christian," to "God fulfilled a *promesa* for me, so I converted," to "God called me to the faith in a special way," to "It is fun, it makes me happy," to "I converted because my husband [or wife] converted," to "We joined the church because we were poor and new in town and needed help." And still others convert to avoid spirit possession and to escape ritual obligation to the *seres* or saints. These reasons were given just as often if not more so than "I converted in order to serve God more completely" or "to save my soul." This variation suggests that belief or internal conviction by itself does not explain—cannot explain on its own—conversion or interest in the church.

According to the church, an individual's spiritual transformation is to be reflected in his or her behavior and also represented by changes in one's material life (clothes, home, and so forth) and in some cases the name by which one is addressed. A change in one's name, category, or title represents a transformation of the self through a meta-statement bearing the message "I am someone else." Through such techniques of (re)classification, converts construct a narrative of difference by the (re)naming of themselves and others in order to create new categories of recognition and valor that uplift believers while reconstituting old identities anew.

As I have shown here, Christian identity is made real through practices of signification that turn on difference as a master trope. Being a *cristiano* in Villa means being different in specific delineated ways that signify positively appraised social values. Because of this association, some observers have

proposed that Pentecostal membership may help converts reinscribe negative identities with alternative categories of worth that resist harmful stereotypes and deflect debilitating labels (see Wedenoja 1980; Austin-Broos
1997; Toulis 1997; Burdick 1998; Brodwin 2003).

Drawing from her work on Jamaican Pentecostals, Austin-Broos (1997)
has made the crucial point that through strict behavioral prohibitions, the
church enables converts to take control of their own self-identity. As self-
proclaimed saints, she argues, Pentecostals in Jamaica are able to wield a
measure of control over their own suffering by claiming moral perfection.
The dysfunctional order of an individual's social and emotional life is not
attributed to the accident of birth or the debilitating social environment
that weaned them, but rather "to a chosen personal history of spiritual and
moral being which can be changed and will be changed only through commitment to a saving God" (Austin-Broos 1997:146). This renegotiation of
meaning endows Pentecostals with the power not only to "image and represent" but also to "valorize subjects through desirable practices" (Austin-
Broos 1997:11). Pentecostals are equipped with and therefore empowered
by a store of Christian symbols framed by a doctrine of morality that they
themselves access, control, and embody. According to Austin-Broos (1997),
the mobilization of this symbolic repertoire was integral in transgressing a
central Jamaican stereotype of being black, female, and lower class—particularly what she calls "concubinage." By permitting a clear break with the past,
Pentecostalism in Jamaica enables followers to forge a new moral identity
that counteracts the dominant stereotype of the unmarried black woman.
By reordering the convert's moral world to allow for perfection to be realized, Pentecostalism breaks with oppressive social ascriptions that criminal-
ize the poor, empowering members to contest their own self-identity.

Similarly, dominant representations of the "mature black woman" in Brazil, according to Burdick (1998), deploy images of the self-effacing black
maid; the affectionate, self-deprecating black mother; and the malevolent
practitioner of black magic (*macumbeira*). Conversion to Pentecostalism,
he argues, has the effect of disarticulating these stereotypes when applied
to the female practitioner. One of Burdick's black female informants proclaimed: "My neighbors were always accusing me of being a *macumbeira*.
Since I passed into the church, I never hear that anymore. They know that
a child of God cannot mess with that stuff" (1998:141). Her identity as a
Pentecostal disarms suspicion of witchcraft because her faith denounces it

publicly. Here, mere association with the church may be enough to dispel the stereotype.[19]

In order to claim the status of respectable *cristianos*, converts must demonstrate their sanctity and convince others of their authenticity according to their proper participation in the faith and not, alternatively, by what they "know" about the divine. It is not enough to have made a personal or rather private change: Pentecostals are required to prove through demonstrative public acts that they are something new and somehow different. As such, I have endeavored to show that Christian identity is negotiated publicly through a variety of signifying practices that are either recognized as valid or invalid by observers. One is either acknowledged to be a serious *cristiano* or not, and these evaluations are always a negotiation. The emphasis Pentecostals in Villa put on the public image of the church shows that Christianity is at least as much a social project as it is a personal one and thus a key component of Dominican social and cultural life in the barrio and beyond.

5

Youth Gangs, Conversion, and Evangelical Moral Authority

In barrios around the Dominican Republic there are many who hold that in order to truly serve God, one must convert to a Pentecostal church. Perhaps the most surprising people holding such beliefs in Villa Altagracia are members of youth gangs called *naciones* (nations). Curiously, these unlikely allies are enthusiastic sponsors of Pentecostal exceptionalism and the holiness claims of converts. This chapter looks at the manner in which Pentecostalism has come to epitomize an ideal form of Christianity for barrio residents as it considers how the church is viewed publicly and the conditions under which it is regarded as a Christian authority from the perspective of popular youth gangs.

I make the case that youth gangs reproduce evangelical authority through the public recognition of Pentecostal exceptionalism. Conversion to the Pentecostal church represents, in most instances, the only feasible way out of sworn lifelong allegiance to a gang. Once a male convert has left a gang for the church, he is no longer a participant in the reciprocal economy of violence that characterizes street life in the gang. Gang members "look after" Pentecostals, whom they see as exemplars of Christian faith and representatives of God on earth. As favored and respected neighbors, remarkable exceptions are made for converts, including absolution of preconversion transgressions, immunity from violence, and freedom from harassment and involvement in street life. Evangelical modes of Christian practice represent for youth gangs the embodiment of Christian morality, and, as such, Pentecostals are revered for their favor with God.

Over the following pages I explore the criteria by which individuals evaluate one another's conduct as "Christian," showing how, by authorizing evangelical themes and validating Pentecostal claims to sanctity, youth gangs contribute to the shaping of an evangelical exceptionalism wherein so-called true converts are recognized as special sanctified persons who are entitled to exceptions, exemptions, and immunities based on their verifiable commitment to serving God and their demonstrable fulfillment of a born-again lifestyle.

I offer ethnographic evidence to show that evangelicalism represents an identity of exception in the streets as it provides sanctuary to converts and, in many cases, immunity from gang affiliation and reciprocal relations of violence—indeed, a fascinating dynamic observed elsewhere in Latin America (see Wolseth 2008, 2011; Brenneman 2012; Smilde 2007). Perhaps most surprisingly, gang members not only respect evangelical Christian sanctity in the streets, but they also defend it. In so doing, youth gangs affirm evangelical Christian themes such as "forgiveness," "sanctification," and "redemption/salvation," bringing abstract soteriological concepts to life in concrete, objectively experienceable ways.

Together, the church and youth gangs fashion a social reality inspired by the doctrinal ideal of transformation from sinner to saint. Converts from youth gangs learn to experience their transformation in Jesus Christ as social possibilities mediated and given immediate relevance by the very institutionalization of relations between the church and the gangs. This in turn validates conversion as a legitimate "way out," authenticating the church's claim to moral and spiritual authority.

I attempt to understand this puzzling relationship between the church and youth gangs in terms of local moral hierarchies rooted in Christian cultural hegemony. The often-heard admonition that "one doesn't play around (or joke) with things of God" highlights the seriousness with which Christianity is regarded locally and the social status it enjoys as the preeminent moral authority in the barrio.

This chapter, then, is about the social status of Pentecostal Christianity, the ways in which it has become a part of everyday life in the barrio, how it has come to represent for a good many residents the ideal form of Christian orthodoxy in the country. The transformative culture of Pentecostal

Christianity is a clearly visible fixture in local neighborhoods, extending beyond the religious sphere to permeate even the most unexpected corners of Dominican society. Here I examine local culture as it is shot through with evangelical themes that seem to come to life not in spite of but rather because of their adoption by various segments of the local community.

Biographical Sketches: José Luis, Danilo, Radames, Angel

José Luis, Danilo, and Radames are three young men who converted to Pentecostalism from transnational youth gangs known in the Dominican Republic as *naciones*. Angel, who is also discussed at length here, is not a *cristiano* but a local leader of a *nación*. I begin this section with several brief biographical sketches to introduce the primary sources for the following discussion.

José Luis was an exuberant twenty-six-year-old completing the equivalent of his second year of high school (he had dropped out in the seventh grade) when I met him in the fall of 2008. He was working as a baker while going to school, and it was his hope to attend the university and study computer repair upon completion of his studies. By almost everyone's account, José Luis had become a well-mannered, clean-cut, and driven young man whose reputation in the community was second to none. However, according to José Luis himself, and those who knew him before his conversion, he was once a picture of deviance and delinquency. His reputation preceded him. Almost everyone I met in Villa knew him to one degree or another. He was notorious for having been the epitome of a gangster, *tíguere*, and "man of the streets." He was equally known for having converted and by most accounts for having turned his life around completely. José Luis, like many other young men I met during my fieldwork, had converted from a *nación*.

José Luis had converted on New Year's Day, 2006, at the annual open-air banquet thrown by Iglesia Evangélica Pentecostal (IEP) just outside the church. He was the first of his family to convert and the only one of his friends who converted that night who remains "in the gospel." He is an active member of the church and enjoys preaching and evangelizing. He was the president of the youth group at IEP and president of his class in school. Perhaps not coincidentally, before converting he was also the local leader of his street gang *los reyes* (also called *los king*, the transnational gang known in the United States as the Latin Kings). José Luis once remarked to me,

"*Dios me llamó para ser cabeza, no cola*" ("God called me to be the head, not the tail"), commenting on his tendency to take up leadership positions in whatever undertaking he pursues.

José Luis rarely went anywhere without his Bible, and he was often giving *consejos* (counseling sessions, "advice") in the neighborhood. I never saw him without a dress shirt, tie, and clean, pressed pants, and he prided himself on exactly how different he had become from his former self.

Pastor Ramón, of Iglesia de Dios (IdD), introduced me to Danilo at the end of 2008. Danilo was a member of another IdD congregation across town and, like José Luis, was once a member of a *nación*. Before converting, Danilo was the leader of *los sangre* (also *los blood*, known as the Bloods in the United States) in Villa. He is originally from Villa but had lived in various towns and cities across the country and was twenty-seven years old when we met. Danilo was always eager to talk with me about his life before converting. I found our talks to be honest and without embellishment. He provided details when prompted, and he tried his best to be forthcoming about his previous life in the gang.

Perhaps the most striking detail about Danilo was the highly visible scars he bore on both his face and arms. His left eye in particular was cloudy and blind, highlighted by a long scar that drew across his brow down to his cheekbone. He had lost his eye to a machete that struck him across the face during a fight. He had a number of other disfigurements on his legs and arms from similar assaults. On his lower back he had a scar from a stabbing that disabled one of his kidneys. Additionally, a few round black scars marked his arm and stomach from bullet wounds that had healed in years prior.

At a young age, Danilo became involved in drugs and the street life. He attributes most of the ten years of his life involved in gangs to his drug use. He began using marijuana at age fifteen and quickly changed to crack and cocaine. According to Danilo, drugs were a central feature of gang life, and drug use was obligatory:

> I said many times "I'm not going to use [drugs]" and it would last a month, maybe even two, but when you are [in a gang] you are forced to use drugs. If I didn't, the others would have seen me as a chump [*pariguayo*], someone who is all talk and no action. Everyone who is in a gang, who is hanging out, has to use drugs. If not, you can't hang

out with them. So, if I was the leader, I was the head, the organizer of protests [*huelgas*] or whatever mischief they went to do, the first person that had to use [drugs] was me because I was supposedly the boss [*el jefe*].

Los sangre have the reputation of being one of the more violent *naciones* in the country. In order to join the gang, one must commit an assault on someone; one must, in effect, spill blood:

> I was in the *nación* called *los sangre*—those that have to cut people. In order to participate in this *nación* one has to at least attack or hit someone with a machete [*darle un machetazo*], otherwise shoot someone. If not, you can't be in the gang. We also had red and blue handkerchiefs, which we used along with two small earrings. This was the signal that we belonged to the gang, but we would hide them so that the police did not see. But even if the police came, they wouldn't say anything because we were a gang; not just one or two people, we were many, and nobody wants problems with a group of people.

As a gang member, Danilo claims he was always armed because he had "enemies everywhere." Usually he would carry a knife, machete, or a homemade gun called a *chilena* for special occasions (planned assaults, or *huelgas*). A *chilena*, also called a *chagon* (shotgun), is an improvised firearm that fits regular ammunition and is made from metal tubing, tape, wood, and other found materials.

While in the gang, Danilo was responsible for leading fifteen people (including women), a small number compared to some of the other gangs around town. Considering the country as a whole, *los sangre* as an organized street gang is quite large. It is, of course, very difficult if not impossible to estimate the actual number of youth belonging to gangs because of their sworn secrecy. Part of this secrecy comes from their constant struggle with police, but it is also maintained by the internal rules of the gang that forbid members from speaking publicly about the organization or their involvement with it.

Radames was once a member of the Trinitarios gang, also known as *DPL* (*Dios, Patria, Libertad*) and *la trinitaria* (the Holy Trinity). He had joined the gang when he was twelve years old. He was seventeen when I met him at IEP in 2008, and he had only been a *cristiano* for five months (he had converted at a *campaña* in Villa). Before joining the church, he had been kicked out of a trade school two years earlier because of his association with the *nación*. He was waiting to matriculate again once his paperwork went through the system.

Radames, like many other young converts that I met, was very enthusiastic about the church, its teachings, and being a *cristiano*. But he also struggled with many of the demands of born-again life, especially the prohibitions that members are enjoined to follow. Radames slept in the church along with Héctor and José Luis and would split time at home with his mother and his two younger sisters. His father lived in New York, and prior to his conversion and subsequent arrangement to sleep in the church, Radames lived on his own with other members of his gang.

It is difficult if not impossible to speak with gang members about being in a gang because of the shroud of secrecy that surrounds them. It was explained to me that if anyone were caught talking to me about the gang or their membership in it, they could be punished, possibly beaten by members of their own gang. However, one local gang leader, Angel, of the Trinitarios, readily spoke with me about the gang, Christians, and pretty much anything I wished to talk to him about. I assume his willingness to speak with me had to do with the fact that he was the man in charge; he was *el jefe supremo*, the local leader of the Trinitarios in Villa.

I met Angel through José Luis, a former member of the rival gang *los reyes*. I had asked a number of my informants if they would introduce me to gang members because I wanted to understand how they viewed the Pentecostal community around town. I had initially asked Radames if he would introduce me to Angel—because they were cousins—but he was unable to set up a meeting. José Luis asked Angel if he would speak to me, and he speedily obliged.

Angel was a skinny eighteen-year-old when I first spoke with him one afternoon in 2009. Angel's younger brother was the only Christian convert in his family; neither he, his other four siblings, nor his parents had ever joined the church. Angel worked in a *colmado* (convenience store) in the capital and had dropped out of school before his first year of high school in order to take a job. In an observance reminiscent of the original Scarface movie (1932), he carried with him a coin that he would flip back and forth from time to time in his pocket. The coin was from the Trujillo dictatorship, with an image of Trujillo on one side of the coin and the Dominican crest on the other. The coin was a gift from his grandmother; he carried it because of the slogan "*Dios, Patria, Libertad*"—the motto of the Trinitarios—emblazoned on the back.

Despite their individual differences, José Luis, Danilo, Radames, and Angel all considered themselves products of the street and shared parallel experiences of violent barrio life at one time or another as gang members in Villa.

Naciones: Dominican Youth Gangs

Transnational youth gangs, referred to locally as *naciones*, are prevalent in Villa as they are in most urban centers around the country. Although street gangs have existed for a long time in the Dominican Republic, it was not until recently, the last several decades or so, that the country saw a prolif-eration of this particular type of youth gang organization (*Clave Digital*, January 15, 2007). Sometimes referred to in the literature as "transnational youth gangs," these groups are international and claim members in coun-tries all over the globe. Today, youth gangs in the Dominican Republic have become a common feature of urban barrios and, according to local police, a major source of delinquency and lawlessness.

Violence is a common feature of gang life, as *naciones* defend territory and are often involved in illicit activities such as drug trafficking, assault, and robbery. Part of what continues the cycle of violence between gangs is the requirement to be on top and to return violence with violence. "If you attack or kill one of ours, then we must attack and kill one of yours" is a com-mon prescription employed by youth gangs seemingly everywhere. Angel explained to me that the Trinitarios have a saying, "*sangre de tu sangre, sangre de mi sangre, sangre que corre de la tuya, va corriendo de la mía,*" which is to say that members see each other as one in the same, organs of the same body. If one Trinitario is cut, the other bleeds, suggesting poetically that if any one of their members is attacked, they are all attacked, and they will defend each other as if they were close kin connected by blood. This potentially endless cycle of violence perpetuates animosity between gangs while encouraging warfare between them. The tit for tat continues until one group agrees to leave things as they are, not trying to one-up the other, finally breaking the cycle for good.

In the context of poverty and high unemployment, the illicit activities of *naciones* may provide urban youth practical means for achieving modest economic gains, but this alone does not explain the appeal of such a lifestyle, particularly because of the dangers and other risks involved with membership. Many gang members will spend time in jail and, at worst, will lose their lives to violence. Most of the former gang members I spoke with had spent some time in prison (anywhere from five days to over five years). A number of my informants, incidentally, converted to Christianity while serving time in prison. While warfare between gangs accounts for much of the violence in youth gangs today, young men associated with *naciones* are frequently the targets of state-sponsored repression and police and military violence.

Most gang members in Villa are young, between the ages of fourteen and twenty-one, a trait typical of street gangs elsewhere (see Vigil 2003:226–227). All members must be initiated into the gang, and initiation rituals differ between gangs. Many *naciones* use violent initiation rites in order to ensure a recruit's commitment to the group and resolve to join. Once initiated, a recruit becomes a member for life and submits to the will of the group and its laws. This commitment for life is de jure if not de facto in practice. Much like the marriage pact, which presumably ties a groom to his bride forevermore (despite the obvious possibility of divorce), in theory a gang inductee is a permanent member of a clique, even if in practice the gang may not be able to guarantee his allegiance forever (many may, in time, sever their ties to the gang through conversion, migration, or marriage as a consequence of aging-out). Young men in the barrio do not join *naciones* with the intention of leaving in old age any more than couples tie the knot with the intention of filing for divorce at a later date. Membership is said to be for life, even if few active gang members are much older than twenty-one. The unfortunate reality is that many gang members are killed or imprisoned before they reach the ages at which they might forsake their gang loyalties in favor of raising a family or pursuing more stable, legitimate forms of employment that offer more security.

The gangs themselves are brotherhoods based on a structure of loyalty and mutual aid providing members with protection, prestige, money, and friendship (and, I think, quite simply something to do), in exchange for complete, undying allegiance to the gang. Youth gangs are typically hierarchical and subject to explicit laws of their own creation. Outside of their own rules, *naciones* offer members a kind of freedom to "do what they want" subject to the laws and wishes of the gang itself (*Clave Digital*, January 15, 2007).

The guiding principles of each gang are held to be sacred ideals. Their laws—in some cases referred to as *la biblia*, or "the Bible"—are said to supersede all other laws, and members are expected to uphold the rules without exception. A member not living up to the expectations of the gang, or any member who is found to have violated one of its laws, is disciplined swiftly. This discipline may only be as stern as a verbal warning or possibly as severe as corporal punishment in the form of flogging or worse; some violations even carry the threat of death. Strict enforcement of gang rules ensures the loyalty and dedication of members and, along with gang signs, tattoos, and signifying colors, consolidates their commitment to shared values and identity, especially in opposition to other gangs.

There are many active youth gangs throughout the country, many of which have come to the island from the United States, including the Bloods, the Latin Kings, and the Trinitarios. Other gangs include *los Pantera, Black and White*, DDP ("Dominicans Don't Play"), *la 42* ("*la forty tu*"), *Amor y Paz, Ñeta*, and the humorously named group *los Talibán* ("the Taliban"). It is difficult to estimate the total number of youth gangs in the country, but some estimates suggest that there are more than sixty. According to my informants, there were some fifteen active *naciones* in Villa.

For Angel and others, being in a gang is about more than just passing time or a way to get respect; indeed, for whatever else being in a gang meant to him, being a Trinitario was a way of representing his Dominicanness and, in Angel's mind, of being patriotic. He claimed to have joined the Trinitarios in order to represent the nation at a deeper level:

Some friends of mine saw me and told me that there were groups representing a nation. They first asked me if I knew what a *king* was. I said no. A *sangre*? I said no. Then they asked me, "Do you know who the Trinitarios are?" I said yes, the Trinitarios were Duarte, Sánchez and Mella. They told me that "this is where we come from, we are Trinitarios, but this is another way of representing *el pueblo*." The Trinitarios here do not rob; they don't attack anyone or anything like that. But the others do. So I got involved when he said to me "I am a Trinitario, and I would like it if you were as well so that when you see abuse, you don't turn away from it, you get involved so that others won't continue to abuse [the defenseless]." And I said great, that's cool, no problem.

For Angel, the Trinitarios exist to protect neighborhoods from the corrupting influence of foreign youth gangs that have come to his country, like the Bloods and Ñeta (Puerto Rico). He suggested to me that the Trinitarios were something good for the municipality because they defended the interests of a free and independent country. While the other gangs sold drugs and perpetrated violence, Angel maintained that the Trinitarios were against such provocations and were concerned with protecting residents from exactly those influences.

The Trinitarios are a patriotic self-consciously Dominican gang and are unique in appropriating national symbols and putting them into service for the gang. Their primary colors—red, blue, and white—correspond to the colors of the Dominican flag (green and black are also used, however inconspicuous such colors may be in the flag itself). The hierarchy, rank, and titles within the gang are based on national heroes, with the founding fathers Juan Pablo Duarte, Francisco del Rosario Sánchez, and Ramón Matías Mella making up the top three positions in the hierarchy. Gang leaders in the Trinitarios are given the title of "Duarte," second in command Sánchez, then Mella, then Luperón, after that Caamaño, and so on—all of them important historical figures of the republic. The gang's motto—"*Dios, Patria, Libertad*"—is gleaned from the national slogan—"God, Fatherland, Freedom"—and can be found prominently displayed on a banner adorning the national crest at the center of the Dominican flag. Each gang celebrates a special day to commemorate their collective ties. *Los reyes*, for example, celebrate on January 6 (on *el dia del los reyes*, or "Three Kings Day"). *Los sangre* celebrate on February 14 (Valentine's Day, no doubt because of the association of hearts with blood). The Trinitarios, for their part, celebrate on February 27—the day of Dominican independence.

As mentioned, the Trinitarios are also known as *DPL* (*Dios, Patria, Libertad*) as well as *la trinitaria* (the Holy Trinity). This triad is a key symbol for the Trinitarios, as *la trinitaria* indexes not only the Holy Trinity—God, the Son, and the Holy Spirit—but also the Dominican triumvirate—Duarte, Sánchez, Mella—as well as the country's three founding principles of God, Fatherland, and Freedom.

It is common for members of the Trinitarios to get tattoos of the flag or the national shield to represent their allegiance to the gang and their country. Radames had the letters DPL tattooed on him, something that at the time, for him, represented in three letters his gang, his country, and his faith. Likewise, Angel had a tattoo of a dove with a clover in its mouth—the dove a popular symbol of the Holy Spirit, and the clover a multivocalic symbol representing the Trinity, the gang, DPL, and Duarte, Sánchez, Mella.

Most of the symbolism used by the Trinitarios—sometimes shortened to the form 3ni—involves the number three, which adds an element of mystique to their guiding principles. Through this mystique the gang takes on an aura of transcendence that serves to unite members and ensure their common allegiance.

Angel saw his *nación*, which he sometimes referred to as an "association," as something good for the country, a group singularly and admirably devoted to the defense of justice in the face of tyranny perpetrated by foreign gangs. The irony of such a take is apparent in the fact that the Trinitarios did not originate in the Dominican Republic at all. Like many other youth gangs, the Trinitarios began as an ethnic prison gang in New York City. Established by Dominican inmates, they were initially concerned with protecting Dominicans from the abuses of other ethnic prison gangs like the Latin Kings (largely Puerto Rican) and the Bloods (chiefly African American). The gang quickly spread from the New York state prison system to New York City streets and neighboring New Jersey in the 1990s and has within a relatively brief period of time become one of the fastest growing street gangs in the New York metropolitan area. It appears likely that the deportation of Dominican convicts back to the island has played an important role in enabling the Trinitarios as well as other street gangs from the United States and Puerto Rico to take root in the Dominican Republic (see Brotherton 2008; Brotherton and Barrios 2009:51, 2011).

An important function of youth gangs in the barrio is the socialization of young men. After all, gangs are primarily male associations committed to enacting or claiming a type of masculinity, especially in the context of poverty, unemployment, political disenfranchisement, and not infrequent cuckoldry—indeed, potentially emasculating conditions for poor men excluded from hegemonic definitions of manhood that include the myth of the male breadwinner. The increasing alienation of male labor in the context of neoliberal economic restructuring, of which the feminization of manufacturing jobs is but one example (see Safa 1995, 2002), has provided perhaps the ideal conditions for the spread of these elective brotherhoods, not to mention the possible stimulus of what Lewis (1990, 2004) has described as the social and economic "crisis" of masculinity facing men in the Caribbean today. Through violence and aggression, gang members earn respect out of autonomous acts of power and agency. Through the submission of other men by violent force, gang members win psychological rewards in addition to the prestige they earn through fear and intimidation of others. Added to that, in all-male peer groups like the *naciones* disenfranchised youth resist their oppression at the hands of the state's tyrannical strategy of *la mano dura* (heavy-handedness) used to combat urban delinquency but disproportionately applied to young male barrio residents.

Perhaps the most obvious symbol of masculinity wielded by Dominican gang members is the ubiquitous machete. Members of *naciones* carry machetes as their preferred weapon of choice. The symbol of the machete has a long history in the Caribbean and is employed in a variety of festivals, religious rituals, games, and theatrical performances. At the same time, the machete itself is perhaps most readily associated with secular work and the backbreaking labor of sugarcane cultivation. As a symbol of labor and difficult oppressive work more generally, the reappropriation of the farmer's tool and the symbol of a farmer's toil as weapons of will and liberating power in the hands of the downtrodden is as significant in the ritual sphere (as in the Rara religious festival in Haiti or the parallel Gagá festival in the Dominican Republic) as it is in the more utilitarian space of the urban streets and barrios (see, for example, Burton 1997 on the symbolism of the sword in Caribbean ritual and expressive culture).

The machete is a masculine symbol par excellence. Used primarily by men in labor-intensive agriculture, the machete is used to clear land for crops and to cut sugarcane. As a field tool the machete is symbolic of men's work (as opposed to the type of work historically performed by women). Because the tool is used for cutting, clearing, removing, or, in another sense, "destroying" other objects, the machete may be linked with another range of cultural symbols associated with men—objects of destruction (compared with objects of creation as female symbols). Linguistically, the term "machete" is most likely a diminutive of *macho* ("male"), an alteration of *mazo* ("sledgehammer" or "club"), which, according to some etymologists, is probably a dialectal variant of *maza* or "mallet," from the vulgar Latin *mattea*, meaning "war club."[1] In a sense, then, originally an agricultural tool native to Central America and the Caribbean, the machete's use value has returned to its linguistic roots in the hands of Dominican gang members, once again being taken up as modern-day war clubs in the service of contemporary urban warfare. Just as the machete in the hands of field workers is used to fell sugarcane stalks, it is used today by urban youth to sever limbs and to cut down male opponents in violent masculine contests over territory, drugs, women, and money, and for the purposes of male goals such as conquest, bravery, reputation, and renown.

The rural field tool in the hands of unemployed urban street kids and teenagers represents a new form of autonomy from the demands of exploitative work and historical ties to the land and its cultivation. With it, urban youth enact a type of masculinity associated with power, strength, and physical domination of other men. It is no accident that just as rural labor is becoming a less viable way of life, such tools would now be used in the urban barrios by individuals seeking to make a name and a living for themselves in the streets.

The machete might be understood as "the poor man's sword." Machetes are cheap and readily available to anyone and are just as good weapons as they are innocuous tools. A macho man not only owns one, but he also knows how to use it. Just in case further evidence is needed to demonstrate a relationship between the machete and masculinity, anecdotal evidence suggests that there is at least a passing association between the machete and the male sex organ. Angel assured me that he had a great big one at home: "*si, en mi casa tengo yo un machete grandísimo,*" he said with a nod and a smile. Of course, the association of clubs and bats with phallic symbolism is also well established in the psychoanalytic literature.

As the local leader of the Trinitarios, Angel's rank is Duarte, but he is aware that he cannot be *el jefe* forever; few gang members are much older than twenty-something, as violence, prison, migration, or other exigencies of street life take their toll. He figures that he will remain in the gang for another four years and retire, so to speak: "Today I am Duarte until death or until I want to be a Christian."

Personal Redemption, Born-Again Exceptions

All of the *naciones* that I became familiar with claim to revere God such that one of the only ways to leave a gang after one has joined is to commit one's life to religious service and convert to Christianity, which usually means to join an evangelical church. According to Radames (who explained to me the particulars of his former gang the Trinitarios), upon entering the gang, new recruits take an oath:

> You take an oath when you join—you say that only death will free you or converting to Jesus Christ. . . . In order to join they give you a twenty-one-day test to enter. After these twenty-one days they give you a role and you swear that if you leave [the gang] they kill you or they make an X on your back. Only if you convert in Jesus Christ are you saved from this. This is what saved me, I converted.

José Luis, a former member of *los reyes*, explained to me that conversion in order to leave the gang was simply a general rule that his gang and others were obliged to follow. Speaking specifically about the laws of *los reyes*:

> [The others in the gang] have to accept [one's conversion] because it is one of the rules that they follow. After that, nothing. They respect [your decision to leave] when you marry and when you are a Christian. If you marry and have your wife and you've separated yourself [from the streets] they respect it because you are no longer involved in those things. . . . If you are a Christian they fully respect it, they don't approach you with gang stuff, none of that.
>
> [After I converted] I went to a meeting with the gang, [turned in my notebook of rules] and they said to me: "What happened?" I said, "Nothing, I converted to Jesus Christ and I feel good." They hugged me and said, "Is it true that you converted? Wow, great, good for you, keep it up!" One takes a side, and I have chosen to stay here, in the gospel.

Conversion is not just accepted as a way out of a *nación*; at times it is even applauded. According to José Luis's description, fellow gang members embraced him when he converted, happily accepting his resignation. This is a far cry from what might have occurred had he decided to leave without proper reason or warning. The rules of the *naciones* are strict; there are few, if any, exceptions. If someone converts and officially renounces the gang, he is held accountable for his decision. If he does not make a full conversion—that is, if he does not remain in the church and demonstrate a convincing transformation—the gang will punish him. From the perspective of the *nación*, you are either serving the gang or you are serving God; you must serve one or the other, there is no in-between. Radames explains:

> Now [the gang] tells me not to leave [the church]. If I leave the church I will have problems with [the gang] because I left them in order to put myself in the church. That is to say, I have to take one of the two things that are required. I am not going to leave [the church]. I am going to stay here.

This, of course, is the same position maintained by the Pentecostal church: you cannot be in a gang and serve God simultaneously. It was exactly on this point that Radames, Angel, and others insisted that in order to leave a gang one had to convert to Jesus Christ and that involvement in the Catholic Church would never suffice as an alternative. They reasoned that if one could party, gamble, fight in the streets, use drugs, or curse—in other words be an active member of a gang—and then attend Mass at the local Catholic church every Sunday, then one could not be a "true Christian." So-called true Christians act like Christians should, which from this perspective usually means that converts follow the prohibitions of the church, regularly participate in congregation activities, testify with regularity, and preach the word of God.

Radames explained that he went to the Catholic church regularly when he was in the gang and that it was not until he joined the Pentecostal church that he was told that it was not okay to do many of the things he was accustomed to doing (such as drinking and pursuing women). Angel echoed this refrain when he suggested that Catholics were too permissive to be considered servants of God. He explains here why evangelical conversion in his gang supersedes any declaration of faith or allegiance to Catholicism:

> [It's possible to leave the gang to join the Catholic Church, but far fewer accomplish this than those who join the gospel.] God is less present with Catholics. Catholics say bad words but *cristianos* remain observant [*se mantienen vigilando*]. . . . The Catholics don't want to have anything to do with us [the Trinitarios]. They think that we are demonic. But when I'm talking with a Catholic I say "No! It is you who is a demon! I am not a demon; maybe I'm going to be more saved than you!" Because I carry God with me everywhere I go. Sure, it is normal for me to slip and say a bad word, but not like *those* Christians.

I don't say things like a lot of Catholics; I don't say things like "these guys are Satanic" or whatever. No. I always carry God with me. Maybe more than them, I'm not sure, but maybe I represent God more than many Catholics.

In his mind, Catholics are just as bad as anyone else. If a man is to leave a gang, he must leave the street life completely, and for Angel and others, the only vehicle for such a departure is the Pentecostal church, because it is stricter and its members "remain observant."

I discussed at length with Radames on many occasions why he thought the gangs deferred to Christianity in this way, and his response was always matter-of-fact:

Because they understand that to convert to Jesus Christ is something greater than what they have. This is what *they* told me. *They* said to me that we respect you in your conversion to Jesus Christ because that's just the way it is, something greater. Also, *Dios, Patria, Libertad* is the motto of the gang. It means Father, Son, and the Holy Spirit. *Dios, Patria,* and *Libertad*, they say that, or *DPL*, which is the same thing.

For the Trinitarios, being in the gang means that only one authority exists above all others (even that of the collective gang itself), and that is the Christian God. Being in a gang does not mean that one serves God per se, but rather that one respects God above all other things and, in the last instance, that one's last recourse is to God alone. However counterintuitive it may seem, for Radames and others, conversion to exit a gang was simply a taken-for-granted fact of barrio street life.

Probing his insight as an unconverted gang leader, I asked Angel why members of his gang were allowed to convert in order to leave despite their presumably binding commitment for life. He answered in much the same way as both Radames and José Luis: "I really accept it because they are with the Lord. If it weren't for him there wouldn't be the *Trinitarios*. He is the one who created us all. Because of him we all exist." Ideologically, the Trinitarios hold *Dios, Patria, Libertad* as their highest principle. Angel insisted that because God came before Fatherland and Freedom in their motto, gang members were obligated to respect conversion and compelled to revere *cristianos* because "Christianity puts God first" and "*cristianos* are with God."

This respect for Christianity, particularly its evangelical iterations, extends beyond conversion alone. Even while Angel refused to speak for other *naciones,* he insisted that the Trinitarios respected *cristianos* without exception. He stressed that they were to be respected above all others because of their proximity and service to God:

> [We respect Christians], it's a Dominican thing. [The Trinitarios] are a Dominican association. The Trinitarios are *Dios, Patria,* and *Libertad.* You have to respect Christianity because it puts God first; they are the only ones with God. . . . The fact is, *la trinitaria* must respect Christians. . . . I respect them; they are with the Great One; they are with Him. One has to respect them. They are with God.

Danilo explains a similar sentiment shared by the Bloods gang that he was a part of before converting. As a member of the gang, he respected *cristianos* because they were, in his words, "representatives of God on earth":

> Before converting I always respected *cristianos.* I never lacked respect for a Christian because I knew that the Christians were the part of God that was on earth. When I would see a Christian person I respected them. I remember one time I was on the corner hanging out with a friend; we were down in La Mella. We were on the corner and a young girl came walking by and the friend who was with me said, "Let's snatch her necklace." And I said to him, "No, not her because she is Christian" and my friend felt bad, but I said to him, "I respect the Christians." . . . I had respect toward the Christians because I knew that the Christians were a part of God in the world. . . . I had a fear of Christians. I never . . . whoever wasn't a Christian I could attack with a machete.

So serious are the rules of the gang in regards to conversion that when a young man converts, he is no longer tied to the reciprocal exchange of violence that attends gang membership. Ideally, conversion provides complete exemption from retaliation. For example, after converting, Danilo no longer worried about the debts he had incurred as a member of the Bloods gang. Allegedly (and, if indeed true, remarkably) all of the crimes he committed against his enemies were forgiven. In Danilo's account, rivals who were looking for revenge abandoned their grudges against him after he joined the church. He insists that if he remained with the Bloods he would have continued to be a target of enemy gangs and at risk of daily violence. Yet his conversion brought with it an exemption—a free pass, so to speak—to a new lease on life. He was, quite literally, forgiven—thus illustrating, to his satisfaction, the promise of redemption assured to him upon accepting Jesus Christ as his savior. His release from the gang became a vivid demonstration of his newfound faith's power to to save the lives of even those ensnared in the most astonishing webs of sin. He understands that his devotion to Jesus Christ is what saved him from certain death and that his identity as a *cristiano* is what ensures his safety in the streets today. Danilo has realized the promise of salvation in terms of his apparent redemption from gang life, a clean slate from which to kick-start life anew.

The Pentecostals in Villa are confident that they enjoy a kind of immunity in the streets that is ensured, if not policed, by the very gangs whose activities they rebuke but whose members they welcome with open arms.

The idea that *cristianos* are exempt from street violence was made clear to me in bold fashion one night during a *huelga*. In Villa, *huelgas* are demonstrations or protests that follow long periods of water and electricity shortages. During such protests, which may last several or more consecutive nights or even weeks, local gangs take over street corners and occupy entrances and exits out of town, preventing people from leaving or moving about. Roadblocks of broken glass and burning tires are set up at intersections to prevent cars from crossing. Businesses close early, and people are implored to stay in their homes. Anyone caught walking about or trying to leave is liable to be stoned, shot at, or chased with machetes. Those not obeying the unofficial curfew become combatants with gang members and others who temporarily assume control of the neighborhoods. Relative lawlessness reigns. Local police are typically far outnumbered and have little recourse to establish their authority. Because I could not leave Villa this particular evening due to the protests, I stayed with Wilfredo, a friend of mine from IEP, at his home in barrio Esperanza. After some time sitting out on the porch listening to gunfire ring out around the neighborhood with unnerving regularity, surprisingly to me, Wilfredo decided to leave the house and go to see if he could find us some food a few blocks away. Considering the unofficial curfew and the proximity of his home to a major roadblock (just down the street), I was concerned that a trip to find a late-night snack was probably not worth the risk. His wife agreed, but despite our pleas to forget about the food, he left anyway. As he walked off into the darkness he raised a Bible over his head and looked back at us declaring with the utmost confidence, "This is all the protection I need. I have my pistol right here." He returned twenty minutes later with his Bible in one hand and a bag of fried chicken in the other.

Although I knew many Pentecostals who often carried a Bible with them, Wilfredo was not one of them. He would bring his Bible to church, but I did not see him with it otherwise. He took the Bible on his walk that night, not out of habit or because he was planning to use it, but rather as a sign to others. The sign was that he was a *cristiano*. The Bible signaled to others that he was neither a combatant nor a threat: indeed, it signaled to others that he was not to be targeted. Wilfredo was confident that if he were identified as an *evangélico*, the young men patrolling the streets with rocks, guns, and machetes would leave him alone. What appeared to me at the time to be an unnecessary risk in Wilfredo's mind was no risk at all. He understood something that I did not: *cristianos* are not to be harmed.[2]

Perhaps I should have known better considering events that transpired only a few hours before. Earlier that evening Wilfredo had held a *culto* at his house, an auspicious gathering occasioned by a series of unfortunate events that had happened the previous week. Toward the end of the *culto* men from the *colmado* down the street, where they had set up a roadblock, came by the house and told everyone to hurry up and finish because they were waiting to start the *huelga* in that area of the neighborhood. After the *culto* finished, the men allowed everyone to leave before commencing the protest. Unfortunately for me, while we were able to leave the immediate vicinity, we could not leave the barrio itself because of other roadblocks that had been set up at the entrances to the main road out of town. What was striking about this incident is that the young men who would later that evening aggressively defend the roadblock on the corner waited for the *culto* to finish and allowed everyone the chance to go home before they began. The protest had begun in other parts of town and in other parts of the neighborhood, but despite this, the *culto* was allowed to finish, and the eighty or so attendees were allowed to depart unharmed.

Likewise, while giving me a ride one evening after a *culto* at IdD, Pastor Ramón explained that he was friends with the most powerful drug dealer in town, and not with a little bit of pride claimed that because of this connection, he was assured that nothing bad would happen to him: "He has said to me, if there is anything that you ever need, come see me and I will take care of it." Ramón said that because of this association, people in town could not touch him. I suspect that Ramón was telling me the truth, though there was no way for me to corroborate his story.[3] It is important to note, in any case, that Pentecostals believe themselves to be exempt from street violence precisely because they are respected as Christian converts.

Looking after Christians

In Villa, *naciones* respect the devout followers of the Pentecostal church. Faithful *cristianos* are exempt from street violence and within gangs find supporters who look after them and look out for their best interests in the streets. Danilo explains:

> Here in Villa Altagracia they respect Christians. Christians are respected. Their homes, the Christians, the evangelicals, the pastors, they are respected. The *tígueres* ought to take care of them.
>
> Here, there is this fear, there is this dogma—the Christians are respected. You can go anywhere and I can introduce you to someone who is of this life [*tigueraje* or gangs] and I say to them: "Look, he is Christian, wherever you see him, take care of him." And wherever you go they are going to look after you because I introduced you. "No, no, he is Christian, he was with Danilo the other day, he is a *cristiano*." They better take care of you because they know that we are the ones who pray for them and that you are the one who can bless them with whatever bread they may have any given day. In other words, the people that are Christian are taken care of.

The idea that being a *cristiano* in Villa means that you are less likely to be harassed and, more than that, that you are likely be taken care of and looked after in the streets is common, and extends to even young women from the church who feel less pestered by men precisely because of their church affiliation. According to Karla: "Around here none of the men cross the line with me. If someone wants to try, their friend will say 'this is the *hermana*' or whatever, 'don't cross the line with her.' . . . Yes, people treat me very well in the street."

Such a perspective is widespread in barrio Francisco; the consensus is that as sincere Christian converts, followers are under the watchful eyes of those around them and that mistreatment of respectable *cristianos* is simply not tolerated.

Seriousness, Fidelity, and True Conversion

As with most religious themes in Villa, Christianity is taken seriously, and conversion is seen as something not to be trivialized or joked with. This idea was repeated time and again by gang members, who insist on treating religious topics, Christianity specifically, with the utmost respect and deference. Christianity, they insist, is serious business; ideally, true Christians are to conduct themselves in a solemn, dignified manner in accordance with respectable values. This is not something to be taken lightly. Membership in a church requires genuine commitment. Angel explained to me that there are some Christians who like both Christianity and the street life, but this, he insists, is clearly a mistake: "No, no . . . for me, that's why I don't convert, I can't be playing around. I don't want to play around [or joke] with the Word of God or with any other thing of God." José Luis expressed having similar reservations the night he converted at a *campaña* two years earlier. While wanting to become a born-again Christian, he was concerned with not taking the commitment seriously. He explains here how he struggled to stay committed because "*uno no puede relajar con las cosas de Dios*" ("one mustn't joke [or play around] with things of God"):

[During the *campaña*] I was sitting cool [*jevi*] with my friends, having fun, laughing, meanwhile people were singing, I was also singing. When the preacher came out they called me up to the front and asked who wanted to accept Jesus Christ today. My buddies with me said, "Hey, let's convert!" and I said, "No, no, I cannot right now, I can't convert, I am not prepared for this." "Look," they said, "Let's do it, you can convert, it's going to go well." And I said, "No way, I don't joke with the things of God, *yo no relajo!*"

After everyone had left that night I said to my friends, those that were from the streets with me, those who converted with me, I said to them, "I have some money and I am going to buy drugs," or whatever, and they said to me, "Look, we already converted, we are already Christians, one does not play around with that." I said, "No, look, I have converted many times and I have not stayed in the gospel." They said to me, "No, you can't do it like that, we already converted, and one mustn't play around with this." Truthfully I was scared. I wanted to be Christian, I wanted to, but I was afraid of what I had to do to be

Christian. [I was afraid] I would not be able to leave the drugs or leave the things of the streets. This was my fear. Each time I got together with one of my friends I would say, "I converted last night, but how come today I don't want to?" With God, *no se relaja*, one cannot joke with things of God because you can have problems.

The trepidation that one should not take things of God lightly because there could be problems is supported by stories such as the one recounted to me by Radames about a man who was punished by God for leaving the church:

There was a man who did not believe that God was real. He kneeled before God and he said to him, "Lord, if you heal my son and my nephew I will convert and never leave the church again." After two days his son and his nephew were healed. The man lasted two months going to the church and then one day he left. After leaving the church he had a bad accident and burned his entire body. Afterward the Lord gave him a revelation: "If you would not have left me, this wouldn't have happened to you."

The idea that something could happen to you is substantiated further by the gangs, who evaluate the fidelity of converts and ensure compliance with the conversion exception by policing the behavior of converted gang members. True converts, those who remain faithful to the church and committed to living a sincere ascetic lifestyle, are acknowledged to be true men and women of God. Those who do not remain in the church after having left the gang are punished—in this case not by God but by the gangs, who ensure that one is sincere or "serious" about his or her conversion.

Cristianos are expected to comport themselves in accordance with the rules of the church, an expectation no less emphasized in the streets. Christianity is considered serious business as it relates to one's salvation and, besides constant vigilance, requires absolute adherence to the gospel. Such stakes require total surrender to an ascetic lifestyle. To play/joke, or *relajar*, with things of God means to not take them seriously, to not accord God the foremost place in one's life. For Pentecostals in Villa, *el relajo* is the opposite of seriousness and as a catchall term denotes a genre of behavior and attendant values associated with the street—the profane domain of *la calle*, the playground of the youthful undisciplined values of *tigueraje*.

Despite being cousins as well as onetime members of the same gang,

Angel did not think highly of Radames. Initially he was happy that Radames converted, but shortly afterward he was concerned that Radames was not acting like a Christian should or taking his commitment to the church seriously. He believed that if Radames did not clean up his act, he could be in a lot of danger. In fact, he was already in danger:

> Well, I was happy that Radames converted, I thought well of it, but there are still some things that I don't like about him. He wants to play. I have had to reproach him many times: "You are a Christian. You have to be in Christianity. Don't stand out. You are Christian, without *tigueraje*, take it easy." He wants to stand out, [he wants to be] Christian in the church and then ungodly [*impío*] in the streets. But I see what's really going on, Radames hasn't realized because he is my cousin. He wants to play [*jugar*] with Christianity and I have some dangerous friends that want to . . . Look, if he wants to get out of it. . . . He is Christian, but if he leaves the church it's going to look very bad, they are going to hurt him. The other day at the *fiesta patronal* they would have done it there because supposedly he was there. They would have hurt him.

Radames had gone to the yearly *fiesta patronal*, a popular festival organized in towns around the country in honor of patron saints. The festivals are usually large street affairs that are thrown by and for residents in a public square. The parties involve several evenings of music (*bachata, merengue, reggaeton*), revelry, and merrymaking. Because of the secular nature of such events, and perhaps too their Catholic origins, *cristianos* are not to attend. Radames had been seen there with friends enjoying himself, but that was frowned upon because he claimed to be a Christian and, more than that, he had left the gang to convert, officially renouncing such earthly pleasures. Angel made it clear to me that one of the only reasons why Radames had not been seriously harmed by fellow gang members was because of Angel's rank and his benevolent desire not to see Radames hurt, but he was concerned that there was only so much that he could do to protect him:

> Radames was in an association called a *nación*, if you leave this association there is nothing else but being Christian. Christian permanently. If you leave Christianity, you die. Here in Villa they don't kill you, Villa is small, they hit you here, leave you crippled. When it comes

we'll see. . . . There are friends of mine that speak to me first, because they have respect for me, I tell them no, I'm going to talk to him, I am going to say to him follow Christianity *tranquilo*, because I know what is happening, I speak with him and he says, "These people are not going to do anything, I am with God," and I think this is wrong, I'm not Christian but still I find this bad. A Christian would find this even worse.

Radames had violated a cardinal rule: if a man decides to leave a gang to become a Christian convert, he gives up a secular life for a spiritual one, in its entirety. The seriousness with which this violation is dealt (possibly physical punishment) indicates the magnitude of such an offense in the eyes of gang members. Radames's grave warning serves as a reminder that the rules of the gang, no less than those of the church, must not be taken lightly. Christianity is nothing to "play around with."

It was José Luis, not Radames, who first introduced me to Angel. I asked Angel what he thought about José Luis and why he held him in higher regard than his cousin Radames:

I know José Luis as *Quico*. I think highly of him. He was a *tíguere*, into drugs, robbing, smoking, he did everything. I don't know how many years he's been a Christian now, but since he accepted Christ I have not seen him go out, or play, but there are many who have left [the church]. Carlito has joined and left, my brother has joined and left, there are many. There were something like four more that entered with him that are no longer Christian. There is another cousin of mine that entered with him but left. Anyway, I think well of him because he has continued being a follower, he has stayed stable, that is why I think highly of him.

It is difficult, as they say, "to remain in the gospel," because of the demands of faith and the requirements of membership. Many individuals convert then leave only to come back and leave once again. José Luis represents the ideal of perseverance: he went from being a brutal drug-abusing gang leader to a pious born-again servant of God. He has thus far remained in the church and demonstrated to others a true conversion. Even though he was a member of a rival gang, Angel respected him to such a degree that he agreed to meet me. Radames, who lacked Angel's respect, was, in the end, unable to do the same for me. At issue here was Radames's unbecoming conduct in light of his conversion. According to the suspicions of those around him, Radames wanted to have it both ways, to enjoy the benefits of church membership plus the freedom of street life. This was unacceptable according to the normative standards of the barrio community, a transgression acceptable neither to the church nor to the gangs.

Christianity and the Gangs

Perhaps it seems surprising that for many of the residents of Villa, Pentecostals have succeeded in representing the church as the foremost Christian authority. Gangs acknowledge evangelical authority almost exclusively when concerning conversion as a viable way out of gang life. They also validate Pentecostal claims to sanctity by permitting exemption from retaliation and violence. By professing the priority of evangelical modes of Christian fidelity and affirming their own unique form of Christocentric values—especially by respecting Pentecostals in the streets by looking out for their best interests ("looking after them") and applauding conversion as a respectable way out—youth gangs make implicit statements about the privileged order of things at the same time they endorse a Christian ethical hierarchy that sees the ultimate service to God in terms of Protestant Christian devotion.

Naciones revere evangelicals and, to this end, contribute to an economy of respect that at once strengthens Christian claims to moral and religious authority while ensuring the gang's own validity in relation to local indices of legitimacy. For local youth gangs like the Trinitarios, Christianity is not invoked simply as a way out of gang life; Christian symbols are used as powerful referents in a politics of representation central to gang identity. In many cases Christian rhetoric and symbolism form the very foundations of gang authority and legitimation—the ideological ballasts used to keep the ship afloat, so to speak. Angel and others justify the regular violence in which they are complicit by invoking the name of God and country. Moreover, through rhetorical appeals to Christian themes of sanctity and redemption, alongside the explicit acknowledgment of Christian moral supremacy, youth gangs in Villa create subjects that will ultimately see themselves as needing to be saved. Instructed to respect Christian authority, gangs produce future evangelical Christians because in time they fashion individuals who will answer the call of conversion and the hail of the evangelist, even as, or perhaps precisely *because* they harden young males into street-savvy *tígueres* ostensibly teetering at the precipice of damnation.

The central importance accorded God and Christianity within the *naciones* can be seen in the folk speech and numerological symbolism of gangs like the Trinitarios. *Naciones* employ a variety of symbols that recruit Christian meaning as a way to grant divine license to their charter, which in turn lends moral legitimacy to their usual endeavors. It also functions to join individual members to one another under a powerful transcendental rubric of divine purpose. Ultimately, what gangs develop among members is a fervor akin to a kind of collective effervescence at the core of religious enthusiasm. In the case of the Trinitarios, the passionate totem-esque devotion to *Dios, Patria, Libertad* is a powerful inspiring locus of zeal that yokes members together in solidarity and mutual interest, just as the very same words function to unite patriotic citizens of the nation-state. The *naciones*, mirroring the Dominican state within which they operate, use Christianity as a legitimizing discourse despite the apparent contradictions in practice. Consider supplementarily the Christian symbolism employed here by Angel to describe the plight of the Trinitarios:

> There is lots of tyranny here within the country, amongst ourselves. That is why we go by everything that is necessary in order to represent God. We follow the Bible, we carry the shield, we carry the flag of freedom and independence.
>
> [When the Bloods and other gangs shoot at us, we try to defend ourselves.] We shoot at them every time they shoot at us and miss. Because they are with evil/Satan [*el malo*], and we are with good/ God [*el bueno*], that is why they will lose. We are always winning, even if some days we lose, if we lose it's because God wants it, but we continue to win because we are with Him, we are going to win because that is what He wants. He knows that when we go out, it is He that goes before us and we who follow.

In claiming to put God first, to fight for good against the powers of evil, gang members construct a sympathetic narrative wherein they are the soldiers of virtue fighting a righteous and just war, cleverly inverting popular representations of urban youth as scourges, delinquents, and obstacles to social progress and community thriving that are regularly propagated by the Dominican media. Within this alternative frame, disenfranchised urban youth take on a vital role in the future of the nation—a role in which they wish to be thanked rather than punished, celebrated rather than scorned.

Were Angel's quote above taken out of context it might erroneously be attributed to an evangelical Christian (minus his reference to shooting, of course). Concerned explicitly with relations of good and evil and the struggles between God and the Devil, it can be shown that gang members represent—if not experience or understand—their daily lives in terms that parallel that of Pentecostal converts who frame their experience based on similar oppositions. Few other groups in the barrio articulate more rigid divisions between right and wrong than the church and youth gangs, and no one imposes more strict rules of comportment as a result. Although it is clear that what constitutes immorality differs greatly between them, the congruence between the church and youth gangs can be seen not only in their strict moralism but also in their critical orientation toward a social reality they together view as corrupt and threatening.

Cultural Opposition and Critical Agency

Naciones are autonomous brotherhoods acting as much within the dominant legal and political order of the country as outside of and against it. With their own leadership hierarchy, rules, culture, and unique social practices, gang members defiantly assert sovereignty and the right to self-determination in bold opposition to the life ascribed to them as impoverished barrio residents. Inculcated from birth with existential ambitions they are unlikely ever to meet and likewise seduced by the richly cultivated desires of popular culture—the diffuse goals of Dominican society ranging from material wealth and happiness, to good health, long life, and leisure—the poor are frequently the social class denied realistic means to obtain the spoils of dominant cultural desire. In situations where material wealth, social status, and political power are made available only to a select few while the desire to possess such assets is diffuse, people on the outside looking in are left to their own creative devices to obtain that which is withheld from them and to seize what is always promised but contradictorily ever kept out of reach. In contexts like these cultures of opposition and critical agency may flourish.

An exemplary illustration of such cultures might be the inner-city street culture of East Harlem observed by Philippe Bourgois in the late 1980s. According to Bourgois (1995:8), street culture, or "a complex and conflictual web of beliefs, symbols, modes of interaction, values, and ideologies that have emerged in opposition to exclusion from mainstream society," offers inner-city youth an alternative forum for "autonomous personal dignity," a cultural creativity, he suggests, arising in response to and in defiance of social ostracism, persistent poverty, and racial segregation. I submit that the *naciones* of the Dominican Republic serve an analogous function for disenfranchised barrio youth by providing a critical space to oppose their marginalization through an alternative value complex where ideals coveted by men-of-the-streets such as individualism, cunning, situational amorality, manipulation, and resolute machismo prevail as prized attributes and chief guarantors of symbolic capital among social equals in the neighborhood (see chapters 6 and 7). By enabling members to earn a measure of respect and to recover a sense of dignity based on alternative moral values accessibly cultivated in the streets, gangs empower the disadvantaged poor by creating winnable everyday scenarios with tangible social rewards.

In a parallel sense then, Dominican street culture exemplified by youth gangs mirrors the culture of reputation values associated with lower-class public street life seen on the island of Providencia, where Wilson (1995) has argued that an alternative value system developed among marginalized men as an adaptive response to their exclusion from elevated forms of social distinction epitomized by the principle of respectability.

I propose that both youth gangs and the Pentecostal church in Villa share in this spirit of critical opposition: both represent contrasting institutional channels that offer voluntary membership alternatives to the deprivation created by the unfilled promises of Dominican citizenship for poor urban residents—both rendered in a cast decidedly divergent from the official political order, envisioning in some cases wildly different versions of the good life (see also Goldstein 2003:203–204).[4] In a system where few opportunities for real progressive social mobility exist for barrio residents, voluntary organizations like the church and youth gangs offer concrete practical strategies for addressing the material and social deficits of living in poverty. Each group redefines for their respective memberships the value of personal transformation, empowering them through substitute modes of prestige and self-fulfillment, and facilitating the achievement of realistically obtainable goals by providing spaces to acheive expertise and mastery for those excluded by the dominant order.

Conversion represents a stepping out, a retreat from the reality governed by man (*el mundo*) in favor of embracing what is described as a spiritual world apart ruled by a just, loving, and generous God who asks only for unreserved submission and exclusive fidelity in return (*el evangelio*). "In the gospel," as believers locate their lives after conversion, followers concern themselves with heightened spiritual matters (the salvation of their souls and sanctified living) and not the everyday profane world from which they seek sustainable lasting escape. Martin (1994:85–86) has described Pentecostalism as a "walkout" from the hierarchical mediation of wider society that "creates an enclave of a people seeking emotional release, personal empowerment, mutual support, and self-government." In the Pentecostal church believers find "a restoration of scarred and fractured relationships, a repudiation of corruption, a discipline of life, an affirmation of personal worth, a cancellation of guilt, a chance to speak and to participate, sisterhoods and brotherhoods of mutual support in sickness and in health, and a way to attain *Santidad Divina* [divine sanctity]" (Martin 1990:83). This exceptional alternative world Pentecostals look to adopt, these "free social spaces" or "protective social capsules" where uplifting concepts of self and new models of initiative and voluntary organization are assimilated, promotes a radical equality among followers in the face of a social order that favors hierarchy (Martin 1990:284). Austin-Broos (1997:237) has keenly suggested that although Pentecostals cannot redefine in and of themselves the social order of which they are a part, they can sustain a critical view of it and at least realize to some extent their ideals within the church itself. The spiritual equality to which Pentecostals subscribe is realized at the level of doctrine—God loves all of his children equally—as well as in practice. Pentecostal churches maintain a relatively egalitarian division of labor with respect to positions within the church and the work followers perform during services (Austin-Broos 1997), while relatively equal opportunities exist for spiritual advancement and mastery through preaching, evangelizing, and other forms of outreach (save for some limitations). Additional parity can be found in the teaching that everyone, no matter one's lot in life, has the potential to receive the gifts of the Holy Spirit, and everyone may be sanctified.

The idea of conversion as resistance or opposition, especially through a voluntary change in identity, is an important leitmotif in Christian literatures everywhere, just as it is in some of the sociology and anthropology of Pentecostalism wherein scholars have noted the radical potential of the egalitarian ethos of the church to provide a communitarian salve for social injustice. Consider the following examples.

Drawing from her work on Jamaican immigrant congregations in Britain, Toulis (1997:206–207) observes that Pentecostalism enables members to deal with the "non-negotiable facts of racism and sexism" by providing them with the means necessary to control their own thoughts regarding themselves. According to Toulis (1997:207), such means are a process of symbolic transformation: "members transform the symbolic code of the wider secular society in which they are disadvantaged and replace it with a new spiritual code in which they are advantaged." Similarly, Wedenoja (1980:39) argues that being a Christian in Jamaica involves identification with a social status and group that implicitly denies or rejects the negative statuses of being lower class, black, African, or Jamaican. In Christ, all human beings are said to be the same. By encouraging believers to see themselves as belonging to a transcendent worldwide brotherhood of the saved, Pentecostals position themselves at odds with ethnic or racial discourses that rely on categorical group membership and ascribed social statuses (Burdick 1998:123).

Critical of traditional hierarchies of authority (especially leadership in the government and Catholic Church) and a society ostensibly mired from top to bottom in corruption and sin, the church—no less than the gang—transforms otherwise disenfranchised residents into emboldened critics of an illegitimate (in some cases deemed satanic) system that renders them politically ineffectual and, presumably, morally and materially impoverished. Through symbolic role reversal, poor unemployed gang members become leaders, strategists, warriors, and businessmen who see themselves as virtuous because they live according to a strict code of ethics.[5] Likewise, through the medium of conversion these same disparaged young men may become spiritual authorities, healers, teachers, moral exemplars, and/or powerful advisers whom their community looks up to with commendable respect. The appeal of belonging to either group is often to be found in their unique ability to create alternative utopian worlds where the unvalued are valued, the victims may become victors, the weak become powerful, the fearful turn fearsome, and the cursed find merited redemption either, as it were, by the Bible or by the sword.

Membership in the church and the gangs is more or less open to anyone, and, once initiated, individual commitment is rewarded with just deserts—indeed, a radical alternative to the confounding arbitrariness and insecurity typical of everyday barrio life in Villa. Although neither could be said to constitute truly revolutionary political movements of a definitive sort, at least as of yet—in both cases the root causes (including actors, institutions, and social structures) responsible for social and material inequities are rarely ever addressed directly, and effective strategies for systemic change are obfuscated by the very impractical political vision advanced by both groups (the focus on individual conversion over systemic transformation; revolution of the self instead of political revolution [Martin 1990:202])—they do represent grassroots modes of resistance in their attempts to redefine for believers and gang members alike the terms of their social and material existence in ways that radically refuse the disparaged condition of poverty. In the church, the most important identity is the one converts alone control through their obedience to God and their ability to convince others of their holiness. A young man may rise to positions of authority in his gang according to his aptitude and ability to *representa bien* (represent well) in his clique, earning the respect of his peers through impressive acts of violence and remarkable demonstrations of shrewd cunning for which he alone is responsible. Angel, who lacked a secondary education, explained that he was chosen to be *el jefe* because of his intelligence and initiative. After proving his astuteness with peers and "making the most contacts," or recruiting the most people for the gang, he was tapped to be leader. In this way he was a self-made man, a leader by his own resolve, not by chance or accident, someone who by the age of eighteen had authority and respect from people his junior and senior who looked to him for direction, not to mention the respect earned from those who feared his capacity for violence. By assuming control of their own representation, representations frequently at odds with the ascribed statuses of poor barrio residents, in taking up positions critical of the established social order, both the church and the gangs create spaces of critical opposition and agency that empower the marginalized despite their inferior structural position.

Conclusion

The gangs and the church function as a sort of alternative national identity, one where members play an important role in the future of the republic.

In a manner similar to the nation-state itself, youth gangs employ leaders in important offices, only in this scenario it is the young men of the barrio who rule and make decisions of import to the community (as a Trinitario Angel *is* Duarte). Their power is not imaginary: real contests over authority can be seen in protests such as the *huelgas* that put gang members in direct and violent confrontation with the state. In response to the marginality, exclusion, and oppression felt by urban youth throughout much of Latin America, Cerbino and Rodríguez (2008) submit that it is no surprise young men wish to create in the form of gangs an alternative political order (within or on the margins of the dominant order) and to imagine a utopian "nation" where they are the ones with political power and influence. Poor urban youth in the Dominican Republic are regular targets of violent state repression and are frequently blamed for social ills they did not create. The gangs have developed an oppositional identity to state and military police, which further marks their external relationship to dominant forms of power but nevertheless figures such brotherhoods as plainly accessible stages for critical agency and important sites of resistance for disenfranchised urban youth.

Like gangs, the church functions as an alternative, intranational association—"a nation within a nation."[6] Not only do church members imagine themselves to be members of a universal brotherhood of Christ, members of a transcendent citizenship united in spiritual equality with like Christians across the world, but they also see themselves as promoting a specific plan of salvation for the future. This "spiritual" or "Christian citizenship" (cf. O'Neill 2010) takes precedence over all other political affiliations, with the laws of Christ thought to be greater than any other earthly rule or dictum. In this scenario, church members are responsible for the salvation of the planet while the fate of earthly souls resides in the hands of each and every benevolent congregant. Members of the church may be poor and therefore politically toothless with regard to the state and the political process nationally, but as servants of Jesus Christ they play what they understand to be a pivotal role in the cosmic future of humanity by defeating the powers of evil and leading humankind to salvation with the help of the Holy Spirit.

Because both institutions have enjoyed a relative spike in popularity over the past several decades, and because both represent important features of cultural globalization and contemporary processes of transnationalism, together they provide a unique lens for analyzing local adaptations to cultural change in the Caribbean and beyond. In the Dominican Republic, these institutions have flourished in the context of widespread alienation and anomie following economic changes beginning in the 1960s, compounded by the fall of sugar prices in the 1980s, and more recently complicated by structural adjustment and neoliberal economic policies of the 1990s and early 2000s (see Gregory 2007:26–30; Safa 1995, 2002). Perhaps not surprisingly, many of the theories used to explain the growth and popularity of the Pentecostal church in Latin America are remarkably similar to those used to explain the growing influence of youth gangs, in many cases connecting their mutual success to compensatory motives driven by social distress and insecurity (Thornton 2012).

The academic literature on youth gangs and the cross-cultural literature on the Pentecostal movement in Latin America have proposed surprisingly similar explanations for the growth of these institutions. Both have been argued to represent contemporary responses to social and political estrangement, the loss of traditional family networks, displacement, social marginalization, and anomie. These are indeed the familiar discontents of late modernity and the effects of neoliberal economic policies that have left many across the globe on unstable ground clamoring to find their way without reliable work or steady income. Deprivation arguments like these are attractive explanations because they appear to connect economic and social changes accompanying the late twentieth century with the concurrent growth and expansion of the church and youth gangs across the Americas during the same period.

While both youth gangs and the church are products of important transnational and global processes at the forefront of cultural changes occurring in the Dominican Republic (see Gregory 2007 for an analysis of globalization and economic change in the country), they both offer realistic options at the local level for social communion, autonomy, self-valorization, and self-determination. Functioning as surrogate kin for barrio youth, both institutions offer alternatives to unstable or ineffectual families, local governments, and/or disaffected communities. Both represent examples of local youth responses to the dislocations of political and economic marginalization where the promises of neoliberal democracy have not been fulfilled for most of Latin American and Caribbean peoples.[7] Both institutions feature prominently in the barrio and represent two clearly lit paths for self-actualization at the local level.

Perhaps the most profound intersection of these divergent domains can be found in the conversion exception itself, where the gang and the church meet in an expression of shared meanings. Conversion as a way out of the gang is an obligatory exception in the barrio and one that exemplifies the reciprocal relations of meaning that obtain between local Pentecostal churches, on the one hand, and transnational youth gangs, on the other. In representing the only explicitly authorized way out of the gang, the conversion exception realizes one of the more fundamental claims of Pentecostal theology: that conversion represents leaving a material world of sin and beginning a new spiritual life with Christ—a transformation so fundamental as to regard one as a new being. By acknowledging the fundamental change that occurs with conversion, youth gangs validate Pentecostal claims to sanctity and deliver the promise of conversion so long as converts maintain their Christianness and continue to demonstrate the sincerity of their spiritual transformation.

Upon joining the church, converts experience forgiveness, spiritual perfection or "sanctity," and the promise of redemption, not simply as abstract theological concepts but importantly as phenomenal reorderings of their social world and radical transformations of its symbolic content. Pentecostals come to experience the objective social rewards of sanctity (that is, through exceptionalism) largely insofar as gang members and others choose to treat them as exceptional, sanctified individuals. Immunities from violence follow from their recognition as exceptional spiritual persons to whom alternative rules are thought to apply. These exceptions are in turn used by the faithful as evidence of their testimony and confirmation of their spiritual holiness. From the perspective of former gang members, conversion quite literally saves them from the vicissitudes of the street by making them exceptional others within the world of violence and uncertainty that characterizes life in the barrio. Importantly, Pentecostal converts come to realize special status, not only among themselves but also in relation to others who are important guarantors of this exclusive regard. In what otherwise seems to be a peculiar and unlikely coalition, youth gangs are important agents in the reckoning of the exceptionalism Pentecostals both claim and in many respects ultimately come to enjoy. While Pentecostal conversion provides sanctuary for gang members seeking release from the street life, gang members in turn esteem converts and look after them in the streets.

Pentecostal discourse creates new categories of difference (such as believer/nonbeliever, sanctified/unsanctified) that draw on existing moral divisions extant in Dominican culture and hyper-recognizes them, making them supervisible, and elaborates those differences in provocative new ways. Through their engagement with the church and its representatives, gang members become sinners, or rather, sinners-in-need-of-saving. So much so that to regard conversion as a viable life option, inevitable for some, has become an integral facet of gang affiliation, the ultimate resolution of the violent freedom one enjoys on the streets becoming the disciplined rule-bound obedience to divine authority in the church.

The conversion exception, as I have shown here, is a part of a larger set of exceptions (including immunities and special considerations) that articulate with dominant orders of moral authority at the core of social intercourse and relationships of power in the barrio. The idea that one does not "play around or joke with things of God" is a reflection of the dominant authority Christian values enjoy in popular culture throughout the country. That born-again Christianity, as opposed to Catholicism, represents the ideal of Christian exceptionalism, regarded as the most genuine commitment to God is a premise cosponsored by youth gangs that recognize Pentecostal conversion as the only acceptable moral alternative to the street life. By acknowledging evangelical Christians, and not Catholics, as representatives of God on earth, in identifying *evangélicos* as "true Christians," as the only Christians "with God," youth gangs endorse Pentecostal claims to moral and spiritual authority.

This chapter has been less about the exceptional status Pentecostals claim for themselves and more about the public acknowledgment of that status and how complex theological ideas are concretized for believers in everyday social situations relevant to converts and potential converts equally. Like the church, the gang is also a foreign import that has had profound effects on local culture, reshaping values in transformative as well as contradictory ways.

The experience of forgiveness that attends conversion from a youth gang becomes a profound confirmation—indeed, a grand realization—of the ethereal promise of forgiveness attending the acceptance of Jesus Christ as one's Lord and savior. Jesus Christ is said to forgive the sinner no matter how wicked his or her life might have been in the past; conversion promises absolution. Even as many of my informants maintained that their previous crimes in the streets were pardoned by Jesus Christ such that they no longer carried the burden of their regrettable acts, they experienced forgiveness as a phenomenal transformation in their interpersonal relationships with others, including with those who at one time wished to do them harm. Compromises like these reflect the widespread acceptance of Pentecostal claims to sanctity, the ideas of rebirth and forgiveness, and demonstrate the gangs' role in giving life to Pentecostal motifs and doctrinal promises of redemption.

This kind of evangelical exceptionalism, however, is not unique to the gangs alone but obtains in other domains of barrio life as well.

Here is where my perspective differs from other commentators on this subject. Some observers, having considered this phenomenon in other parts of Latin America, have attempted to understand the relationship between gangs and the church as well as the conversion exception by focusing almost exclusively on the gangs themselves, independent or outside of the social contexts in which this symbiotic relationship derives meaning.

There is a temptation from decontextualized perspectives to interpret the conversion exception as an opportunistic strategy of the gangs to ensure that members who leave will not represent a threat to the future thriving of the gang. The conversion exception, from this perspective, appears to be a strategic social contract between the gang and ex-gang members alone, with the gangs providing for freedom under the condition that converted gang members remain in the church and demonstrate their Christianness by keeping to their own affairs.

While such perspectives are explanatory to a point (and are by no means false), they do little to explain why Protestant conversion, rather than some other religious or secular ritual, became one of the only viable exceptions. They do not explain why evangelical Christianity, and not Catholicism or some other religious faith, provides the only way out. They also do not explain why a lifetime membership exception in the form of conversion exists in the first place.

This is not the only realm where conversion provides for an escape, of course. There is another parallel, explored earlier in chapter 3, that involves Pentecostal exceptionalism in quite a different location: that is in the realm of magic and service to the spirits. Similarly there, a viable way to break out of the bonds of reciprocal service to the spirits or saints is to become a pious evangelical convert. As a Protestant, the spirits may no longer possess or enter the head of a once-loyal devotee. Additionally, believers often cite conversion as "the only way out" of drug and alcohol addiction, a relationship of dependence that is thought only to be broken upon accepting Jesus Christ into one's heart.

Seeing as conversion fulfills an exception to gang membership in much the same way that it does in other domains of social and spiritual life—as a ritualized "safe space"—this particular ethnographic detail indicates far more than the preservational concerns of the gang alone and instead hints at a more diffuse state of affairs wherein the propositions of the church, that conversion transforms and sanctifies the individual, are accepted and made real for individual converts but have also become a social fact for the communities in which they live.

If we begin with the church and understand the conversion exception as a dynamic aspect of relations owing in large degree to the logics of discontinuity and dualism at the core of Pentecostal cultural frameworks, we can better see the conversion exception as rooted in the key Pentecostal notion of transformation that has today become a mainstay of barrio life in the country.

Far from being a marginal sect or fringe cult, today Pentecostal churches have come to play an important role in the day-to-day lives of barrio residents, both Christian and non-Christian alike. By choosing to focus on youth gangs, ostensibly the least obvious group of individuals to help discuss Christian moral authority, I hope to have demonstrated the meaningful ways in which Pentecostalism has shaped local culture in the contemporary urban barrio and advanced itself as a moral and spiritual authority among Christian denominations locally.

Residual Masculinity
and Gendered Charisma

I left Nagua around the age of sixteen and moved to *la 42*, in Capotillo [a depressed area of Santo Domingo, notorious for crime and violence]. You know what they move there, right? Anything and everything; it's a drug cartel. I arrived there as a *jovencito* with little experience. I had many dreams. I allied myself with the *tígueres* in the neighborhood; the *tígueres* there are ruthless. When I arrived it was something else. There were many people there who knew me from Nagua and they said that they were going to kill me, because, you know, I was involved in the vices, the games, the drinking, the gangs. I remember like it was yesterday.... I made a lot of money selling drugs there in Capotillo. Lots of money, but I would drink it.... We would go to the club and, you know, we weren't thinking about anything.... I was young.... With machete in hand I would go out on the streets with my gang to fight. I knew how to "dance" the machete. Even on the twenty-fourth of December I was in the streets. I remember going up and down the barrio with a machete in hand and a bag of drugs in the other. Selling to people, and waiting for other gangs....

When I converted to the gospel the Lord immediately cast away my problems. I accepted the Bible and I began to give testimony that God had indeed transformed me. Now I go to Capotillo, where I once sold drugs, and I preach. Where I used to sell drugs, now I go and I speak against drugs. When I go there the men say, "But my God, you are different. You are much younger now! You look much better now, what is happening?" And I say that I have Christ now; because remember, I used to spend thirty days a month in the streets, "smashed," with a machete in hand and with a .38 at my side. So now when I go there the men they say, "But you are much younger now!" It's that I have Christ and I'm not in sin.... Since converting I am a serious man, I work more, I am soon going to have ten years in the gospel. I go to where I used to sell drugs, I preach and go with my Bible and nobody desires to do anything bad to me, nor do I desire to have other women. God has done a cleansing in me.... God has told me to be an example for other drug addicts and I want to be an example to other drug addicts. I want to go to different countries and testify to God, because there are people who are in this life that don't believe that they can change. I preach that there is still hope; everything is not lost.... I was a drug addict and now I am free. I was a *machetero*, a *bandolero*, and today I am free.

Juan Carlos

This chapter considers men, masculinity, and charismatic authority. Above is a selection from the conversion narrative of Juan Carlos. Limited space here prevents me from detailing his testimony in its entirety, but I have included particulars that have become commonplace in the conversion narratives of Pentecostal men in urban barrios throughout the country. Through these testimonies, Juan Carlos and others like him claim a certain type of authority and male prestige that is critical, I propose, to the ways in which he and other male converts legitimate their transformation in Christ and shape their new identities as Christian leaders and as men of God.

In what follows I argue that male converts in the Dominican Republic reconcile the apparent antinomy between Pentecostal Christianity and barrio masculinity by exploiting their former identities in the streets as admirable and exemplary machos. Through detailed narratives of sin and redemption grounded in the particulars of their preconversion lives as so-called *tígueres* (or "macho men"), converts articulate and assert their maleness and at the same time satisfy the esteemed conversion ideal of transformation from sinner to saint. Those converts who demonstrate the greatest reversals of fate, those who best exemplify a personal transformation from severe depravity to unquestioned righteousness, are often attributed the most prestige and recognized as charismatic ideals and spiritual leaders in the faith community.

Men and Conversion

For some time now scholars studying Pentecostal Christianity in the Global South have acknowledged the transformative and liberating aspects of the church for women and the significant manner in which membership empowers them in new and in crucial ways (Martin 2001:54; Cucchiari 1990; Brusco 1995; Austin-Broos 1997; Chesnut 1997; Burdick 1998). The prevailing view has been that the movement appeals, in general, more to women than to men. Noting that, on average, women tend to represent the largest percentage of believers worldwide (Cucchiari 1990; Chesnut 1997; Martin 2001; Miller and Yamamori 2007), a number of studies on Pentecostalism have proposed that certain aspects of the church may advantage women over men and cite evidence that conversion improves gender relations for women, particularly in the domestic sphere, and provides for greater autonomy from and equality with men (Robbins 2004a:132; Brusco 1995; Smilde

1997; Mariz and Machado 1997). The anthropologist Elizabeth Brusco (1995) has gone so far as to describe the movement as a form of "female collective action," and the discernable benefit that membership affords female converts has prompted one commentator to remark, "if there is a 'women's movement' among the poor of the developing world, Pentecostalism has a good claim to the title" (Martin 2001:56).

There are several features of the Pentecostal message that seem to resonate most with female converts—in particular, respect for the nuclear family and marital bond and the demonization of behaviors and practices associated with the male prestige complex (for example, promiscuity, adultery, hypersexuality, drinking, gambling, violence, lewd and lascivious behavior, and so forth) (Burdick 1993; Brusco 1995; Austin-Broos 1997; Chesnut 1997, 2003). Considering the latter, Brusco (1995) has argued that Pentecostalism "domesticates" men by demanding that they give up *machismo* and turn their attention and resources toward the home, the traditional center of female authority. Such a change benefits women, who, with the support of the church, can demand that their spouses be faithful and contribute money to domestic concerns that a husband would otherwise spend on himself and his close friends (Brusco 1995). At the same time that men are enjoined to leave the profane world behind in exchange for a spiritual career in the church, they are asked to submit to the authority of God, surrender the freedom and autonomy of the streets, and commit themselves anew to home and family. This reorientation appears to provide an incentive for women to convert, even as it creates an antagonistic scenario for the conversion and retention of men.

This "reformation of *machismo*" is the source of considerable ambivalence for men in the church as well as those on the outside looking in. Pentecostalism's ascetic moral commitments drive away many potential male converts by prohibiting behaviors that are valued primarily by men and asking them to take up seemingly feminizing positions and attitudes upon joining the church. The autonomy men are asked to give up upon conversion is experienced as a significant loss (Martin 2001:55), and the repudiation of traditional sites and methods of male bonding is viewed as a formidable challenge to converts locally.

Men in the Dominican Republic, for example, often find renunciation of the street and its associated values the most difficult obstacle to becoming and remaining a Christian. The freedom to pursue transitory relationships with women and to act on sexual urges, as well as to get together with friends to socialize over alcohol and popular music, is an important part of young male identity that believers are asked to forsake upon conversion. As Flaco from Iglesia de Dios (IdD) told me: "It is very difficult to be a Christian. How should I put it? Look, when you go out with a group of friends who are not Christian the first thing they want to do to celebrate is to drink beer, to drink alcohol, and flirt with women [*mujerear*], and do that kind of stuff. But you mustn't. It is very difficult. You want to hang out with your friends but you can't do those things." Moreover, he lamented the fact that he was prohibited from responding to the advances of women he liked: "It is difficult too when you are in a group and there is a girl who likes you, but she's not a Christian. You are a Christian and the Bible says that this relationship cannot be. It makes it difficult for you because sometimes the girls are·pretty and you even like them, but in order to be right with God one must reject it. It hurts you to reject them, but you reject the majority." Pressure from peers to socialize over a beer or to share a rum with friends at a *colmado*, to flirt with women, or to sing along to popular *bachatas* proves to be too great for most; the allure of the streets and the trappings of a pervasive form of Dominican masculinity known as *tigueraje* (a masculine persona associated with street culture) are usually more than enough to dissuade men from participation in a community that, according to some locals, "just doesn't like to have fun." In Brazil, Chesnut (1997:111) observes that male camaraderie in drinking and "whoring" is such an integral part of masculine identity that converts who withdraw from this type of male socializing often have to deal with considerable taunting and mockery from their former friends, who view them as having surrendered to their wives' authority. Even years after conversion, men in Brazil still find the temptation to indulge in "vice" to be one of the most difficult aspects of conversion and of keeping the faith (Chesnut 1997:111–112). In Brazil, as in the Dominican Republic, conversion is less appealing to and perhaps ultimately more demanding for men. At the same time, if men are able to make a full conversion, to break with "the world" completely, they stand to gain more in the way of prestige than women, who are thought less in need of saving and for whom the path to redemption is thought not as steep.

At issue here is the challenge of giving up common modes of socializing and the familiar signs of popular masculinity in exchange for a bona fide Christian identity. In the Dominican Republic, Pentecostal Christianity is emphatically opposed to *tigueraje*, a lifestyle and attitude associated with the extreme traits of masculine street culture—namely, slyness, aggressiveness, carousing, womanizing, infidelity, and various kinds of delinquency (de Moya 2002:114n.7; Padilla 2007:134). A *tíguere*, someone who embodies or recalls these personal qualities, is the quintessential *hombre de la calle*, or "man of the streets." He has a way with words, and with women, and embodies the values of public male culture found in bars, *colmados, discotecas* (nightclubs), and pool halls.[1] *Tigueraje*, in this sense, represents exactly those attitudes and behaviors condemned by the church and considered brutish and morally disdainful by followers.

Although a term typically reserved for the lower classes, the notion of *tigueraje* is, to a degree, central to the construction of masculinity for men of all social classes (Padilla 2007:134). A master of self-promotion and self-preservation, a *tíguere* is a hustler and a savvy, street-smart macho-man of the highest order. According to Krohn-Hansen (1996), he is a "survivor in his environment," and, through his own cunning, he is able to "emerge well" from any situation (Collado 1992). Not unlike Wilson's (1995) men of reputation on the island of Providencia (Padilla 2007:134), the *tíguere* persona in the Dominican Republic likely represents creative resistance to domination and reflects a subaltern response to exploitation and the scarcity of respectability. Derby (2009:186) characterizes the *tíguere* as the "classic dissimulator, someone who gains access to a station above his own through dressing for the part, through the appropriate style, but also through being bold, a smooth talker, and having a 'predatory masculine' presence." He is an aggressively enterprising person, if not a social climber, and characteristically defiant of his social position and ascribed social status. Admired for his cunning and yet disdained for his methods, the rebellious and wily Dominican "tiger" contrasts sharply with the submissive image of repentant sinner, who, with outstretched arms and complete humility, comes to the feet of Jesus, on his knees, and begs for forgiveness. While a *tíguere* is the archetypal individualist (Derby 2009:187), relying on himself and his skills alone to get him through any situation, Pentecostals, alternatively, rely on the will of God and the power of the Holy Spirit alongside a community of the faithful to overcome everyday challenges and to negotiate the difficulties of life, attributing any success or prosperity to their steadfast faith in Jesus Christ. According to believers, the *tíguere's* opposite is the Christian man, *el hombre serio*, a man of God who shuns worldly desires and rejects the pleasures of the flesh in favor of spiritual pursuits and the higher path to salvation. It is believed that when a man truly converts, he ceases to be a *tíguere* and becomes a man of God. For many men in the Dominican Republic, then, their very masculine identity is experienced as an obstacle to becoming a Christian. As I was assured time and again by believers, one cannot be both a *tíguere* and a *cristiano* simultaneously; after all, they personify distinct moral perspectives.[2]

Yet despite the antinomy between *cristianismo* and *tigueraje* and the potential that exists to be stigmatized as unmanly, and while the comparative literature on Pentecostalism in the Americas suggests a marked appeal for women (Chesnut 1997:22), Pentecostal Christianity still attracts men to its flock. Services at Iglesia Evangélica Pentecostal (IEP) and IdD are regularly dominated in number and in enthusiasm by men, and I frequently observed services where men represented more than 50 percent of the congregation in attendance. In fact, men were recurrently passionate and the principal participants at most evening services, and sermons often focused on topics that were directed solely at them.[3] According to local congregants, alcoholism, delinquency, promiscuity, drug abuse, and gang affiliation are persistent problems that confront the men in town to a far greater degree than the women. Consequently, many local churches focus their efforts on the evangelization, retention, and spiritual education of young males, who are commonly denounced by Dominican society as "delinquent" and who are perceived by the Christian community to be in particular need of salvation.

Although most men find the demands of conversion daunting, many clearly do not find them insurmountable. Some of their concerns are mitigated by taking up formal leadership roles in the church (Austin-Broos 1997:123) and asserting a more authoritative status in the domestic sphere as formal heads of the household (Chesnut 1997). As pastors, deacons, and evangelists, men assume institutional positions of power in the church that may counterbalance or compensate for the loss of esteem, authority, or respect in "the world." As church leaders, they exercise considerable influence over congregations and local neighborhood politics, and the prestige of their institutional roles provides for more than a modicum of deference and generalized public approval. Even while women find equality with men in the Spirit (Martin 2001:54; Brusco 2010:81)—that is, equal access to the spiritual gifts and graces of God—men continue, on the whole, to fill official leadership positions in the church and to wield institutional authority. With respect to the nuclear family, a Pentecostal husband may adopt a more patriarchal stance toward his wife and children. According to Chesnut (1997:113), conversion takes a man from being "king of the street" and makes him "master of the household." Legitimated by Pauline principles of patriarchy (Martin 2001:54), conversion solidifies his authoritative status at home (Burdick 1993:114) with the support and sponsorship of the church. With this institutional backing, men may exercise more authority over the domestic sphere provided that they fulfill the moral expectations of a Christian husband and father.

Just because a man converts does not mean that he will be seen as less than a man. This is due in large part to the fact that converts commit themselves to alternative definitions of masculinity based principally upon culturally specific notions of respectability. By demanding that congregants respect the sanctity of marriage, secure employment, pursue homeownership, and provide for their families, Pentecostal identity empowers congregants to claim respectable status, albeit within the limits of their socioeconomic position (see Wilson 1995:103). In championing the ideals of respectability, converts are able to associate themselves with the dominant values of family, fidelity, and seriousness that are not prominent in the street but which represent trenchant and desirable hegemonic ideals (de Moya 2002:114–115; Wilson 1995). Cultivating values distinct from that of the street, Pentecostal men replace *tigueraje* with the ideal of "seriousness," or what I call *el serio*: a value orientation characterized by a telos of work, order, discipline, honesty, responsibility, reliability, maturity, industry, decorum, integrity, and moral fortitude. Their relative prosperity and respectable status, validated by their material possessions, employment, marital status, and fulfillment of social obligations, becomes the standard alternative with which to measure a man's worth in the barrio.

Residual Masculinity and Narratives of Sin

Nonetheless, even as men in this context may come close to respectable status the more fully they embrace the church's teachings and conform to its standards, they cannot, as largely poor, undereducated, nonwhite Dominicans, fully claim the respectability reserved for the upper classes. Furthermore, even while a man in the church may assert authority over his wife and assume positions of influence over congregants in the church, he cannot be certain of his status with peers in "the world" who continue to operate under the values and precepts of the street. As a result, the symbols of male identity represented by *tigueraje* continue to be important markers of maleness among converts just as they are for their unconverted male associates. Consequently, even while Pentecostals strive to attain prestige based on a new set of values rooted in respectability, they do not abandon the street completely. The powerful modes of sociality that shape Dominican men in the barrio and the practices that give meaning to their gendered identities do not cease to be relevant upon conversion but continue to hold sway over converts and the ways in which they understand themselves and the world around them. The difficulty in assimilating Pentecostal norms and a novel born-again lifestyle may be seen in the high incidence of backsliding or disaffiliation in evangelical churches (Gooren 2010b:124), particularly among men (Bowen 1996:73).

One way of reconciling the conflict of values between the church and those of the street is through the development of testimonies that function to parlay male prestige from the streets and transform it into personal charisma and masculine identity in the church. This is possible because converts retain, as part of their new identity as Christian, an important residual identity based on their previous lives as "sinners." Developing and promoting this former identity becomes as important to converts and the production of their evangelical identity as the maintenance and promotion of their new identity as saint (or "sanctified believer"). Pentecostal Christians substantiate their identities as former sinners through testimonies and conversion narratives that give an account of their preconversion lives. By invoking their previous lives as *mujeriegos* (womanizers), hustlers, thieves, and gangsters—indeed, their former lives as *tígueres*—male converts assert their manliness and claim authority in the streets without transgressing the rules of the church. The enduring or "residual" identity buffers the potential loss of respect by constituting these converts simultaneously as both men of the streets and saintly men of God.

Consider briefly the rhetorical work accomplished by the following selection from Renato's testimony:

Look, I had something that we call here "open" or "informal" relationships. When I say this I mean, "fuck them and leave them." I had a few relationships like this. I don't want to say a number because I don't know exactly how many. . . . I'm one of those people who loves to party. When hanging out, I had a real problem with this. . . . As for more "formal" girlfriends, I only had two. But from the streets, that were not formal, that I didn't bring home, I believe there were many. I had a "sack" of them, *muchísimas*.

Rhetorically, Renato's confession accomplishes several noteworthy ends. First, by discussing his former relations with women as overwhelmingly successful, he characterizes himself as someone who excelled at one of the most valued measures of barrio masculinity—the pursuit and conquest of women. Interestingly, he models this accomplishment with the metaphor of a sack—a receptacle to collect his countless sexual triumphs. In so doing, he essentially "saves" the meaning of these achievements for later when he resignifies them as sinful and brought to an end as a part of his conversion testimony. Second, by framing this behavior as something sinful and that no longer characterizes his new life today as a *cristiano*, he fulfills the Pentecostal imperative of moral transformation, even as the symbolic value of his former accomplishments with women (and success as a *mujeriego*) bleeds into his new identity as Christian convert. Here Renato claims the associated prestige of success with women, marking himself as manly in the language of the barrio without actually transgressing the rules of the church. He represents himself as someone who has *voluntarily* relinquished women in favor of a higher calling, and thus establishes himself as both moral victor and chaste, humble Christian follower.

> You know, I was from the streets. . . . Before I was a Christian my thoughts were always in *tigueraje*. . . . My life project used to be *tigueraje*. That is what I knew, that is what I saw everyday. Machetes, fights, this and that, I saw this everyday. My head was programmed. I used to practice the machete. I knew how to wield it. I knew how to make an illegal gun, a homemade firearm. I believe that if I had not become a *cristiano* I would be dead or on file in every part of the country. I have been close to death two times, but thanks to God I don't appear in any police reports.

Such admissions are important to the ways in which believers constitute themselves as legitimate Christian converts and simultaneously as authorities in and of the streets. Converts are encouraged to develop precisely these kinds of stories in conversion narratives in order to demonstrate the positively miraculous transformation in Christ that is promised by conversion and achieved through the power of the Holy Spirit. The restraint that Renato alleges to show in denying himself opportunities to collect more women for his "sack" demonstrates the strength and maturity of his faith and is commended by his congregation. His successful transformation from "ladies' man" to "man of God" shows that change is possible, even for the most unlikely sinners. His claim to experience and success in *tigueraje* and his victory over such vices through conversion and the power of the Holy Spirit permit him to claim authority on matters of the church as well as those of the streets.

I was introduced to Juan Carlos through a friend. Before converting to the gospel, Juan Carlos claims to have been known as *el verdugo*, the "executioner" or "tyrant." He limped from repeated *machetazos* (blows from a machete) to his legs, and he had been stabbed numerous times in the back, which had left gnarly scars. Juan Carlos was thirty-eight years old when I met him in 2009, but the hard life of drugs and violence had taken its toll, and he instead looked to be in his mid- to late forties. At age thirty, he was caught and arrested in the city of Higüey for drug trafficking. He spent three years in prison in Higüey and then La Victoria, the most notorious prison in the Dominican Republic. He converted while in prison in Higüey and ministered to inmates while interned at La Victoria. Today he calls Pantoja (a municipal district just outside the capital) his home and paints furniture to get by. His mother, his brother, and his wife have all converted since hearing his testimony. Juan Carlos claims to have received the gift of preaching and evangelization from God subsequent to converting, and he is held in high regard throughout the area as an evangelist. He lives relatively simply and certainly has not made it rich off his conversion, but his testimony has made him a person of respect in the barrios of Pantoja. Juan Carlos's testimony of extreme hardship, of a violent street life, immoral and dissipated in almost every way, not only defined him as a man-among-men but also made him the perfect example to others of the power and virtue of conversion. Today he claims to be nothing like he was before and gives all of the credit to Jesus Christ and the power of the Holy Spirit. Juan Carlos's testimony detailing the wicked and debauched state of his previous life gave him the spiritual credibility he needed to be a leader in the church and established his credentials in the streets that he needed to be respected in the barrio as a whole.

Both Juan Carlos and Renato, along with other male converts, shield themselves from accusations or suggestions of femininity through similar narratives of sin and violence. By emphasizing the wickedness, brutishness, and indeed "manliness" of their preconversion lives, converts assert their masculinity and resist the feminizing potential of church membership.[4] Recalled in testimony but forged in the streets, male converts retain the enduring male prestige that was earned primarily in their preconversion lives, but which they carry forward in their testimonies and narratives of change. If successful, respected Pentecostal men are referred to as *varón*, a title of esteem that serves to underscore their maleness and acknowledge their achievement of respectable status (the term "*varón*" literally means "male/man").

José Luis exemplified the transformation from quintessential *tíguere* to model Christian follower and was able to translate this image of reform into considerable prestige within the local faith community and significantly beyond it. Having spent the better part of his youth on street corners selling drugs and gang banging, José Luis transformed his *tigueraje* into spiritual legitimacy through his testimony—the lyrical representation of his transformation from drug-addled gang leader to Bible-toting evangelical preacher. José Luis embodied the ideal of conversion since his previous life in the streets could be represented in such a way as to exemplify the backward and destructive nature of "the world" and frame, in contrast to it, his new life in the gospel, where he no longer embodied fear, violence, and intimidation but instead joy, charity, and submission to God. In exemplifying the Pentecostal ideal of transformation from sinner to saint, he was considered by many to be a spiritual leader and barrio hero, and was granted a great deal of prestige both in the church and in the streets.

> Before I converted I was a failure. Before converting I had the opportunity to study at a technical school (I am a repair technician in welding), but afterward I was running in the streets. I was a *tíguere* in the streets. I used drugs, I robbed, I mugged people; I did *everything*. I was the leader of a gang. I had my own clique. I belonged to a gang called *los kings*. My life was nothing before knowing Jesus Christ. I did

countless things that maybe God did not like, but after I met Christ, now I am different. . . . Before, the most important thing for me was to have a .45, to be in the streets causing trouble, to have the biggest drug point in town. That was my vision before, but not now. Now I'm Christian and things are very good. Now my vision is to finish school and to study at the University. I have everything under control.

José Luis's testimony appealed to those in the streets with whom he identified himself. His history as "one of them" formed a symbolic bridge of identification that he used to connect with the gang members and drug dealers he wished so very much to save. "They listen to me," he insisted. "They listen to me because they know who I was. They know that I wasn't always a *cristiano*, that I was once a *tíguere* from the streets." His friend Héctor concurred, "There are people who see me, José Luis, and other young men who have converted and they say 'truly God is real.' They say 'look at that *muchacho* over there, you should be like him.' And I say to them, 'I have allowed God to do his work in my life and I want you to permit God to do the same.' They see a transformation in us."

José Luis's exemplification of the Pentecostal ideal of transformation paved the way for esteem ("respect," or *respeto* in the local idiom) wherever he went. Even Héctor, who otherwise was more articulate, better educated, and equally involved in the church, was simply not as popular and did not garner the same regard as José Luis, whose transformation was considerably more stark and by comparison far more astonishing. He went from being a ferocious gang leader who exemplified the ideals of *tigueraje* to becoming a popular spiritual leader virtually overnight, and the sheer sinfulness of his past provided that his conversion would be seen as extraordinary, exceptional, and divinely inspired. He was what others describe as a living testimony, an exemplary illustration of God's transformative power and infinite grace. He represented the Christian ideal and was frequently cited as an example to others of right Christian practice and the remarkable power of conversion.

As José Luis's case illustrates, as well as many others, because of the unique emphasis on conversion and the considerable value put on personal transformation in the Pentecostal church, those individuals whose lives demonstrate the greatest change as a result of conversion are regarded as the ideal and most coveted converts since their unlikely conversion best illustrates the transformative power of God. These exemplary converts are seen as more unique than others and their transformation more extraordinary because of the apparent unlikelihood of their conversion in the face of such terrible sinfulness. They are understood to be closer to God, or to have a special relationship to him; they are said to be living testaments of Jesus's infinite mercy and are frequently said to reflect his grace in their lives. Celebrated as Christian ideals, they are awarded the respect and authority reserved for leaders in the faith. They are invited to lead congregations of their own, to evangelize in public squares, to testify around the country, and to lead spiritual retreats.

This particular dynamic creates an incentive to represent one's previous life to have been as broken, as sinful, and as debauched as possible so that one's conversion appears all the more miraculous and divinely inspired. This is most readily apparent in the testimony of converts who attempt to extend or exaggerate their transformation in Christ and embellish the conditions that led to their successful conversion experience. By highlighting the acute sinfulness of their previous lives, converts claim the legitimacy associated with championing the transformation ideal, all while maintaining respect in the streets.

A characteristic feature of popular male conversion testimonies in the barrio is not so much that they give an account of sin per se, but rather that they recount overwhelmingly successful campaigns of sin. Male converts do not just emphasize the sinfulness of their pasts, they underscore their mastery of ungodliness with measured detail and no small amount of embellishment. Renato did not just pursue women from time to time, he *sacked* countless numbers of them; José Luis was not just a member of a gang, he was a gang leader; Héctor was not just an abuser of drugs, he was a prominent seller; Juan Carlos was no mere drug dealer, he was a notorious drug trafficker; and so on. Even individuals whose previous lives seem less mired in sin are quick to insist that, for example, they did not just drink the occasional beer; they were, in point of fact, alcoholics. Juan Carlos, Renato, José Luis, and innumerable others testify to more than just being bad: they profess to have been *really* bad, indeed, exceptionally accomplished sinners. Despite the fact that José Luis claims to have been a failure before converting, he was not a failure from the perspective of the street and norms of *tigueraje*, which he at one time championed like no other. He rose through the ranks of his gang by excelling in the streets, not by failing in them. The same went for Juan Carlos, whose criminal record and some may say street savvy made him a *tiguerazo,* or "top dog" among his friends. These individuals were no mere sinners—they were above all *successful* sinners. I do not wish to suggest here that all converts necessarily offer untruthful or exaggerated testimonies.[5] Rather, I want to point out that believers have a choice of how they represent their previous lives, selecting what details to highlight and foreground and which details they wish to be vague about and to avoid. These expository accounts bear directly on the image of reform converts look to promote through their impressive descriptions of sin and redemption.

Protestant conversion narratives have been observed to follow a standard formula wherever they are encountered (Gooren 2010a:93; Brereton 1991); this context is no different in that regard. The most successful narratives follow some variation on the following theme: lost or broken soul finds Jesus Christ through divine intervention, converts, and a sinful life is transformed into a sinless life in the service of God. A typical conversion narrative describes the bad or negative state of a person's life before his or her conversion and the fundamental transformation that has occurred since accepting Jesus Christ as one's savior. The testimony explains how one's conversion to Jesus Christ changed him or her from a sinner to a saint, a nonbeliever into a believer, an immoral being into a moral one. While the structure of these testimonies tends to be shared, the content—the character and quality of sin, for example—is open to creativity and variation. It is up to the convert to decide how he or she wants to represent his or her sinfulness and subsequent transformation in Christ, so long as the theme of redemption endures.

It is relevant to note that the categories of sin that are emphasized by male converts in this context are somewhat circumscribed. Converts construct testimonies that describe their previous lives as sinful, but not infinitely so. The degree and quality of sins professed are constrained by cultural norms of civility and local standards of humanity. One does not often hear, for example, that a person was physically abusive to his wife, that he was a rapist, that he abused children, or that he was responsible for killing others—nor, in a totally different sense, that he had engaged in homosexual relations or visited male prostitutes. Although these examples are all considered sinful by the church, these offenses are not culturally approved outlets for aggression or youth and do little to authenticate a convert's macho image. The cost of confessing such sins, it would seem, appears to be too great. Rather, converts draw on images of the ubiquitous *tíguere* in order to construct a persuasive and compelling narrative, in part because the moral ambiguity of such a character (alluring yet distrustful, admirable but immoral) provides the ideal material to invoke a sufficiently wicked persona (with the added benefit of being unquestionably masculine) while remaining within the acceptable bounds of deviant behavior.

To recapitulate, through narrating stories of past sinfulness and demonstrating a profound transformation from profane worldliness to ostensible spiritual perfection, male converts fulfill the cultural myth of forgiveness and redemption and constitute themselves as spiritual and moral leaders. By demonstrating a miraculous triumph over sin, converts characterize themselves as special recipients of divine grace and favored subjects of God. Only by emphasizing the backwardness of their preconversion lives can reformed sinners be said to have truly overcome the darkness and to have epitomized the biblical trajectory from sin to sainthood. This transformation is most apparent and awe-inspiring when it can be shown that a convert was particularly wicked before converting and that he has only truly turned his life around with the aid of the Holy Spirit. The greater the transformation, the greater the prestige, with those who demonstrate the most profound reversals of fate accorded the highest regard. With these credentials, converts are enjoined to share their testimony with the world, empowered to lead as exemplars of the faith and as recognized spiritual authorities—or, as believers maintain, as living testimonies and God's representatives on earth.

Spiritual Authority and the Cultivation of Negative-Charisma

Max Weber defined charisma, or what he called "charismatic authority," as legitimacy based on exceptional or extraordinary characteristics exhibited by or imputed to a particular individual. Borrowing from the original Christian conception of charisma (or *charismata*) as denoting the gifts of grace conferred by the Holy Spirit, in Weber's sociological formulation charisma became a property of one's personal character that is regarded by others as "a manifestation of endowment with, or possession by, some divine power" (Shils 1965:200), or as Parsons (1964:668) rearticulated more generally, "the quality which attaches to men and things by virtue of their relations with the 'supernatural.'" What separates charisma from, say, simply prestige, or some other form of legitimacy, is that it derives authority because of its supernatural/divine (and therefore utterly extraordinary) provenance.[6] As extraordinary individuals produced by divine favor or grace, the men referred to here become charismatic ideals, not simply through positive affirmations of piety or necessarily through reception of charismatic gifts (charisma in the original sense), but, importantly, through a miraculous moral transformation and the apparent triumph over wickedness. In representing this transformation as severe and fundamental (through testimony and conversion narratives), converts cultivate a kind of legitimacy that might be referred to as "negative-charisma" (cf. Aberle 1966).[7] Only by characterizing their previous lives as particularly depraved and ungodly (as negative or in negative terms) and emphasizing the distance from or absence of the divine—in fact, the inverse of positive charisma—can converts truly shape amazing, awe-inspiring testimonies of exceptional and exemplary value and lay claim to the distinction of special divine favor. If believers are appraised for their triumph over wickedness, then the greater their former wickedness, the greater the miracle of their perceived triumph, and thus the greater their charisma as recipients of that divine grace. The charismatic authority derived by converts through popular narratives of former sin may be called negative-charisma because legitimacy in this context is constituted as much by assigning negative value to one's previous identity as sinner as it is to assigning positive value to one's present identity as sanctified believer.

Conversion narratives are an important site for the legitimation of spiritual authority, indeed charismatic authority, because they establish a convert's relationship to the divine and set the terms for his or her future as a recipient and possessor of God's grace. Without a "good testimony," converts will not be baptized in the church and cannot become full members of the congregation. They must demonstrate, alongside a convincing personal transformation, that God has miraculously changed them for the better. Although tales of sin are a necessary component of any testimony, they are not sufficient on their own and must be accompanied by a verifiable moral reformulation. As narratives, tales of sinfulness may be manipulated in ways that other more embodied forms of charisma may not, yet if former sin is not redeemed by present sanctity, the stories go for naught. Individuals like José Luis, Renato, and Juan Carlos define themselves as "true Christians" and claim spiritual authority by cultivating negative-charisma in their testimonies while at the same time achieving a sanctified born-again identity through their manifest moral and spiritual transformation. As one local deacon maintained, "There are people who, even after some time, you see them and say 'no, there has been no change.' If I speak to you the gospel and I live doing things that are not like a person who says they are Christian, then I have not converted. It is to be convinced that Christ is the Lord that changes us and transforms us." Such persons are living evidence of God's transformative power.

The Pentecostal emphasis on spiritual and moral transformation creates the conditions under which negative-charisma becomes salient and converts may exchange the transgressions of the past for spiritual legitimacy in the present. This unique emphasis means that individual transformation, more than piety or virtue alone, is part and parcel of one's charismatic authority. Given this, it is doubtful that negative-charisma will be encountered in religions not driven by conversion or predicated on profound personal change. Should one wish to become a priest in the Catholic Church, for example, his past history as a sinner is likely to be de-emphasized. He would gain little by calling too much attention to his former misdeeds; in fact, his authority in the church may be compromised rather than strengthened or affirmed should revelations of fantastic sinfulness be made public to parishioners. Unlike the Pentecostals discussed here, his spiritual authority is one based largely on the perception of *inherent* piety rather than on the perception of *achieved* piety and the impressive conquest of mortal sin.

Pentecostal Christianity has been described as a "charismatic movement," not because a powerful magnetic leader dominates an excited following (which is often what Weber's concept of charisma is invoked to explain), but because of the significant emphasis on spiritual gifts (again, charisma in the original sense) and the primary importance put on the direct experience of the divine (see Robbins 2004a). Without conventional ecclesiastical mediation, every member of the church is understood to have equal access to the power of the Holy Spirit in addition to direct, unmediated communion with God. Consequently, unlike other charismatic movements addressed in the literature, the Pentecostal church cannot properly be described as an organization of simply leaders and followers: all believers are potential recipients of divine grace, and thus all are potential bearers of charisma.[8]

By making the faith's greatest assets available to every believer, regardless of his or her office or station, Pentecostal Christianity looks remarkably egalitarian. Any member may claim divine inspiration or favor and need not possess formal qualifications to preach, evangelize, consult, et cetera. Absolute authority by any one individual seems always to be mediated by this fact. And yet despite the apparent equality between the faithful—everyone, after all, is said to be equal in the eyes of the Lord—real differences obtain between average, unexceptional followers and those who stand out in the faith as spiritual leaders (preachers and others who are looked to for inspiration and guidance). It is plain that some individuals are regarded as having more grace than others and have set themselves apart from their fellow congregants as exceptional or "extraordinary" in this regard.

José Luis and Juan Carlos are extraordinary because of the spiritual transformation they are said to embody by virtue of God's favor and the distance they have traveled to conquer sin. Their miraculous salvation from the clutches of evil entitles them to exceptional status and special regard among the faithful. As persons endowed with charismatic authority, they are not to be followed or obeyed so much as they are to be held up as examples to others—Christian ideals to be emulated rather than served. Pentecostals lead by example, and through their example they become moral and spiritual leaders in their communities.[9]

These leaders, then, are considered spiritual authorities insofar as they are sought out for advice, healing, preaching, and evangelizing, and are generally recognized as special agents or representatives of God on earth (regardless of their institutional position or official role in the faith community). As certified "technicians of the sacred," they are conferred a unique prestige and authorized to administer the Word to others and, by dint of their distinction, to lead by example. José Luis's charisma is evident in the respect he commands in the barrio, in the sincerity with which people seek out his advice and guidance, in the responsibility with which he is entrusted, and not the least in his status as a favored preacher and evangelist.

By drawing on Weber's extension of charisma as a type of legitimacy, one that is intrinsically tied to the numinous or divine relation, and acknowledging at the same time the dynamic range of that relation (from spiritual gifts to miraculous salvation), the concept of charisma provides a useful analytic for identifying a kind of spiritual authority in the church, that something resulting from divine favor that makes one a member of an admired few, a spiritual elect who lead by example and inspire a community of believers.

Many studies that invoke Weber's charisma tend to focus on the character of powerful captivating leaders rather than on the form of legitimation that renders their authority salient and valid. In the Pentecostal context, charisma identifies more than just the extraordinary magnetism of dominant leaders or the familiar graces afforded by God; at its most dynamic, the term locates a form of legitimation whereby any individual based on his or her real or perceived favor with the divine is attributed special or extraordinary status. It is in this sense that the individuals discussed here are charismatic, not merely because they are the products of divine grace but, importantly, for the varied and creative ways in which they leverage their favor with God in the service of their own legitimacy as Christian elect. Men in Dominican barrios are charismatic, not by the gifts of grace alone, or even at all, but by establishing themselves as exceptional converts through extraordinary testimonies of sin and redemption. For these male converts, the cultivation of negative-charisma (legitimacy established by way of negative terms and associations) becomes a crucial site for the manufacture of spiritual authority in the church and the comprehensive achievement of a born-again identity as exemplary men of God.

Gender and Charismatic Differentiation

I conclude with a few comments and observations related back to gender difference and differentiation vis-à-vis Pentecostal conversion in the Dominican Republic. A very significant difference between male and female testimonies in the barrio is that women do not emphasize the same qualities or degrees of sinfulness as men. This is due chiefly to the fact that sinfulness, as defined locally by the Pentecostal church, is by and large a sphere of male activity. Because men presumably drink, smoke, and fornicate more than women, the process of repentance appears to be more full for them (although, as I mentioned, certain sins are forbidden to them as unmanly), and forgiveness and salvation take on a greater force and significance (Mintz 1956:409). This is not to say that women do not sin, only that the transgressions of women tend not to be seen as severe as those of their husbands or brothers.

A notable consequence of this particular constellation of relationships, when considered in the context of urban barrios in the Dominican Republic, is that Dominican women are not as free to claim what I have referred to here as negative-charisma and the prestige associated with exemplifying the conversion ideal. While women can and certainly do sin according to the church, their sins are frequently understood as of a different order than those of men because they are thought incapable of the most deplorable offenses. While promiscuity and prostitution may be transgressions that women escape through conversion, they are rarely if ever broached in testimonies where cultural norms of decency do not allow for the airing of such sins publicly. It is quite unacceptable to most barrio residents for women to proclaim a past history in the streets, apart from a mere passing association with its freedoms (women's symbolic association with the home and the values of respectability prevent it). Women here simply do not have the same liberties to extend, exaggerate, or even profess a range of sinfulness that men are not only free to acknowledge but also are actively encouraged to develop and promote.

However, witchcraft, sorcery, playing the lottery (gambling), and insolence toward one's husband, along with laziness, lack of ambition, and cavorting or visiting with spirits, are all popular and indeed "suitable" topics of female testimonies that I have encountered in the Dominican Republic. These confessions are typical in the barrios, where women are commonly the purveyors and consumers of Afro-Dominican and Haitian religions (in addition to Catholicism) and where poverty, unemployment, and patriarchy antagonize and regularly victimize female residents. The solicitation of saints in the Catholic Church, for example, and the invocation of spirit beings in the context of Dominican *vodú* are activities demonized by the church that become the popular sins of female converts.

The differences in the social symbolic value of male and female testimonies are significant to the diverse ways in which men and women claim spiritual authority. With former sinfulness as a special path to legitimacy all but closed to them, women approach other avenues to authority and upward mobility in the church. For example, women are quick to gain respect and renown in congregations by leading prayer groups and by conducting the church's outreach and charitable endeavors. But perhaps more notably, women are perceived to be more attuned to spiritual matters. It is widely held throughout the Caribbean and Latin America that women are "more open to matters of the spirit" and that their predominance in congregations is a function of their "greater sensitivity to the Spirit" (Chesnut 2003:142). In the congregations that I observed in the Dominican Republic, women were more likely to be "slain in the spirit," just as they were more likely to be possessed by malevolent spirits. As several scholars have noted, while men routinely monopolize formal institutional positions of authority in the church, women, who are largely excluded from such positions, tend to claim the authority of inspiration through reception of the Holy Gifts such as speaking in tongues, healing, and prophecy (Robbins 2004a:132; Cucchiari 1990:693–694; Martin 2001:54). While reception of the Holy Gifts represents the most viable way for women to access spiritual authority in the church (Brusco 2010:81), for men it appears to be through negative-charisma and exemplary fulfillment of the Pentecostal conversion ideal. Not associated, like women, with an inherent calling to the spirit, young Dominican men derive spiritual authority in the church by recalling the wickedness of their preconversion lives and satisfying the Pentecostal ideal of transformation from sinner to saint.

Men are able to claim divine favor relative to women by establishing themselves as exceptional converts miraculously saved from evil. By making their amazing transformation the locus of their legitimacy, male converts acquire charisma in lieu of spiritual gifts and the embodied spirituality that has become for women the primary source of their religious authority. Of central importance to Pentecostal identity is the path believers took to become Christian and the fundamental difference that they now exhibit as a result of their conversion. The emphasis on moral transformation serves to exclude women from the holy grail of Pentecostal deliverance because they cannot exemplify the transformation ideal to the same degree as men. As a result, women are imputed less authority than men, even if they participate more in congregations, demonstrate greater religious knowledge, show more evidence of charismatic gifts, and are considered less likely to leave the church or to backslide. This is not to suggest that women do not have charisma, only that due to certain religious and cultural restraints they are less likely to be imputed the same authority associated with conversion and developed in testimonies as men.

The type of charisma associated with conversion and cultivated in testimony, then, is by virtue of cultural considerations to a large degree outside the grasp of female converts. It explains why men tend to exaggerate their conversion narratives more than women and why they tend to communicate qualitatively different testimonies. It also helps to explain the unequal distribution of a certain kind of authority within the church (along lines of gender) without relying entirely on reductive appeals to the "simple fact" of patriarchal domination. There is more of an incentive for men to exaggerate their conversion stories as well as fewer restrictions. The authority they gain in doing so is readily apparent in any congregation where many of the most prized converts—and the most prestigious among them—are former drug lords, gang members, thieves, and tyrants of the streets. It should be no surprise that the most charismatic Pentecostals that I came to know had the most tumultuous pasts, mired in bloodshed and sin, and whose testimonies frequently took on impressive airs of fantasy.

The cultivation of negative-charisma is, perhaps counterintuitively, directly related to the promotion of spiritual authority and legitimacy in the church. In an exchange where the worst become first, so to speak, the most depraved sinners become the evangelical select. By exemplifying the conversion ideal, Pentecostal men in the barrios of the Dominican Republic justify their position in the church, validate their spiritual claims, and establish themselves as Christian elites. An artifact of this production is the residual prestige that converts gain when performing their conversion narratives for others. The hypermasculinity attached to their former identities in the streets functions to bolster converts' masculine qualities in the church and counter the feminizing potentials of evangelical piety. Like the Dominican masculine culture hero the *tíguere*, male converts are perceived as having overcome great odds to become victorious in spite of considerable disadvantage; succeeding where others failed, the convert "emerges well" from the depths of sin to triumph with God by his side.

Pentecostal Social Currency and the Search for Respect

Wherever one goes they give you respect.
Arturo

In this chapter I am concerned with the tangible ways in which Pentecostal converts in the urban barrio experience their evangelical identities as symbolic capital in the form of prestige. Local Pentecostal churches make male and female converts "respectable" by promoting values of respectability and, in so doing, furnish poor and otherwise marginalized men and women with access to forms of status and prestige from which they are typically excluded (Simpson 1978:154; Burdick 1998; Brodwin 2003).[1] I also consider here a specific constellation of values in Dominican society that render respect for devout Christian converts and structure the moral economy that affords them conditional distinction.

For the Pentecostal community at Iglesia Evangélica Pentecostal (IEP) and Iglesia de Dios (IdD), *respeto*, or "respect," is the most cited benefit of conversion and is the predominant idiom through which converts experience the positive social rewards of evangelical Christian identity in the barrio. This particular concept of respect is dynamic, referring both to the prestige one earns as a *cristiano* as well as to the experience of sanctity that converts cultivate as part of their personal transformation in Christ. I refer to this type of prestige as a form of Pentecostal social currency that is awarded on the basis of a convert's ability to embody time-honored cultural ideals associated with the "good Christian," such as "the benevolent and sacrificing neighbor," "the reformed and redeemed sinner," and "the dutiful and loving wife."

Respect is not given freely: this form of prestige is dependent upon proving the sincerity of one's convictions by meeting the demands required of the faithful; converts earn respect according to their perceived faithfulness and unwavering satisfaction of behavioral prohibitions. Converts must earn respect and thus warrant the esteem that may be bestowed upon them as favored servants of God. Salvation, likewise, is understood in equivalent terms—it must be earned. Converts are implored to follow strict rules of comportment in order to be sanctified; only by fulfilling the gospel and the word of God will their eternal salvation be ensured. Positive social regard confirms for churchgoers their achievement of sanctity and the promise of salvation through a new life in Christ. Churchgoers experience the otherwise intangible idea of sanctity in the form of respect from their local community, positive social regard that can be experienced objectively. For example, in addition to the exceptions made for them by gang members and others, for Pentecostals in Villa, the admiration they claim to receive from their acquaintances, the titles of deference they acquire as converts, and the newfound trust they earn from family and friends are various instances of the respect they now enjoy as self-proclaimed sanctified men and women of God. In turn, believers interpret this public regard as confirmation of their spiritual transformation and achievement of holiness. While, for example, converts can never be positive that what they are doing will ensure their salvation, or that they have indeed achieved sanctity with any certainty—their own internal battles with sin always seem to contradict spiritual perfection—they can experience the "success" of conversion tangibly in the form of prestige (experienced here in terms of "respect" or positive social regard), confirmation of one's truly divine transformation. It is likely that for this reason, evidence of the Spirit in one's life takes on considerable value for believers along with the physical, demonstrative aspects of the faith, which seem to confirm, at least among their peers, their relative achievement of genuine piety. The inner-worldly asceticism promoted by the church would be relatively meaningless to converts if they could not see positive changes in their daily lives. The church joins with other popular religious institutions to offer immediate solutions to everyday problems of barrio life such as poverty, jealousy, witchcraft, and illness. Conversion may not always be instrumental or compensatory; believers in any event must decide for themselves how membership in the church is helping improve their lives. As long as the answer is affirmative, and believers determine that the benefits bestowed by the faith are *vale la pena*, or "worth it," in the end, they are likely to remain in the church, and if not, they always have the option to leave.

Earning Respect

> There is a respect, you know that when you are in "the world" many people respect you because you were who you were and you could at any moment, you know. . . . There are people who convert and nobody respects them in the barrio and you know why? Because they keep doing illicit things and people don't have respect for them. People say, "This guy is a fraud, a charlatan." But when a *tíguere* sees that you have converted truthfully they say, "Wow! This was a *tíguere* and he truly converted." They are going to respect you. More than the respect God puts in you, because now God puts respect in them. You can go places where people say bad words and they will say, "*Varón*, please excuse me." I say, "Wow, but who am I?" Thanks to the grace of God they want to offer you a soda, they want to offer you a juice; they invite you in and ask you to pray for them.
>
> Juan Carlos

For the Pentecostal community in barrio Francisco, the tangible rewards of salvation are experienced as respect from those with whom they interact. Members of IdD and IEP consider the positive regard they obtain from their peers to be the most salient and practical benefit of Christian identity. One young woman from IdD insists that "the greatest advantage to being a Christian is that people respect you." In fact, most of my informants, without being prompted, describe their experience in the church as eliciting respect from others. For Héctor, the newfound regard his conversion occasioned was a personal triumph, an achievement almost immediately apparent in his dealings with others and, in particular, his relationship to law enforcement:

> There is a respect and consideration in the neighborhood [for *cristianos*]. Before I became a Christian, the police did not respect me. They treated me as if I was a criminal. After I accepted Christ, I would say that they see in me something like a divine authority; something to which they owe respect. One time there was a [police] raid here in

Villa and there were protests. I was there, speaking with a man (and I had my Bible with me but it was hidden) and the police force they call SWAT (who are very dangerous) came and took the man I was [speaking] with away. He was riding his bike around without papers and I wanted to speak on his behalf but they put him in a truck and they didn't say anything to me, just *"varón,* go home!" They didn't even see my Bible because I had it behind me. They knew that I was Christian and something that is a part of God. I have gone, and other Christians have testified that they have gone as well, to dangerous places and the authorities don't have a problem with them—without them having to say anything or even to identify themselves. They don't do anything. They see something distinct in you.

Héctor's transformation to a Bible-toting Pentecostal permitted a new relationship to local authorities that he has come to understand in terms of respect—specifically, respect for Christian authority. The divine admiration to which he refers is embodied—acknowledged not because he announced himself to be Pentecostal (or because he revealed himself to be holding a Bible), but rather, in his appraisal, because of a divine essence (in his terms, *"algo distinto"* ["something distinct"]) attributable to God that presumably demands recognition. This respect, like God's grace, is thought to be tangible and something that, according to Juan Carlos, "God puts in you." Indeed, that very same "something" that Héctor proposes makes one distinct and "something to which [others] owe respect." It is "thanks to the grace of God" that Juan Carlos is treated differently today, that he is treated with respect by his community. In attributing this new regard to their spiritual transformation and to the grace of God in their lives, Juan Carlos, Héctor, and the rest of the faithful in barrio Francisco come to experience sanctity in terms of positive social rewards like trust, confidence, admiration, and renown. For converts here, the achievement of sanctity and the experience of grace are understood in terms of respect and the public regard that follows from true inspired conversion.

This respect, although it could be understood analytically as a type of charisma, is not conceived of solely as God's grace (even if it is often so attributed). Pentecostals see their reformed deeds and disciplined conduct as important genres of ethical behavior that elicit respect—a product of inward changes inspired by God, but ultimately executed by the individual believer (see chapter 4). This is different from the authority they might acquire as a result of their achievement of the conversion ideal and positioning as divine favorites as discussed in chapter 6. In that scenario, only a select few become charismatic exemplars (living testimonies exalted for their improbable transformation). For the rest (and not excluding those select few), positive social regard in the form of respect is the popular idiom through which they come to experience and understand their spiritual transformation in Christ and their public identities as Christian converts and redeemed sinners.

In order to understand how Pentecostals come to experience their Christian identities as important mantles of respect, let us first consider the tangible social rewards that converts claim to receive as a result of their spiritual transformation. In practice, Pentecostals in Villa understand respect in a number of ways, particularly related to how people treat and relate to them as individuals. If strangers listen to them preach, it means that they are respected. If others seek their help or advice, it means that they respect them. If acquaintances refer to them by titles of esteem (such as *varón, hermano, hermana,* and so forth), then they are respected. In the same vein, if people show consideration for their beliefs and the prohibitions that they follow, they feel respected. This was impressed upon me repeatedly when church members discussed the advantages of being Christian converts.

Pentecostals in the barrio are happy to describe their dealings with non-Christians as relationships of respect because they will refer to them as *varón, varona,* or *hembra.* The term *"varón"* literally means "male," as in *"un hijo varón,"* meaning "a son." When used in reference to an adult, the term emphasizes the virility of the man and takes on a sense of reverence. To refer to someone as *varón* is to emphasize his masculinity, but it is also, above all, a term of respect. While anyone may be referred to as *varón,* it is frequently used as a term of respect for *cristianos,* an acknowledgment of their status as serious, respectable Christians. Women may be referred to as *varona* as a similar term of respect, in which case it does not mean "a mannish woman" but rather a respected (or respectable) female. Karla explained to me that in school, the other students respect her because she is Christian. She knows this because they call her *varona* or *varonita*: "In school [they respect me a lot], they call me *hermana, varona, evangélica,* it's *jevi* [cool]! It's cool when another girl asks you for advice and she goes and follows the suggestions that you gave her." On occasion women in the church are also called *hembra,* which tends toward the female equivalent of *varón* for women ("*hembra*" means "female").

Another form of regard bestowed upon the faithful is the respect others show in consideration for their beliefs and the prohibitions that they follow. This takes the shape of abstaining from the use of obscenities when in their presence and offering them a nonalcoholic beverage like a juice or soda instead of beer or rum (see Juan Carlos's quote above). Even Angel, the local gang leader we met in chapter 5, confessed that he tries not to use obscenities when in the company of Christians:

> When I am speaking with a *cristiano* I try not to say bad words. But if I am talking with a person who thinks that they are a *tíguere* then yes, they come out, I say them. But when I am speaking with disciplined people, I try not to say any bad words.

The discipline to which Angel refers is a frequent characterization of respected Pentecostals, recalling the ideal of self-restraint and obedience to God. To show such restraint, to exhibit self-discipline, to be obedient to God, is to be godly and to demonstrate one's religiousness or, simultaneously, one's "seriousness" and commitment to a spiritual calling.

Additionally, people show their respect for *cristianos* by listening to what they have to say. I am continually impressed by the patience and gratefulness that meets evangelists in the streets of Santo Domingo. In the capital, it is not uncommon to receive a pamphlet or flyer from an *evangélico* in passing, often on the street corner or en route in public transportation. It is more likely to see bystanders accept and read what is given to them than to see them reject it outright or to throw it away. People listen to sermons given on street corners and are likely to attend special church events like *campañas* and *retiros* even if not affiliated with the faith. Often *campañas* are occasions for entertainment as well as reflection for locals who enjoy listening to sermons and singing along with the catchy, inspiring music. When events like these occur, especially when they take place at the center of town in public squares, they tend to be the main attraction, bringing believers and nonbelievers together for an evening of communion.

This kind of regard for Pentecostal faith is seen in other contexts as well. It is not unheard of for *colmadónes* to close for several hours in order to accommodate a special church event being held in the streets nearby. In Villa, whenever there are large *campañas* or *retiros* at the center of town, in the park, or on a stage in the vicinity, the *colmados* in the area turn off their sound systems until the events come to a conclusion, effectively sharing the aural landscape with their rather vocal critics.[2] According to one informant, they once even held a church service inside a *colmadón*!

Pentecostal churches play an important role in the barrio for non-Christian residents who seek healing, prayer, and advice about a range of issues. Domingo spoke with pleasure about the respect extended to Christians in the neighborhood: "Well, at least in our community the Christian life has earned respect and acceptance. For whatever difficulty there may be, the community looks to *cristianos* to come and pray [for them]. And when someone wants a favor from the Lord, they always look for Christians to intervene, to intercede on their behalf, for them to pray. At least we have earned the respect [of the community]." This role is taken seriously by members of the church, who see themselves as vital agents for peace in the neighborhood. This has encouraged a number of church members to take up important positions within neighborhood councils called "*juntas de vecinos*" as well as unofficial roles as spiritual guides and mentors. According to Juan Pablo, who along with Denny (the president of the *junta*) was a member of the neighborhood council, as council members they are empowered to take action if they observe something of detriment (such as drug dealing) occurring in the neighborhood. Juan Pablo believed that others trusted Christian converts with positions on the council because they are deemed to be honest and are seen as responsible leaders in the neighborhood.

Pentecostals are expected to be trustworthy, and for many converts the newfound confidence of others is an advantageous boon. Flaco explains that being a *cristiano* ensures that he will be trusted:

When you are Christian the people in the neighborhood trust you. When you are not a Christian you can go to a house and maybe the parents or grandparents will look at you strangely and they may say, "What is this guy up to?" You could be there for whatever reason but they don't have much trust in you because you are not Christian. When you are Christian and you go to a home, they welcome you, everyone trusts you, everyone defends you. It is not very common for those who are not Christian to gain trust. Wherever they go Christians are given more trust: at work, at the University, at school, in high school, they give you more trust.

Karla believes that because she is baptized and is a member of the church, her mother has more confidence in her, and, as a consequence, permits her to do many of the things other parents forbid their daughters to do:

> If I were not a *cristiana* my mother would not let me sleep over at a friend's house. I am certain of that. I can stay two or three days at a friend's house. I can go to visit a male friend at his house too. They can come visit me also without any problem. But if I were not a *cristiana*, I am very certain that my mother would not [allow it].

José Luis also understands his newfound respect in terms of trust. In particular, he marvels at how today he is admitted into people's homes without the suspicion or worry that he will hurt or rob them:

> Before they respected me out of fear.... They were afraid that I would take their television if they let me in, that I would take the fan, that I would steal whatever thing in their home.... They were scared. Now they respect me more; now its "*varón de Dios*" ["man of God"]; "How are you *varón*?"; "Look here *varón*"; they call me José Luis.... On one occasion I was thrown out of a house. [After that] I was not allowed inside or on the patio. After [I converted], I [was allowed back in]. I sat on the sofa, they said to me, "*varón*, here you have all the trust that you want; look in the fridge, there is juice; have some juice; here is the remote control, turn on the television." That is to say, I didn't have the trust that I have now.

The faithful are expected to be trustworthy. Some people prefer to deal with evangelicals in business deals or ventures because they believe they can rely on them not to take advantage of the situation or to rip them off. Several observers have found that Pentecostal asceticism renders members hardworking and reliable in the eyes of employers, thus making them eminently employable over others (Willems 1968:197; d'Epinay 1969:133; Maxwell 1998:354; Robbins 2004a:136; Smilde 2007:6). This is an ideal, of course, and people in the church are neither universally nor uniformly trustworthy, but the demands of the faith impose additional sanctions on believers who violate the code of truth—particularly the directives not to lie, cheat, or steal. Under such constraints, *cristianos* who show themselves to be serious converts will be extended more confidence than those who do not.

God, it is said, opens many doors to the faithful, and converts in Villa recount enacting this popular metaphor by literally entering homes through doors that were once closed to them as nonbelievers. The confidence of others is interpreted as a consequence of the spiritual transformation and the degree of sanctity a follower has achieved through his or her unwavering commitment to the faith. Trust comes to be experienced as the newfound confidence family and friends extend to them as redeemed sinners. Like the gates of heaven that open wide to embrace the sanctified, so too the doors of the local community appear to swing ajar, receiving with open arms the most dedicated servants of God.

Congregation and Prosperity

Several studies of Pentecostal economic behavior have pointed out the potentially positive financial rewards of conversion. A key debate in the academic literature has been determining "the extent to which Pentecostal-charismatic Christianity plays a role in establishing the 'Protestant ethic' in today's converts similar to the one played by Calvinism in Weber's account of the development of capitalism" (Robbins 2004a:136; see also Weber 1992). Emphasis on the conservative values of thrift, honesty, and hard work, combined with ascetic values that discourage wasteful spending on alcohol and leisure while simultaneously promoting investment in the household to the benefit of the nuclear family, may prove useful in ushering converts into advantageous modern forms of accumulation and consumption that at best lead to upward mobility and at worst stave off abject poverty (Willems 1968:197; Annis 1987; Brusco 1995:125, 142; Robbins 2004a:136–137).[3]

Along with fostering habits and attitudes congruent with modern capitalism, Pentecostal churches tend to appeal most (though by no means exclusively) to the poorer sectors of Dominican society, and it is to them that evangelizing efforts are addressed. This is typical of Pentecostal Christianity elsewhere. Mariz (1994), for instance, has characterized Pentecostalism in Rio de Janeiro as a cultural strategy for coping with poverty. A conservative moral frugality prevails in faithful households who convert discretionary income into productive savings and capital to make additions to the home, buy a car, or invest in other material symbols of status and financial well-being. Nevertheless, concerns of the faith are not reducible to economic concerns alone. At the same time, it would be foolish to assume material considerations do not factor into the strategic decision-making processes of religious actors; yet we run the risk of a dangerous reductionism if we see religion or religious choices as following solely from calculated financial interests. One issue is that it is not altogether clear how significant the economic advantages to conversion are (Robbins 2004a:136–137), though a few scholars have made the case that, at least for some, the doctrine provides a code of conduct that guards against falling further into destitute poverty (Maxwell 1998:351), with the church community tending to rally in material support of those in dire financial need. Moisés, the man who first introduced me to IdD, was quite candid with me when he explained that the reason he joined the church when he moved to Villa was because his family needed help: "I have to be honest, [we joined a church] because my parents were without work. My dad had a business but it went under. We had problems, many economic problems. You know that when you have problems you always look for help, a word of comfort, so you go to the church." It is not uncommon for the congregations at both IEP and IdD to support members of their community from time to time either by taking up special donations or by arranging services to assist building projects, food and clothing acquisition, day care, or transportation depending on an individual's specific needs. Converts in Villa, no less than elsewhere (see Smilde 2007:7), do not shy away from explaining their conversion in terms of the perceived economic, social, and personal gains associated with church membership. It is worth noting that converts themselves frequently report that joining the church has improved their financial situation. They attribute their good fortune not just to divine providence but give practical reasons to boot, usually pointing out that they no longer spend their money on alcohol, gambling, or *brujos*. In Villa, neither pastor at IdD or IEP could be said to have made more than a basic living off his or her work in the church. Both lived like most of their congregation, not appearing to enjoy superior material prosperity. Pastor Ramón put this in terms of sacrifice and understood his role as pastor to guide and to educate people about the true nature of Christianity through his example. Few other congregants were better off. In fact, material prosperity as an explicit goal of faith was an idea expressly discouraged from the pulpit of both churches.

The concern for material gain is not foremost in the local Pentecostal discourse that I observed in Villa. Material prosperity, if it arrives, is perhaps an unintended artifact of fidelity (though sometimes interpreted emically as a reward for fidelity) but never mentioned as a spiritual pursuit or goal in itself. Prosperity theology, or the teaching that God provides material prosperity to those who need only to ask for it, while present on the island, particularly in churches such as the Universal Church of the Kingdom of God (a neo-Pentecostal organization established in Brazil popularly known in the Dominican Republic as *Pare de Sufrir*, or "Stop the Suffering"), has yet to garner widespread support or following (though it has gained some popularity in parts of the country), I suspect in part because of the cultural emphasis on work and individual responsibility often associated with local definitions of proper participation in Protestant faith. The Pentecostals whom I got to know criticized *Pare de Sufrir* precisely because it claims to offer a "quick fix." Consider Josefina's mixed feelings about the church in her remarks from a conversation one afternoon in her kitchen:

> Look, in my opinion, this church isn't bad, but I do not think that one should talk as if everything is pretty when in reality it is not. For example, they sell things to people there to "stop the suffering." The church is telling people something that is not true, that is not the way that things are. When I converted my life changed. However, there continue to be difficult moments in my life. There have been moments as a Christian that I have cried for things that have happened to me and I have felt bad. There have been times that I want to be alone because sometimes in life there are difficult moments. So, *Pare de Sufrir* says whatever the problem, if you want to change your life go here, if you want to stop the suffering, easily, even if you do not believe in God, if you want to stop the suffering you make an offering. I think that they should speak to people about a plan of salvation, and not talk to people about stopping the suffering because there will always be suffering in this life, because life is not the color of roses.

Josefina and others reject what they perceive to be the premise of *Pare de Sufrir*: that people need only to come to the church, make an offering, and be free of problems thereafter. To benefit from true faith in Jesus Christ, congregants at IEP and IdD believed that members had to congregate, pray, and worship alongside others in addition to following the letter of the Bible (which, as we have seen, means regular adherence to prohibitions). *Pare de Sufrir* is suspicious to many in the community because it did not require membership, moral accountability, or ascetic discipline. It is viewed as a place where people do not have a community and are not accountable to others, a place where the ultimate goal of salvation goes unheeded in favor of the immediate satisfaction of worldly pursuits. Allegedly, visitors think they can go to the church one day, fix their problems, leave, and not be subject to reconciliation with Jesus, much less the moral policing of a congregation. On more than one occasion it was preached at IEP that this is not how God works and that such an approach is ultimately not amenable to living a genuinely holy life. Life, to the contrary, is understood as suffering and requires constant discipline of individual desires and regular edification in the church in order to maintain a path to salvation. The idea that one can "stop the suffering" was an affront to members of the community in Villa who understood their route to salvation in terms of sacrifice and suffering. Domingo echoes Josefina's statements by explaining that suffering is a necessary part of being a Christian: "To be Christian is to suffer," he explained to me one day, "it is to endure the suffering that Christ endured, to endure it within our lives."

The emphasis on "congregation" as an essential component of correct Christian practice, according to local Pentecostals, means that one is part of a collective with a communal responsibility to the image of the group (to keep up appearances), the salvation of others (through evangelism), and the mutual support for one another in his or her respective paths with God (through *consejos*). The congregations of IEP and IdD reject the doctrine of prosperity—the teaching that believers need only ask to be blessed with riches to receive them—mainly because it ignores this emphasis on communality and interdependence between believers. Also, it appears to work under the assumption that suffering can be eliminated in this life, a presupposition refused by Pentecostals in Villa. While churchgoers understand their conversion as bringing better things to their life, frequently respect, *el gozo* (joy), and spiritual sanctity, at IEP and IdD they rarely if ever connect this with extravagant material gain. At most, congregants testify that they have been blessed with a beautiful home since accepting Christ as their savior, but explicit claims of making it rich off of Jesus are reproached and regularly preached against in both churches.[4] It is also clear from conversations with congregants that without accountability to a faith community and the edifying support of fellow members alongside regular doctrine classes, the most important aspect of the faith locally—personal transformation—would be nearly impossible to achieve on one's own; Satan and the temptations of the world would be much too great to escape.

El Serio and the Values of Respectability

In order to earn respect converts must act "respectable." In addition to being trustworthy, the Pentecostal faithful cultivate identities based on qualities associated with the good Christian such as charity, chastity, modesty, temperance, kindness, and humility. According to the declaration of one seasoned member of IdD: "As a Christian, one has to walk decently and dress decently so that they treat you with great respect. . . . I have learned how to obtain respect and that to be a Christian is a great and good thing." Decent or respectable behavior constitutes the primary means of ensuring the respect of peers and embodying a born-again identity.

Respectability, defined here as a complex of cultural values rooted in hegemonic Christo-European ideals (Wilson 1995), is exemplified by the principal moral focus of the Pentecostal faith and the behavioral norms advocated by the church. In addition to promoting family, fidelity, and probity as capital values, the church endorses the parallel ambitions of monogamous heterosexual marriage, secure and gainful employment, as well as home-ownership and personal qualities reflecting saintly virtues. Economic prosperity, orthodox Christian morality, principled solemnity, and a particular kind of familial stability are trademarks of respectability in the Dominican Republic and are confirmed by an individual's material wealth, employment, marital and residential status, decorum, and honorable public reputation. For obvious reasons, then, values of respectability are always more easily championed by members of the upper classes, for whom meeting this ideal is relatively effortless. Locally, this sense of respectability is captured by the notion of "*ser serio*," or "being serious." I call this idea of seriousness "*el serio*" in order to compare it with another dominant contrasting mode of moral conduct in the barrio—that indexed by the term "*el relajo*," introduced in chapter 5.

El relajo is the opposite of seriousness and is often attributed to the behaviors and values of the street, *la calle*, and that of *tigueraje*. Associated with the terms "*el coro*" and "*la chercha*" (party/hang out), "*el relajo*" (joke/joking; "unseriousness") is a derivative of the verb "*relajar*," which means to relax or to ease. When one hears the oft-repeated adage "*con dios no se relaja*," or "one mustn't play around [or joke] with God," there is a sense that one is being cautioned not to "rest on one's laurels" or to "slack off" when dealing with spiritual things—topics that are not to be taken lightly but are to be regarded as serious.[5] I liken *el relajo* to the idea of "play" within African American orders of behavior where play, according to Abrahams (1983:54), is not distinguished from "work" so much as "respectable" (or in this case "serious") behavior. Joking or play behaviors are judged to be inappropriate for the home, where they are considered rude and destructive to family values; in the streets, they are not only permitted but are also cultivated as a means of status acquisition. In contrast, *una persona seria* is a mature, disciplined person committed to work and responsibility who leaves the values of play and jest to the dominion of the street and the diversions of the *tíguere*, who, according to his nature, flaunts unruly behavior in defiant opposition to the principle of stratification concomitant with respectability.[6]

El serio is marked by maturity, discipline, work, and family, and *el relajo* by youth, freedom, play, and friendship. Their respective key values could be summarized as a series of binary opposites such as home/street, private/ public, work/play, honesty/trickery, self-restraint/self-dissipation, hierarchy/equality, and religious/secular.[7] In this way, *el relajo* and *el serio* reflect dominant value orientations in the Dominican Republic that are analogous to Peter Wilson's model of reputation and respectability and which parallel dualisms exaggerated in the *dos mundos* worldview of Pentecostals, the Manichaean moral divisions they regularly apply to their experiences.

A widely applicable analytic used to describe the particulars of social organization on the island of Providencia, Wilson's original theory was an attempt to explain the apparent fractures found in Caribbean social systems and to reconcile two prevailing analytic models—pluralism and functionalism—that have dominated sociological and anthropological debates about the Caribbean region (Besson 1993:15). According to Wilson (1995), the values of reputation, championed by men, reflect values typically associated with lower-class public street culture and represent an indigenous (local or *creole*) response to domination and the scarcity of respectability. Respectability, on the other hand, rooted as it is in the Eurocentric colonial social structure, reflects the predominant values of social hierarchy, order, and upper-class Christo-European culture. According to de Moya (2002:113), these two distinct, at times opposing yet complementary ideals—reputation and respectability—constitute guiding principles that dominate most political and social life in the Dominican Republic. The ethnographic evidence

I provide here further demonstrates that Wilson's model has comparative utility across the Caribbean and can help elucidate a deeper understanding of Dominican moral values and their relationship to local Christianities.

Wilson declares that the principle of stratification subsuming all others in the Caribbean is the principle of respectability (Wilson 1995:9). I propose that in the Dominican Republic, the conflict between reputation and respectability values—between *el relajo* and *el serio*—reveals itself to be a struggle between practical and ideal moralities, respectively. In the barrio, where respectability is a social ideal out of reach for the majority of male residents by virtue of their class status, reputation values like that of *tigueraje* and the allied values of *el relajo* predominate among male groups. So-called men-of-the-streets cultivate practical alternative values such as individualism, wit and cunning, situational amorality, and hyperbolic machismo as conciliatory substitutes for the prestige they are denied by their exclusion from respectability. Men earn prestige among their male peer groups by excelling in *tigueraje*, an attainable goal for those otherwise excluded from mainstream respectability.

In the barrio, *cristianos* and *tígueres* are paragons of *el serio* and *el relajo*, respectively, and are typically opposed in kind. Just as *el relajo* is the negation of *el serio*, one cannot be both a *tíguere* and a *cristiano* simultaneously. The *tíguere* is representative of what Pentecostals call *el mundo*, the profane world of sin, while *cristianos* regard themselves as otherworldly representatives of an elevated spiritual realm, *el evangelio*. While *cristianos* may be associated with domesticity and self-discipline (obedience to God and submission to the law of the gospel), the *tíguere* epitomizes the freedom and unruly "wild" of the urban public, free to roam the streets, his undisputed domain, and to pursue sheer unmitigated self-interest (*tigueraje*).[8]

As such, the forms of respect derived from *tigueraje* differ greatly from those within the model of respectability to which Christian converts aspire. Being a *cristiano* in Villa means discipline and austerity; embracing seriousness and the values of *el serio* means following the prohibitions and not "playing around." Statements like this one, from Juan Carlos, are indicative: "Since I converted I am a serious man, I work more." A *cristiano* is to be a *persona seria* who champions the values of respectability through hard work, self-discipline, responsibility, and fidelity to the gospel. *El hombre serio*, the respectable (Christian) man, achieves his position of moral authority not merely by claiming to be principled but by enacting the ethical ideal.

Renato too considers himself a devout Christian and necessarily a serious man on account of his fidelity: "I am known for being serious and for being a Christian. Everyone knows that I am Christian, that I attend the church, and that I am a serious person." For Renato, in order to be considered a *persona seria*, to be a respected person, an individual needs to follow the rules imposed by the church and to "walk a straight path":

> For me being serious comes from inhibiting yourself or staying away from the things that you see are bad. So if you inhibit yourself things and walk a straight path, without twisting yourself, without looking from side to side, for me this is the concept of *ser serio* [being serious].

Through self-discipline and restraint—by following the prohibitions of the church and "inhibiting" his worldly desires—Renato is regarded as a serious, respectable man of God and, accordingly, demands respect from his peers. It is within this restraint that he achieves sanctity. In embracing the conservative values of respectability and aspiring to meet the ideal of seriousness, Renato aligns himself with the dominant hegemonic ideal, and must, as a consequence, forsake the street and *tigueraje* that afford a different kind of regard based on alternative (if at some level similarly constituted) values.

As we learned in chapter 5, Christianity is considered serious business as it relates to one's salvation and requires complete allegiance along with constant vigilance. Such stakes require total submission. For Pentecostals in Villa, *relajar* is to party with alcohol and sing salacious songs as if one has no fear of God. It is to curse and to speak crudely; it means to hang around bars and street corners, to not take seriously one's religious commitments, to skirt moral obligations to family and community, to trivialize that which is profoundly sacred.

According to Nicol (who had joined the church, left for a short while, only to return again), her friends accepted her conversion because—or rather, only when—she was serious about it:

> [My friends] were okay with [my conversion] because they accepted me as a *cristiana*—they did not accept me for playing around with the gospel. If I am a Christian I cannot leave the church and go hang out with them and party. I already left the church [before] and they understand this.

If one follows the prohibitions closely, and others see that you take the rules of the church seriously and are not doing what you should not be doing—that is, doing what the *impios* or *mundanos* are doing—you may be accorded respect as a Christian convert.

The gist of this dynamic was aired in theatrical fashion by a popular comedic film release in 2009 entitled *Cristiano de la Secreta*. In this, one of the biggest Dominican film releases of the year, an evangelical man attempts to live two lives: one as a *cristiano* and the other as a *tíguere* by acting on desires that are forbidden by the church. He must hide his Christian identity from friends in order to flirt with women, go to the bar, sing, dance, et cetera. Much of the humor in this comedy is based on the ruse wherein a Christian succumbs to the temptations of the world and attempts to enjoy the pleasures of *el mundo* while keeping his identity as a convert secret from others. He is ultimately unsuccessful, primarily because he cannot do both; the two identities are fundamentally opposed—he is either a devout *cristiano* who does not do those things, or he is a *tíguere*, a man of the world who is permitted to do those things. The main character realizes in the end that he will be accepted for who he truly is, a *cristiano*, and that he need not be a *tíguere* to gain acceptance or approval (or, in terms of the film's narrative, to win the woman of his dreams). The film reinforces the normative idea that Christianity is to be regarded as serious and, above all, an important calling in life that demands fidelity and respect from believers.

To the degree that Pentecostals are able to follow the rules of the church and demonstrate to others that they are serious Christians, they are considered *gente disciplinada* (disciplined people). Sonia, for example, proclaims with the church: "I don't want anything to do with the pleasures of *el mundo*, the pleasures of the flesh. You have to govern the flesh." It is within such governance, in the discipline of desire and the refusal of worldly indulgences, that *cristianos* achieve the spiritual goal of sanctity, remake themselves anew as reformed sinners, and, in their hopes, gain the respect of others.

Social Sanction and "True" Believers

Respect is closely tied to the perceived genuineness of conversion. A true conversion elicits positive appraisal; a false conversion, or *mal testimonio* (bad testimony), can provoke the opposite, instead drawing disdain and hostility. The principal resentment held by Dominicans against Pentecostal churches is the effrontery of converts whose boasts of spiritual expertise belie the sincerity of their religious convictions.

Not everyone can be accorded deference and admiration, of course; these are social commodities that have value only insofar as others do not have them but wish to possess them. People desire to be looked up to, to be respected and acclaimed. Pentecostals see themselves as representatives of the divine to whom others may turn for help, coveting the designation of spiritual authorities ahead of their neighbors. As individuals, they want to be recognized for their accomplishment of spiritual ideals not easily achieved. In so doing they secure the confidence and admiration of their community based on a generalized respect for the achievement of Christian fidelity.

However, this respect is not given freely. Self-proclaimed *cristianos* are held to a higher standard they themselves impose and others share in policing. Converts are under the watchful eye of their congregations just as much as they are by their neighbors and the public at large. It is unlikely that churchgoers will be regarded with esteem if they do not live up to their declarations of spiritual perfection. Those who come up short may be shunned or ridiculed, with the greatest criticisms leveled at backsliders and those who have "lost their way." Consider Radames's concern that if he were to slip back into his old ways he would not be able to face the fact that he had told people one thing, only to turn around and do the exact opposite in the end: "It doesn't take much to go back to drinking and doing the things you used to do, this is what I am afraid of. I am afraid that someone will say to me [disapprovingly]: 'After you talked about the Bible so much, now you leave the church.'" Virtually everyone knows what is expected of local evangelicals—what they can and cannot do, for instance—and do not let them claim the respect associated with Christian fidelity unless they follow the rules. This is especially because of, as I hope is clear by now, the diffuse sentiment that one does not "play or joke with things of God." A true believer follows the prohibitions and "acts like a Christian should" by appealing to the ideal of seriousness and championing the values of respectability.

Fidelity to this form of Christian identity has an exchange value within an economy of respect because it is difficult to maintain. To be an estimable *cristiano* in the barrio requires great discipline and vigilance; the demanding requirements of church membership can be taxing. Ultimately, these challenges serve to be obvious deterrents to conversion or longevity in a congregation (see Wilson 1994:108). Being a *cristiano*, for some, is simply too much work and personal investment, a commitment requiring too great a sacrifice. Why uproot a relatively stable life in order to join a congregation in search of salvation, an amorphous and confusing theological concept that only truly gains legs or takes on any real significance to converts after they have been in the church long enough to learn what it means? The benefit is not always clear to outsiders; the trade-off is not always apparent.[9] Converts young and old speak about the great benefits that come with being a Christian—namely, respect. But for many of them, it is difficult to remain in the church or to follow the prohibitions as they should. For the young men and women in barrio Francisco, it is difficult to stop listening to their favorite *bachatas* or to cease going out with their friends to clubs and bars. Most people are unwilling to make the sacrifices in their personal lives required to become Pentecostals; it is a significant commitment and considerable lifestyle change. It means giving up a great deal of freedom. Anecdotal evidence suggests that most people who convert after a *culto* or during a *compaña* do not remain in the church. It is typical for people to convert multiple times before eventually staying long enough to be baptized, if returning at all. José Luis, for example, had converted several times before finally sticking with it, as did many others.

If converts make the transition successfully and are able to remain within the fold of a congregation, if they "separate themselves from others," constitute themselves as serious spiritual persons, as representatives of God on earth, they will be respected as *hombres* and *mujeres de Dios*, men and women of God, whose spiritual transformation occasions esteem from their communities.

When a *cristiano* does something un-Christian or separates from the church, he or she is considered *descarriado*, "lost" or "gone astray." The term itself comes from the verb "*descarriar*," which means "to lead astray" or "to put on the wrong path." The expression is used by *cristianos* to refer to a time when they themselves or other faithful were not doing things that were pleasing to God, when converts backslide or return to their previous lives in the streets after converting. There is an obvious if not even explicit connection to *la Oveja Descarriada*, or the "Parable of the Lost Sheep," as told by Jesus in the New Testament (Matthew 18:12–14 and Luke 15:3–7). The term also has related cognates such as "*descarrilar*," "to derail" or "be derailed," as well as "*descarado*," meaning "shameless," and "*descaro*," meaning "audacity" or "insolence." People who convert but then leave the church only to come back again refer to their time away as *descarriado*. The concept of *descarriar*, or backsliding, constitutes an important discourse within the evangelical community I observed in barrio Francisco, where it served to create distance between the church and converts who were struggling to abide by the faith. In a strict sense, the notion of *descarriar* has to do with fidelity to the church and the evangelical Christian community; the very idea of *descarriar* is antagonistic to the notion of seriousness and being compliant with the rules and norms of the church.

There is a respect for following the rules of the church. Those Christians who are considered *descarriado* stop going to the church for reasons of shame or embarrassment as well as out of respect for the church. I was told the story one day of a man in Villa who was making a staggering 10,000 Dominican pesos a day selling drugs. When he converted he stopped selling drugs, embraced the church, and became a fine example of a devout follower. However, when the money ran out, it was explained, the call of the street proved too great, and he left the church and returned to selling drugs. What is significant about this story is that the man did not try to remain in the church and continue to sell drugs. He was well aware of the moral conflict and respected the church such that when he returned to selling drugs, he cut his ties with the faith and stopped attending *cultos*. For many, this is the preferable course of action. Unless they are *sinvergüenza*, or "shameless," if converts are *descarriado* they will cease going to church services until they resolve their conflict and can recommit themselves to the faith. Some people convert one day, realize they have made a mistake the next, and leave the church the following day rather than carrying on as if they were being faithful to the congregation. Followers are implored not to have "one foot in the world and one in the church"; the faith requires total commitment. Fidelity and sincerity are therefore necessary qualities of any respected *cristiano*.

It is not uncommon to hear people criticize evangelicals for being hypocrites or charlatans. Churchgoers failing to fulfill public expectations of comportment are mocked and offered up as reasons for why Pentecostals are not the spiritual authorities they claim to be. A convert who participates in something that the church disapproves of is probably considered *descarriado*, but for the public he or she appears to be a two-faced *cristiano*, someone who is not who they claim to be.

Ultimately, *cristianos* are held to a high standard of behavior they themselves insist on setting. If they do things that others know Christians are not supposed to do, they may be sanctioned through gossip or rumor. Gossip and rumor function to temper Pentecostal claims to superiority and spiritual perfection. Churchgoers' claims of holiness are tolerated as long as they are seen as making significant sacrifices in their daily lives in the name of spiritual perfection. But while Pentecostals are allowed to claim a certain degree of prestige related to assuming an evangelical identity, there is a limit to how much. Even though conversion may provide relative social ascent, gossip and rumor limit ambitious advancement by prohibiting any meteoric rise in status through social sanction. Charges of infidelity are leveled at church leaders with some predictability, and accusations of theft and corruption by greedy, conniving pastors are not uncommon.

Snobbery and self-importance among evangelical Christians tend to be antagonistic to the public. Droogers (1994:47–48) observes that Pentecostals sometimes feel a certain pride or even superiority toward the rest of society because of their special personal relationship with God, which gives them the confidence of being "on the right track." In Villa, such followers are challenged regularly in public debates over their knowledge of the Bible and their claims to spiritual perfection. Many people perceive *cristianos* as acting like they are better than everyone else, assuming (and sometimes even claiming) that they are the only ones who will be saved. Evangelicals have been accused of claiming to be "*la botellita del desierto*," or the "the water bottle in the desert," which is to say that they claim arrogantly to be the only people with the answer to salvation. Believers are aware of such claims, and many actively work against those criticisms (my informants, for example, claimed not to make such assertions). In any case, the public checks these claims by chastising backsliders and challenging grandiose claims of superiority. Few regular members of the church can declare spiritual or moral authority over others because they run the risk of alienating themselves from the neighborhood community, their friends, or their coworkers. As such, few that I came to know make it a point to preach to strangers. José Luis pointed out that he knew who was open to the gospel message and who was not and that he did not push the issue with those he considered "not yet ready for the Word." This took the form of not preaching to his neighbors or coworkers. Proselytizing at one's job could cause strain or division in the workplace if pushed too far or if a church member is too openly critical of another's behavior. For my informants, it was enough to represent Christianity through their actions so that others might "see a better way."

The demands placed on people who claim respectable Christian status are great, and a language exists to talk about those who do not live up to the expectations of the church and the public at large. Christianity is serious business in the Dominican Republic and conversion regarded as a serious matter. Where the spiritual realm is concerned, things of God are not to be taken lightly, and there is little room to play around with the sacred authority of the divine.

Conclusion

I was truly surprised by the assertion of many of my informants that there were devious segments of the population who claimed to be Christian so that they could obtain the benefits of membership. I did not understand what this meant until much later, when I learned that such claims were tied to a discursive conflict over who were to be regarded as true Christians. The benefits about which they spoke were not "salvation of the soul" or the favor and protection of Jesus Christ, but rather practical rewards like the trust and confidence of one's neighbors, the admiration of one's friends and family, and respect in the streets.

I have attempted here to trace the practical benefits of Pentecostal identity that converts claim to experience as a result of their conversion and faithfulness to the gospel. Most prized among these rewards is regard experienced in the form of respect from friends, family, and neighbors. Respect comes from demonstrative fidelity to the Christian faith (both its prohibitions and its stipulations) and achievement of "seriousness" through conformity to the esteemed values of respectability. Today Pentecostal Christianity has become an important index of respectability at the barrio level and therefore an exceptional resource for social distinction. Whether or not converts become financially successful or improve their economic situation as a result of their conversion, social benefits accrue to the faithful nonetheless in the form of prestige, whether they are blessed with material prosperity or not. Pentecostalism envisions a just God who ensures a world where even the poor will get their due (Simpson 1978:239). Although the conservative economic values of the church may lead to improved material conditions, the real payoff for believers may not be in the here and now but in the hereafter with the imminent return of Jesus Christ. However, it would be short-sighted to assume that deferred gratification in the next life alongside Jesus Christ is a worthwhile goal for converts who need immediate relief and answers to health and happiness today. The opportunity to compete for prestige, to vie for esteemed offices in the church, and to win acclaim (Simpson 1978:239) is an invaluable resource to residents of Villa, and in all likelihood the most appealing carrots proffered by the church.

Christian moral values predominate in the barrios of Villa and to a greater or lesser extent the country as a whole. While marriage, financial stability, and homeownership remain attractive ideals for most citizens, they are difficult to attain for the majority of Dominican men and women who cannot seem to access the same cultural capital available to their white, rich, and entitled Dominican compatriots. The irony, of course, is that even while Pentecostal asceticism offers respectability to converts and a viable alternative to *tigueraje* locally, the faith itself still lacks prestige in the eyes of the upper classes since it is viewed as a popular church, an institution for the poor and popular classes, and not an elite religion (see Droogers 1994:47).

While Pentecostal churches make certain forms of symbolic capital available to barrio residents based on the prestige associated with achieving respectability, the capital gained, while significant, is not spectacular, and social mobility is limited by the durable class divisions that structure Dominican society from within. It should be made clear that negotiations over status and prestige that occur in the economy of respect that I have outlined take place at the local level and between social class equals. What individuals gain is a kind of Pentecostal social currency that may be exchanged locally among neighbors and peers, but has less value outside the context of the barrio. In truth, local Pentecostals are probably as likely to become rich as a result of conversion as they are to become famous. The social rewards of conversion are relative and negotiated locally, tending to coalesce around relative status claims to moral and spiritual authority.

After converting, Radames asked José Luis what he should pray for now that he was a Christian:

At the beginning, if I didn't know how or what to pray for, I would ask José Luis how it is that one should pray. This was the first thing that he told me: "Ask God that people respect you in the streets, ask God to keep your testimony, ask God to protect you, to have dignity, respect people so that they respect you, because you have to respect them for them to respect you."

Now people respect me. Even those who before wanted to start problems with me. Now they say to me, "*Varón, dios le bendiga!*" and that's it! They can see the angels that exist around me. I can't see it, but they can see it because the Lord covers us. When you say to him "Dear God, I want you to protect me in a special cover," the respect for you will be greater than before.

For Radames and other young faithful at IEP and IdD, respect becomes the principal confirmation of authentic Christian identity, confirmation of sincere, genuine conversion and concrete evidence of spiritual transformation. It is through respect that Pentecostal converts come to experience their conversions as personally fulfilling and socially efficacious and through respect that the faith is recognized as a legitimate, formidable spiritual force in the neighborhood.

Conclusion

The Politics of Christian Identity

When asked about the character of Altagracianos, one resident submitted: "[Villa] has always been identified as a religious town, it even has a religious name: Villa Altagracia. Almost everyone believes in something. If someone says they don't believe they're called crazy because here everyone believes in something. People have always identified themselves by something. There are some who do not identify themselves with any [particular] religion but they believe in God." In a concurring statement, one local pastor declared: "In the barrios, the people look for God." We might consider these characterizations generalizable to the country as a whole; after all, Santo Domingo, the original colony and today's capital city, is named after a Spanish priest and founder of the Dominican religious order, Saint Dominic de Guzmán, and the nation itself, of course, was christened in honor of this very same order. Institutions of faith have played ample roles of consequence throughout the history of the country; perhaps no other single institution has had a more profound impact on Dominican culture and society than Christianity. Historically, the main driver of Christian cultural change in the country was Catholicism, from the highest rungs of officialdom down to the everyday practices of the masses; today Protestant Christianity, led by local Pentecostal churches overwhelmingly directed by believers at the grassroots level, is steering Dominican Christianity and popular religious culture in new directions.

And yet despite the country's deep Catholic roots and celebrated Catholic heritage, alternative Christianities—in particular, evangelical Pentecostal-charismatic varieties—have carved a vital and enduring space into the religious landscape to such an astounding degree that, for many barrio residents, it is the *evangélicos* and the Pentecostal church, not the *católicos* and the Catholic Church, that epitomize the ideal of Christian religiosity. Even those critical of so-called Protestant *sectas* must contend with the very real impression Pentecostalism and other anti-Catholic denominations have had on the configuration of belief at the local level. Whether or not individuals acknowledge evangelical Christianity to be the preferred form of divine service, they often concede as much by recognizing conversion as a valid ritual transformation and a sign of exceptional devotion. By accepting conversion as the "only way out," by respecting *cristianos* for their orthodox fidelity to God, it would seem that even in dissent the opposition today is helping the evangelical church move old cultural furniture into noticeably new arrangements.

We have considered several examples from Villa Altagracia of just how Pentecostal Christianity has established itself as a formidable Christian authority in the barrio and how, despite its early marginality, it has won for itself demonstrable legitimacy and wide-ranging respect. This has been accomplished in no small part thanks to signifying practices of orthodox fidelity that have come to be acknowledged by the community at large as an exceptional example of Christian devotion. Why else would conversion exempt believers from lifelong vows to serve the saints, provide them sanctuary from gang violence, or grant them respect in the streets? More than legitimacy, evangelical faith communities have acquired a sizable measure of spiritual authority that at one time in the country's history belonged solely to the Catholic Church.

With no religious commitments of my own, I myself have no horses in this race, so to speak, and do not want the arguments presented here to be read as either some kind of endorsement or condemnation of any religious group, Christian or otherwise. I have attempted here with sincere diligence to be sensitive to the complexities of the topic at hand, to sketch out the nuances of evangelical identity in the barrio fairly, and to outline the everyday negotiations over spiritual authority as they are manifest in social practice and find their elaboration under the constraints of Catholic supremacy. My attempt to highlight the relative triumphs of Pentecostal Christianity in local communities despite Catholicism's historical dominance is based upon my desire to understand the ways in which the urban poor put their religion to work in their everyday lives. By clarifying the status of the church as it stands for believers on the ground, I hope to have refined our understanding of how members of this once peripheral institution have earned respect in "Catholic Dominican Republic," and how in turn they are transforming the very idea of Christianity in poor urban neighborhoods like barrio Francisco.

Pentecostalism is no longer a marginal faith: it is an exceptional one that is simultaneously an integral feature of the local religious milieu, inseparable from the daily life of barrio residents by asserting itself as a Christian authority. The church, conversion, and converts themselves play an inseparable role in the spiritual economy at the local level and are remarkably vocal protagonists in the drama of everyday religious and social life extending far beyond the pulpit. In a matter of just fifty years Pentecostalism in the Dominican Republic has grown tenfold, a development that has no doubt made indelible impressions on the country, its culture, and its people.

Although barbs are sometimes exchanged between national leaders of the Catholic and Protestant Churches, both institutions have managed to sow amicable if not courteous relations. This speaks, I believe, to the broader acknowledgment of Christian culture as a social fact in the Dominican Republic and acceptance of Christianity broadly as the preeminent cultural and moral ideal in Dominican society irrespective of denominational affiliation. Both institutions, having joined forces under the standard of Christian orthodoxy (even if envisioned in different terms respectively), have found a common adversary in African- and Haitian-derived religion. When not cooperatively combating the influence of purported sorcery and witchcraft, both churches may, from time to time, be seen collaborating on social initiatives aimed at eradicating poverty and homelessness or defeating drug addiction, crime, and domestic violence. Betances (2007:3) observes that today the Catholic Church collaborates with evangelicals on political mediation and natural catastrophes but keeps its pastoral programs separate.

Believers themselves consider both Protestant and Catholic Churches to be peddling similar merchandise in a relatively narrow religious market where religious consumers are perceived to be more or less Christian— right or wrong, better or worse—but ideally Christian nonetheless. Here Protestant and Catholic believers clash over what will count as appropriate or "true" devotion to God and not, crucially, over the social status or value of Christian identity itself. For this reason, ritual performance and the "doing" of belief have become a crucial space for spiritual differentiation, as doctrinal differences are less immediately apparent to believers who all, ostensibly, share basic tenets of the faith and similarly identify as "Christian." Emphasizing identity through practice rather than pronouncement—deeds over declarations—Pentecostals in the Dominican Republic look to challenge Catholic authority and to embody diffuse Christian ideals through public contests of moral and spiritual distinction. This can be seen in the very public testimonies, spiritual campaigns, and evangelizing missions that community churches regularly employ, not to mention the micropolitics of preaching the Word and demonstrating divine favor through spiritual gifts, healing, and miraculous conversions.

Parsing Relations with the Divine

The contrast between local Catholic and evangelical perspectives on the proper form of ritual practice (particularly that of prayer) is borne out in their diverse views on exchange and reciprocity with the divine revealed in supernatural petitions known as *promesas* and *propósitos* for Catholics and Pentecostals, respectively. These two distinct approaches to divine solicitation reveal important conceptual differences between Christian believers locally. A *promesa*, literally a "promise," is a Catholic vow made to a saint (sometimes to God). It is usually a promise to carry out an act of devotion if and when a saint fulfills the given request; in this way it is not unlike a token of gratitude or an act of thanksgiving. *Promesas* are made by all manner of Catholics, from those who are more or less orthodox to those who practice even the most heterodox forms of popular Catholic devotion. Once a *promesa* is made, there is no obligation to carry it out until the petitioner's request is fulfilled. *Promesas* may be compared with similar yet in several important respects very different vows made by Pentecostals, known as *propósitos*. Like *promesas*, *propósitos* are appeals made directly to the divine. For Pentecostals, that means to God alone, and, like the *promesa*, *propósitos* can be made for just about anything, from healing a sick family member to securing a lucrative job. The difference is that the pledged act of devotion is performed *before* the request is granted—not after. In this arrangement, the supplicant makes a *propósito* with God—for instance, to pray for three straight hours a day until his or her appeal is answered. Put another way, the fulfillment of a devotee's request proceeds from the devotional act. The Pentecostal faithful may enter into any number of *propósitos*. Although it is not something to share with others (they are considered to be private, personal oaths to God), *propósitos* are made for reasons such as finding a spouse, healing a sick family member, or converting a neighbor or friend. Becoming a Christian convert constitutes a generalized *propósito* with God that one will be saved if he or she continues to live a righteous life in the service of Jesus Christ. Some of the more popular *propósitos* that I observed were those made to God in the hopes of finding a wife. Typically, *propósitos* of this kind are made by recent male converts and are vows to sleep in the church until God provides them a spouse. Other common acts of devotion include the promise to pray daily until a request is granted, to hold vigils in the church, or to attend a spiritual retreat. When *la pastora*'s daughter was sick, she did a *propósito* that sent her to a retreat in San Cristóbal, where she prayed for a month until her daughter got better. In order to "erase" the sin of a gang tattoo he had gotten while with the Trinitarios, Radames spent three days "in *propósito*"—praying and fasting in the church. Radames, as well as José Luis, Héctor, and others, had a *propósito* to sleep in the church until God provided him with a wife. *Propósitos* may involve abstaining or doing without something until the request is met. Radames explains how a *propósito* is made: "You say, 'Dear God, I have a *propósito*, and I will stop doing this or that until you fulfill it for me.' So I stop doing this or that until he completes for me the *propósito*." According to Radames, "It inspires you, gives you the knowledge that God is real, that he is the truth." *Propósitos* are encouraged by the congregation and are thought to have real results. Yamilca, a member of Iglesia de Dios (IdD), believed that she influenced her ex-husband's conversion to Christianity through the *propósito* that she had taken for this purpose, along with prayer and fasting she directed toward this goal.[1]

Promesas and *propósitos* are analogs based on fundamentally different assumptions about the relationship between ritual and efficacy and reciprocity with the divine. The difference between them is slight, but crucial. The *propósito* assumes a kind of reciprocity with the divine that effectively puts the onus on the individual solicitor—the idea being that if I work really hard through prayer and fasting, this or that will likely happen for me because God is good and listens to his faithful children. Here the responsibility for effective results resides with the sincere piety of the individual and the outcome of prayer, fasting, or some other act of devotion (and is therefore strikingly optimistic). Alternatively, the *promesa* assumes a more detached ethic, one that requires the devotional act only *after* the wish is granted; thanksgiving is only required if the requested services are rendered. Pentecostals assume that the actual practice of devotion, if earnest, will dispose God to answer their prayers and fulfill their petition, and if not, it is because God has another plan for them. They must be devoted; they must carry out their devotion in order to be heard—that is to say, through acts of piety and thanksgiving performed *prior* to God fulfilling their request. The Catholic *promesa* assumes no such correspondence. The solicitor makes a vow with the hopes a saint will fulfill a request and is only motivated to do anything if things work out for him or her in the end (a strikingly pessimistic stance). *Propósitos* require a degree of initiative that reflects the powerful individual ethos of the Pentecostal message. This ethos emphasizes individual and social transformation through purposive action on the part of faithful believers. Although never assuming things will change for the better, faithful converts commit themselves to sincere devotion with the confidence that God will reward their loyalty and faith. When good things do happen, God's grace is credited, but, and here is the critical point, the result is necessarily tied to personal changes and the acts of devotion undertaken by the individual solicitor—rewards always follow devotional acts. The supplicant's devotion is inevitably connected then with God's gift of grace, even if God is viewed as the autonomous agent of recompense. Conversely, if and when a *promesa* is fulfilled, it is not associated with individual devotion or piety because that act must always follow satisfaction of the original appeal. Beyond the simple initiation of the vow, Catholics assume no individual responsibility for its outcome and thus are only obliged to repay the divine request when the appeal is granted. Catholics, in general, do not assume they have any control over what the divine will do but pray that they will receive the help they need. Indeed, appeals to God are not always answered, and for this reason the intercession of saints is sought since there is little to nothing a mere parishioner believes he or she can do; they are at the will and mercy of God.

Besides the obvious ritual differences between Pentecostals and Catholics in the neighborhood, a closer look reveals substantial conceptual differences in the ways in which the two groups visualize the role of individual devotion, the fruits of fidelity, and appropriate reciprocity with God. The differences highlight distinct models of and models for proper relations with the divine and reflect distinct attitudes regarding the correct form and function of Christian devotion. In Pentecostal Christianity, spiritual rewards are the return for devotional piety; in Catholicism, devotional rites repay divine favor.

Achieving Legitimacy and Cultivating Spiritual Authority

As I am reminded time and again by my informants, their most effective tool of evangelization is their "way of being": their actions, their behaviors, their embodied testimonies, and not, for example, their words, best intentions, or theological virtues. In the barrio, living testimonies always seem to hold more weight than the spoken word. You cannot force people go to church, believers concede; people must want to go on their own, and, according to the faithful, only the power of God can change one's heart.

Several themes emerged by examining Mariela's story in chapter 3, among them, the dependent interconnected relationship between religious institutions as well as the predominance of a Christian moral framework in casting religious life in the barrio along a continuum of orthodoxy. Certain hegemonic values tied to Christianity's historically dominant position have structured the play and elaboration of difference with regard to heterodoxy and religious pluralism at the local level. While Christianity as a hegemonic cultural ideal reigns supreme, who will exemplify this ideal is a hotly contested point of fact that is regularly debated in the course of daily interaction.

Because they share a familiar spiritual universe, believers of all kinds are able to engage one another in strategic debates over the meaning and morality of supernatural beliefs and practices. This engagement, enabled by the mutual intelligibility of diverse beliefs across local faith groups, shapes relations of conflict and exchange in the religious field and, more instructively, demonstrates how evangelical forms of Christianity are able to converse with and, as a result, to transform the local cultures (their customs, norms, and so forth) within which they have become an integral part. Many Dominicans have come to respond to Pentecostal claims of spiritual authority because they already acknowledge Christianity as the height of spiritual legitimacy. This can be seen in the matter-of-fact way in which Christianity is accepted as a spiritual and moral ideal, regardless of church affiliation. Furthermore, conversion may become a likely route among several along any believer's potential religious path because of the way in which intersecting local beliefs channel the faithful here or there. One is likely driven to serve the saints or called to the feet of Jesus Christ as an outcome of overlapping accounts of spiritual agency coupled with an accommodating cosmology that legitimates and constitutes their mutual elaboration, no less their reciprocal concessions. Young men and women in the barrio take up conversion as a viable solution to the problems of the contemporary world because it remains an attractive and accessible option to them within their horizon of possibilities. Cultural institutions like the church, the street, and youth gangs circumscribe the social possibilities made available to barrio residents. The church has become a strategic resource to maneuver within the confines of meaning available to residents of the urban barrio, enabling them to claim new forms of agency and authority where few opportunities for advancement exist.

Achieving a measure of moral and spiritual authority in the barrio is accomplished by embodying Christian ideals already privileged around the country and by demonstrating fidelity to those ideals through embodied ritual practices that inscribe believers as holy. Proof of spiritual transformation and conformity with the rules of the church has become the currency of choice among believers in the trade for prestige, with genuine conversion the price that converts must pay to be rescued from the entanglements of gang life and the vicissitudes of spirit devotion. As we saw in chapter 6, those individuals who can best exemplify the conversion ideal stand to gain the most esteem. Through their miraculous transformations they are recognized charismatic leaders who exercise vast spiritual authority among the community. The elevation of Christian identity as an achieved status in the evangelical churches has complicated Dominican Catholicism's historical tendency to ascribe Catholic or "Christian" identity to Dominicans at birth by virtue of infant baptism or simply by way of cultural tradition. What makes a true Christian and who gets to decide are contentious issues that have important implications for the experience of being and becoming Christian in the Dominican Republic. It is in this area that evangelicals have perhaps made their most noteworthy progress.

Christian Identity Politics

In the Dominican Republic, and in other settings dominated by Catholicism or strong mainline churches, Pentecostalism marks Christian difference as a meaningful category of social distinction. Where and when it arrives in these contexts, it forces local communities to confront the fact of Christian pluralism and the possibility of being the right or wrong type of Christian in potentially new ways. Being a Christian, and what that signifies, suddenly has a meaning different from what it had before the expansion and entrenchment of Protestant churches into communities throughout the island. Pentecostal discourse about "being Christian" invites not just a situation where people can be the right or wrong type of Christian but also produces a condition of possibility wherein one cannot (by virtue of his or her conduct or conviction) be considered a true believer. In scenarios such as this, the church attempts to mark behaviors that would disqualify individuals from claiming an authentic Christian identity. This exact strategy is largely at the base of Pentecostal attempts to wrest authority from the Catholic Church. Emphasizing identity through action rather than belief or declaration, Pentecostals have challenged the Catholic Church in its claim to authenticity and by extension have cast doubt on Catholicism's legitimacy, seeking in turn to represent the Christian ideal themselves by offering up conversion as the orthodox exemplar within a sometimes confounding maze of heterodoxy.

The establishment of Pentecostal and other evangelical churches in barrios across the Dominican Republic has created the opportunity in local communities for people to choose what kind of Christian they want to be, along with providing a language to distinguish between them, moral criteria with which to evaluate them, and license to recognize or refute them. In addition to igniting contests over the meaning of Christianity and inciting competition between faiths, Pentecostal culture opens the door to public debate about how Christians should act and what they should believe. In effect, local Pentecostals have changed the terms of public debate about what it means to be Christian, shaping the public's view of conversion, Christian morality, and Christian identity par excellence. By proffering authenticity as the gold standard of legitimacy, Pentecostalism positions itself on the offensive; its efficacy derives not from its stipulations alone but from its active criticism of others and its unceasing repudiation of competing faiths.

An important crux of Pentecostal identity claims is that they profess more than just "We are Pentecostals and this is what we believe"; crucially, they declare, "We are *true* Christians and this is what *real* Christians *do.*"

Christian identity politics, or the complex of relations relating to and concerned with the definition, status, and reckoning of Christian identity, is a principal product of Pentecostal cultural change in countries formerly dominated by Catholic hegemony. In the Dominican Republic, Christian identity politics result from the persistent social contest over the definition of true Christianity and the charged local debate over spiritual authority. The success of a subordinate, marginal Christian group today is dependent upon its success in negotiating these politics in an effective and convincing way.

One effective strategy deployed by the Pentecostal church has been to conflate the practice of Catholicism with Dominican *vodú* (see Brodwin 1996:171). As we saw in chapter 3, Dominican Catholicism's sometimes murky relationship with the exercise of magic and the practice of *vodú* is seized upon by the evangelical community and leveraged as proof of the Catholic Church's illegitimacy as a definitive champion of orthodoxy. The all-or-nothing rubric of Pentecostalism, for another example, proposes the impossibility of being just "a little bit Christian" and exposes the often syncretic Catholicism to its critique and reproach. Accordingly, if someone is found to have "one foot in the church and one foot in the world," that person is not acknowledged to be a true Christian and is not accorded the respect or exceptional regard reserved for the genuinely faithful. Even when rituals like baptism are employed to acknowledge the truly devout, conduct remains the primary measure of authenticity; the specter of social sanction ensures that even the pious remain so over time.

We might consider a third example as well. In chapter 6 we learned that through testimony and the exemplification of the conversion ideal, savvy raconteurs are transformed into charismatic ideals regarded as extraordinary paragons of divine grace by virtue of the distance they have traveled to conquer sin. By empowering individual believers to claim moral and spiritual authority based on how bad or sinful their lives were before, and not on how virtuous they used to be, the church inverts traditional models of legitimacy that confer authority by means of formal ordination to titled clergy and credentialed leadership born out of seemingly just deserts. In so doing, average followers of the faith are authorized to claim moral and spiritual authority above and beyond what is typically afforded to individuals of their social rank. The poor become leaders, healers, teachers, and exceptional spiritual others, valued for their accomplished faith despite their social status. Pentecostals in Villa, armed with amazing testimonies, encyclopedic knowledge of the Bible, and elaborated Christian ways of being, challenge the Catholic monopoly on Christian authority.

In an ironic twist of fate, the Dominican Republic's very Christianness—its history of Christian domination, its professed orthodoxy—is exactly the quality that betrays the Roman Catholic faith and the long tradition of Catholicism in the country. Unable to offer exceptional status to the masses or spiritual power to the poor, the Catholic Church cannot furnish individual believers in the barrio with the respectability and renown promised to them as pious evangelical converts. By achieving what Pentecostals call holiness or sanctity, converts from all walks of life are empowered to claim moral authority otherwise denied to them as largely poor, disenfranchised barrio residents. This vaunted quality of Christianness, remote and out of reach for so many, becomes attainable insofar as converts are able to succeed at being "serious" born-again devotees. Add to that the spiritual gifts and respect from peers that follow from sincere conviction, and it becomes evident that the poor are empowered as leaders of the faith according to their own accomplishments.

One response of the Catholic Church in the Dominican Republic, as it has been abroad in so many other countries in Latin America, has been Catholic charismatic renewal, or the Catholic adoption of Pentecostal devotional elements like conversion, faith healing, and speaking in tongues (for a review of the Catholic charismatic renewal movement, see Csordas 1997, 2007). If you ask Pastor Ramón, however, it is not just the ecstatic aspects of the faith that are appealing to believers but the austerity of the Pentecostal church that drives the increasing adoption of its elements in other churches:

> The Pentecostal movement has had great growth, today surpassing other churches in places where no traditional churches exist. In some places, if there are churches at all, they are Pentecostal. So other churches have had to say, "We have to live a more austere life. We have to separate ourselves a little bit more." I believe that after people enter the movement where sanctity of the human being is promoted—and the word "sanctity" means to separate oneself, to separate oneself in

order to look for God in a more effective way—there is more emotion because the people get excited and the emotional part makes people change.

This quality of separation and distinction, of austere religious devotion, of emotion and transformation so important to followers, as we have seen across the preceding chapters, cannot always be replicated elsewhere, especially where ideas about sanctity require the distancing from and denial of sin. The Pentecostal emphasis on transformation in particular enables successful (if sinful) men of the streets to transfer their prestige to the church in spiritually productive and personally rewarding ways. The doctrine of conversion is therefore a powerful rejoinder to dominant Catholic beliefs in the fundamental necessity of sacraments and the intercession of saints to the flourishing of individuals' spiritual lives. Without an emphasis on redemptive, ameliorative identity, the local Catholic Church will continue to struggle to appeal to contemporary barrio residents searching for respect in a dehumanizing exploitative world. Class is a powerful social divider, and the division of labor in the Dominican Republic is such that few can access the resources (socially, politically, or economically) necessary to move up the social ladder. Many dreams are built (and dashed) on the hope of playing professional baseball in the United States because it represents one of the only familiar ways that poor Dominicans have to exchange a life of poverty for one of considerable economic prosperity. Worst of all, far too many women are cajoled or otherwise manipulated by predatory traffickers into various forms of prostitution or sex work as a way out of rural poverty. Options are bleak for poor Dominican men and women. Weber identified long ago the appeal of salvationist religions to people at the margins of society who stand to gain the most from "redemption" and of becoming someone else, so to speak (see Weber 1963). Pentecostalism has become, for barrio residents, a strategic identity for moral renewal, a symbolic cloak for exceptional self-re-creation, if worn correctly. Converts embrace the strict rules of the church because through them they may achieve the respect only a miraculous spiritual transformation can afford.

Ultimately, the role of Pentecostalism in the Dominican Republic is a social one as much as it is a religious one. The focus of sermons and Bible classes tends to coalesce around pragmatic concerns of daily life and managing behaviors and relationships that are more material than spiritual. Even when sermons drift toward millennial futures and the mystical saving graces of God, the message is almost always driven home with a practical grounding in the everyday lives of the community. Congregants learn how to navigate the moral terrain of life as a Christian through Bible classes and peer counseling. People go with what works and, as the data that I have provided here suggests, the church is an accessible institutional option for dealing with life's challenges under the redemptive auspices of divine intervention.

I became interested in this topic not because Pentecostals in the Dominican Republic claim to live exceptional spiritual lives apart but because so many others have decided to accept such claims as social facts. The Dominican Republic today is still Catholic in undeniably important ways, but the success of Pentecostal churches at the local level demonstrates an important shift in popular religious enthusiasm and a swing in the balance of spiritual authority for those historically denied it. Pentecostal churches today are ubiquitous across the nation. Every barrio is likely to have not one but several churches serving the neighborhood community. Pentecostalism's grassroots engagement with everyday folk treats individual believers as potentially powerful spiritual actors and equips them with the tools necessary to assist in their existential quests for meaning as much as their more pragmatic but equally fulfilling search for respect.

Notes

Introduction: Pentecostal Cultural Change

1. In the Dominican Republic, just as elsewhere in Latin America, the term used to denote Protestants is "*evangélicos*," commonly translated as "evangelicals" (Annis 1987:76; Kamsteeg 1998:9; Stoll 1990:4; Brusco 1995:14–15). The term usually encompasses Seventh Day Adventists and Jehovah's Witnesses along with Pentecostals, Methodists, and Baptists, as well as many mainline Protestant churches. This generalization is not unproblematic as it subsumes a considerable amount of theological diversity into one blanket term, potentially confusing cross-cultural comparison. For one thing, not all Protestant churches are evangelical. Furthermore, while all Pentecostal groups may be evangelical, not all evangelical groups are charismatic; that is, they do not all hold the gifts of the Holy Spirit to be a doctrine of central importance to the faith. Robbins (2004a:119, 122–123) has noted that scholars working on Pentecostalism in Latin America often use the term "evangelical" to refer to groups that for comparative purposes would more profitably be called Pentecostal-charismatic Christians (in this way distinguishing between, say, Pentecostals and Fundamentalists); and Bastian (1993) is critical of the reductionism inherent in conflating diverse religious phenomena under the blanket term "Protestantism." Despite the potentially disparate denominations subsumed by the term "*evangélico*," I retain the folk terminology along with the customary English translation to refer to Pentecostal Christians here because it is what believers call themselves and indicates the identity with which they look to mark their differences from Catholics. It may be helpful to add that conventionally the term "evangelical" refers to a tradition of believers who, despite their internal variation, share several important traits in common with one another—namely, theological conservatism, emphasis on the "literal" interpretation of the Bible, personal salvation, and evangelism (Stoll 1990:4). Churches sharing these generalities, along with preferences for conversion and adult baptism, are what I refer to here as "evangelical," along

with Dominican Pentecostals who, in my experience, find these distinctions to be most relevant (see chapter 4).

I tend here to use the terms "Pentecostal," "*cristiano*," and "evangelical" as more or less synonymous throughout. I do so in part for convenience's sake as well as to communicate the meaning and usage with which Dominicans employ these terms. Of course, depending on whether someone is referring to a male or a female Christian in Spanish, they would say *cristiano* or *cristiana*. Again, for convenience's sake I have used *cristiano* throughout (instead of *cristiano/a*). I have followed this same general rule with other Spanish words as well, choosing the masculine form over the feminine, but I could just as easily and happily have done the reverse. When obviously referring to a woman I have tried to be consistent in using the feminine adjective form.

2. The precise figures, however, are difficult to ascertain. People often convert, leave, only to return to the church again and again. Adherents otherwise maintain various levels of affiliation or involvement with the church that make their exact numbers none too clear. Should official statistics count frequent attendees at religious services, regular tithing supporters of the church, or, sensibly, only baptized members of a congregation? These are only some of the issues. That being said, perhaps the most provocative estimates project that the number of Pentecostal charismatic believers worldwide will surpass one billion before the year 2050 (Jenkins 2002:10).

3. See Betances (2007:220–225) for a detailed discussion of more specific numbers and further citations of survey figures. Although official membership numbers appear to be relatively low, the number of what Betances calls "affiliates," or members who are not yet official members, is considerably higher. According to Mariano Sánchez, former executive director of CODUE (*Consejo Dominicano de Unidad Evangélica* [Dominican Council of Evangelical Unity]) with whom I spoke back in 2009, 15–20 percent of the country adhere to Protestant faiths if nominal church affiliation is counted along with people who were members at one time and who have not taken up other religious commitments since. A Gallup poll from 2006 determined that 18.2 percent of the population identified as practicing evangelical Protestants. The same poll found that only 39.8 percent identified as practicing Catholics (see these and related numbers on the Dominican Republic referenced at "The Association of Religion Data Archives" website [http://www.thearda.com/]).

4. David Smilde's work is a notable exception to these studies. His book *Reason to Believe* (2007) considers data collected among men and demonstrates the imperative to consider both men and women when examining evangelical conversion. Smilde concerns himself with the question of why (and how) men

convert and the slippery related question, "if people can decide to believe, why doesn't everyone?" Even while our investigative concerns are dissimilar and our questions oriented differently, our shared focus on men reveals some notable correspondences between Venezuelan and Dominican evangelicals.

5. For other tendencies to discount Christianity in anthropology, see Robbins (2003a, 2007), and for the tendency of academia to represent conservative or "fundamentalist" Christians as problematic or "repugnant," see Harding (1991).

Chapter 1. Orthodoxy and Christian Culture in the Dominican Republic

1. I do not wish to overstate the passionate role of crusade at the expense of dismissing the clearly provocative profit motive. Rodríguez León (1992:43) put it this way: "While it is true that the Crown of Castile had a genuine evangelizing intent with regard to the new lands, it is no less true that conquest of America was inspired by commercial gain."

2. See Rivera (1992) for a more expansive discussion of the political and religious conquest of the Americas in what he calls "a violent evangelism."

3. The notion of a continuum of religious variation is important here as it allows us to approximate the overlapping zones of diverse religious forms encountered in the Caribbean and to be faithful to the qualities of internal variation that characterize the plural, heterodox religious settings typical of polyethnic multicultural Caribbean societies (see Drummond 1980; Burton 1997; Alleyne 1980).

4. A particularly striking example of late has been recent efforts aimed at denying citizenship rights to Dominicans of Haitian descent (see, for example, "Dominicans of Haitian Descent Cast into Legal Limbo by Court," *New York Times*, October 24, 2013). The Dominican Republic's own relationship to racism and racial discourses is admittedly complex. For several admirable attempts to disentangle the complicated issues surrounding Dominican racial identity, see, for example, Candelario (2007), Simmons (2009), and Mayes (2014).

5. For an interesting discussion on the politics of this display, see Thompson (2002).

6. Although never realized, Lundius and Lundahl (2000:579) cite a 1929 proposal from the archbishop of Santo Domingo to erect a huge monument to be called *El Cristo de la Frontera* (Christ of the Frontier) in commemoration of a treaty that officially established the border with Haiti: "It was intended to be an ultimate sign that the Dominican Republic had been won for the True Church. It also appears that it was intended as a way to ward off the devil, who apparently had his abode across the border [in Haiti]."

7. Along with some tax exemptions, until very recently (2013) Catholic weddings were the only religious marriages recognized by the government, although

anyone could be married in a civil ceremony (U.S. Department of State, "International Religious Freedom Report," 2005).

8. The Catholicism practiced by the masses is in many respects quite far removed from the Roman Catholic orthodoxy observed by resident clergy and espoused by the Vatican in Rome. Described by observers like Lundius and Lundahl (2000) as "popular religion," the Catholicism practiced in much of the country takes the shape of a cult of saints, attributing miraculous power and everyday wonders to the accessible and useful heavenly beings. Lundius and Lundahl (2000:339) propose that present-day Dominican popular religion derives in large part not from the exalted and sophisticated Roman Catholicism of the conquistadors, but rather from isolated Spanish settlers and the common man taking part in the conquest, "uneducated and with his roots in rural society and peasant religion." They enumerate five significant practices that derived from medieval Spain: "pagan" features that were connected to peasant farmers who were concerned with fertility; though not exclusively, the desire for intermediation between a supreme yet distant God and human beings by the saints; the Spanish practice of building *ermitas*; the presence of the Devil and/or a particular conception of evil as embodied or represented by the Devil; and the establishments of *cofradias* (lay confraternities).

9. Historically, Haitian *vodou* has been the victim of fantastic sensational literary accounts and harmful stereotypes propagated by both the domestic and international media (see Hurbon 1995). The effects have been no less harmful to similar religious beliefs in the Dominican Republic.

10. An indicative example, among quite a few, appeared in *Clave Digital* in March 2010. The local weekly newspaper ran a story about a Haitian accused of witchcraft in a province of Santiago. The accusation so infuriated local residents that authorities had to shut down the "*centro de espiritista*" of the Haitian immigrant who was accused of "perverting the youth with satanic rites and *vodú*." "The practice of *vodú*," explains the article, "generated violent protests in the community whose residents, supported by Catholic and Protestant churches, as well as other popular organizations, took to the streets and blocked off traffic on the main highway connecting Santiago with Puerto Plata." The accused man was arrested by migration officials and later released. "However, migration warned the alleged sorcerer [*hechicero*] not to continue practicing *vodú* in the area or, otherwise, his [identity] documents would be taken away and he would be expelled from the country." The accused man is quoted as accepting "*con tranquilidad*" the dismantling of the center but maintained that the practice of *vodú* was not evil, "because it is a part of Haitian culture" (*Clave Digital*, March 16, 2010, my translations).

11. More than enough has been said about the antagonistic relationship that the Dominican Republic nurtures with Haiti (e.g., Hoetink 1985; Fennema and Loewenthal 1987; Sagás 1993, 2000; Wucker 1999; Heredia 2003; Howard 2001; Martínez 2003; Martínez-Vergne 2005). Samuel Martínez makes the crucial point that this hostile view tends to be one-sided: "the Dominican obsession with Haiti is an unrequited passion: Haitians do not regard Dominicans with anything like the same feeling as that of Dominicans looking upon Haitians" (2003:83). I do not want to delve into this complicated issue here, but suffice it to say that so-called voodoo practices are both the target of anti-Haitian rhetoric and constitutive of racist discourse in the Dominican Republic.

12. For the best and to my knowledge one of the only examples of social science writing on Pentecostalism in the Dominican Republic, see the work of Marcos Villamán (particularly 1993a, 1993b, 2002). On the history of Protestantism in the Dominican Republic, its missionary history, and its geographical expansion, see Wipfler (1966), Lockward (1982), Platt (1981), Alvarez Vega (1996).

13. For a good discussion of evangelicals and national politics in the Dominican Republic, see Betances (2007).

Chapter 2. Villa Altagracia: El Pueblo Caliente, El Pueblo Profético

1. The website has since been taken down.

2. In the interest of confidentiality, pseudonyms have been used throughout to protect the identity of my informants.

3. Eight thousand people died in traffic accidents in the Dominican Republic over a six-year period from 2003 to 2009 (*Clave Digital*, May 7, 2009).

4. Safa (1995, 2002) has noted the stark transformation of the gendered division of labor brought about by the introduction of export manufacturing jobs, an industry that chiefly employs women.

5. Many of the nicer homes in Villa remain from the prosperous time of the sugar mill and when the *zona franca* was most productive and offered lucrative jobs to managers and administrators at the higher ends of the employment hierarchy. Most of these homes are restricted to a few specific barrios.

6. "*Culto*" means "worship" and refers to any service or ceremony of religious worship. It can be used to refer to such worship in any number of contexts and across religious communities—both evangelicals and Catholics "*hacen culto*." In the Pentecostal church *cultos* are daily services held at the church, and the term is applied to any occasion of public worship. When Pentecostals in Villa "*hacen culto en la calle*," they hold a church service or special *campaña* (spiritual campaign) in the streets to attract the public.

7. I also conducted fieldwork in Pantoja/Los Alcarrizos and Santo Domingo but with far less sustained engagement with communities there.

8. Because of the singular nature of independent churches, in the interest of confidentiality I have chosen to use a pseudonym in place of the actual name of the church.

9. A *retiro* is a spiritual retreat and can be anything from a handful of church members fasting and praying for an afternoon to a large gathering of hundreds of worshippers at a designated place. *Retiros* can be held in public spaces like parks or squares, or they may be held in hospitals or prisons.

Chapter 3. Pluralism, Heterodoxy, and Christian Hegemony

1. Although today Mariela recounts her story in terms heavily informed by her evangelical conversion, we would be wise to focus on the content of her story rather than the shape of its retelling. Even though her story takes on a narrative arc familiar to evangelical testimonies, I have found no reason to question the basic facts of her account or to dismiss the particulars of her story as nothing more than a projection of her current beliefs. This task is admittedly difficult. It is, however, the challenge inherent in all interpretation, and of the translation of experience in general. I cannot understand my past apart from my current perspective and my subjective way of seeing the world today, both of which are, as a matter of human experience, subject to continuous reformulation and thus to ambiguity. However, I do believe that we can try. Mariela tried, albeit in her own way. For this reason, I believe we can trust her account just as we would our own, with the understanding that no viewpoint is completely objective or outside of the foibles of perspective and the temporal conditions that train our recollections and personal historical accounts. Her story is, in any case, a familiar one to the Dominican Republic, a typical tale of spiritual discovery and transformation, one that should be read as generalizable to a good many women and men who find themselves drawn to serve the saints and who find healing in the power of the supernatural (see, for example, Schaffler 2004).

2. The term "*seres,*" or "*beings,*" refers to a type of supernatural entity familiar to the Dominican Republic. Also called *misterios, luases/loases* (*luá* singular and likely derived from the Haitian *lwa*), *sanses* or *sanes* (colloquial plural of *san* or *santo*) (Deive 1992:170; Davis 1987:64–65; Patín Veloz 1975), also *santos* or *santos magicos* (saints or magical saints). The names can vary by region and from person to person and are not always used consistently but generally refer to the same entities, so-called *vodú* spirits (see Patín Veloz 1975; Deive 1992; Jiménez Lambertus 1981; Davis 1987; Alegría-Pons 1993; Ripley 2002). As a Pentecostal today, Mariela relates her experience with the *seres* as having been a relationship with demons.

Though she would from time to time refer to them in more neutral terms, such as *seres* or *santos*, it is her current practice to refer to them as *demonios*, or "demons." I reproduce her own words here in order to more accurately represent the way in which she wishes to recount her story and reflect upon her own past. It is important to point out that she did not always see these spirit beings as demonic (something she readily admits). Her conversion to Pentecostalism informs her current regard of them as categorically evil. Today she is adamant about the fact that she mistook the true nature of the *seres*. In line with her evangelical beliefs, she now maintains that they were always demonic; she just failed to recognize their true provenance before converting.

3. The idea of "sending sickness" is widespread throughout the Dominican Republic, as in Haiti (see Farmer 1990). Among several forms of harmful magic used to make people sick are the *envíos, despachos de muertos*, and magical weapons called *guangás*. According to Lundius and Lundahl (2000:268), "a *guangá* may be anything, organic or inorganic, but most common is the *enviación* (consignment), a magically prepared parcel buried in the path of the one you intend to hurt." They are considered particularly powerful and can seriously harm or kill a target victim. More generally, *guangás* are enchanted objects that have been made "poisonous" by a *brujo* through magical means, which upon contact with someone will cause a desired effect, usually illness (Métraux 1972:285; see also Simpson 1940, 1954; Deive 1992). An *envío* is also considered to be powerful black magic and involves enchanting a target with the spirit of the dead or deceased (*los muertos*). The victim suffers for a protracted period of time and can die from it if it is not diagnosed in time and the spirit of the dead not removed from the body quickly. Spirits of the dead are sent upon a person for reasons of vengeance or envy and can cause the involuntary possession of the targeted person, which may result in madness or serious physical illness (Schaffler 2004:7; Deive 1992:249).

4. Her path from illness to spirit-mediumship might be termed *adorcism* (compare with *exorcism*), where the possessing entity is placated by accommodation rather than expulsion (de Heusch 1962). I. M. Lewis (1986:123) suggests that adorcism in some contexts is more attractive to women, particularly as an effective mode of resistance to male domination. Mariela's strained relationship with her husband would support this interpretation. Her conversion to spirit medium no doubt strengthened her position with regard to her unfaithful husband, who as a believer in the power of the *seres* was likely impressed, perhaps as a result even "reined in," by her transformation into a convincing diviner with powerful spiritual allies.

5. This is not, however, universal. Several converts whom I came to know had

been possessed after conversion. Everyone is potentially a target of demonic possession if they are not careful. Congregants are instructed to be vigilant and to pray that the Holy Spirit gives them strength to resist demonic advances. The stronger and more experienced they are in the gospel—that is, the greater their faith—the less likely they are to succumb to such powers. For example, only the most experienced followers are directed to perform exorcisms or sent to destroy altars, the thought being that if a believer is not mature enough spiritually, evil spirits can possess them upon coming into contact.

6. Not irrelevant here is the observation that Mariela might have used her diagnosis as a way of challenging her husband's infidelity. This is evidently quite common across spirit possession cultures the world over. Several interpreters of spirit possession globally have identified the idiom of possession as an effective tool in negotiating relationships of inequality or oppression, especially for women and society's disadvantaged (see Lewis 1966, 1971; Boddy 1989, 1994; Bourguignon 2004).

7. Ideas that connect witchcraft, illness, and animosity are possibly derived from traditional West African assumptions about the close relationship between misfortune and social conflict (see Mintz and Price 1992:45).

8. This admittedly complex evolving sentiment toward the spirit world evinced by converts, along with their changing perceptions of evil, is elegantly parsed by Jacobson (2003) in the context of Puerto Rican popular religion in Cleveland, Ohio.

9. This is ironic considering that many of the magical beliefs in question, such as the conjuring of demons, love magic, devil pacts, and the demonological witch concept itself, probably come not from Haiti or Africa but from colonial and precolonial Spain.

10. Both Patín Veloz (1975:144) and Davis (1987:115, 128) insist that while many believers view the *misterios* and saints to be one and the same, the "actual" correspondence is not equality of identity but one of patronage, something seemingly more akin to the relationship between humans and the divine. *Misterios* from this perspective are helpers or messengers of the saints, who are their patrons and who stand in hierarchical relation to them as benevolent powerful protectors and providers. Davis (1987:128) quotes an informant who said, "Belié Belcán is not San Miguel. Belié works with the power of the saint. Belié worships [*adora*] San Miguel. . . . It's like a president who has an exclusive minister who represents him. When San Miguel cannot be somewhere, Belié goes in his place" (my translation). There are believers who no doubt explain the correspondence between Belié Belcán and San Miguel in exactly these terms. However, it is just as clear that others consider them as nothing more than different names for the

same being or at most different aspects of the same identity. Deive, for instance, is uncertain about the extent of identification between the saints and *seres*, unsure of whether there is a true "assimilation" or whether it is a simple correspondence by analogy (1995:224–225). The problem lies in the fact that it is common for practitioners to claim to work with and be possessed by saints—not *misterios*—and they are often ignorant of any other identification, affirming that they work with saints alone. At the very least, the relationship between the *seres* and *santos* is, according to Patín Veloz (1975:144), a "chaotic" one. In any case, perhaps more important for our discussion here is that the subservient relationship of creole identities to dominant Catholic saints is further evidence of a very clear assent to Christian domination in the local religious milieu (Davis 1987:115).

11. The Bible, for example, is employed across the continuum in myriad ways by diverse believers. That the word of God is powerful is not questioned, rather, how the Word is interpreted and utilized is the primary site of disagreement. For example, whether a psalm is to be properly used as a spell or a prayer is one such area of discord; that the Bible can be used to invoke a spirit or to exorcise one is another.

12. The term *"vodouista"* is clumsy and imprecise, not to mention the fact that an insignificant few actually use it to describe themselves or even apply the term *"vodú"* to their own practices. This can be seen in the more common routine locally of referring to these same beliefs as *santería* and believers as *caballos, servidores de misterios,* or *espiritistas* (see Davis 1987:65).

13. This statement is more contentious if applied to Haitian *vodou*. Several observers have proposed that Catholicism and *vodou* in Haiti, while representing complementary institutions, remain parallel, separate religions (e.g., de Heusch 1989). In arguments like these, Catholic or Christian elements are viewed as ancillary dimensions to the primary operations that follow from non-Christian elements of ritual within the *vodou* complex. I find some of these interpretations difficult to substantiate in light of the ardent fidelity to Catholicism expressed by practitioners and specialists alike. While few if any practitioners would be able to practice *vodú* without Catholicism, it may be the case that in Haiti such possibilities exist. In the Dominican Republic, however, the profound and intimate links joining Catholicism and *vodú* are many and utterly tangled such that one could make the argument that while the syncretism characteristic of Haitian *vodou* may appear to evince an aggregating, "mosaic" effect (where the separate elements of Catholicism and African-derived religion never truly mix [see Herskovits 1938:130]), the syncretism evident in Dominican *vodú* is much more in line with the idea of fusion or "blending" implied by the notion of syncretism as

synthesis where elements of distinct religious traditions appear to have melded without maintaining any clear differences (cf. Desmangles 1992).

14. Named Basílica Catedral Nuestra Señora de la Altagracia, the basilica houses a supposed miraculous image of the Blessed Virgin Mary and is the foremost pilgrimage destination for Catholics in the country, who gather there every year to honor the republic's patron saint on her feast day, January 21.

15. Not to mention the practical difficulty in defining the differences between Haitian and Dominican variants of *vodou*, especially when encountered beside one another in the same locale with participants from both countries. While generalizations may be made about the differences between Dominican and Haitian versions of *vodou* (e.g., Patín Veloz 1975:142; Deive 1992; Lundius and Lundahl 2000:375; Andújar 2007:166–170), in practice it can sometimes be difficult to distinguish the two. How does one make the distinction between Dominican and Haitian *vodous* when a given ceremony is performed in the Dominican Republic? Does it matter if the participants are Haitian or Dominican, or what about both? This is not to say that there are not important differences (as mentioned earlier, for example, Catholicism is put considerably more forward by Dominican practitioners), but when invoking *lwa* who are called upon in both countries (for example, Tiyán Petró/Ti Jean Petro [Deive 1992:177–178]) and are performed in possession in similar ways, how do we know if we are dealing with one or the other? And does it matter? It should also be added that in most cases the distinction is not made by believers themselves, other than to regard Haitian magic and spirits to be more powerful than their Dominican counterparts and to acknowledge that at times the spirits are called by various names. Jiménez Lambertus (1981:175) proposes, rightly I think, that Haitian and Dominican *vodú* are regional variations of the same religion. In the Dominican Republic, it is believed that the magic encountered in Haiti and performed by Haitians is more powerful (Andújar 2007:167), but not that the spirits with whom they deal are unrecognizably different. Moreover, my own reading of the religious festival known as *el Gagá* is that it differs only slightly from its ostensible precursor in Haiti, *Rara* (compare McAlister 2002 with Rosenberg 1979 and Aracena 1999). Although the degree of correspondence and divergence of *vodou* practice in Haiti with that of the Dominican Republic is as yet still uncertain, it represents a potentially fruitful object of future inquiry in its own right. Consider, for example, the delightfully thought-provoking claim of Lemus and Marty (2010:53) that when possessing a devotee, the majority of *luases* or *vodú* spirits in the Dominican Republic speak Spanish with a heavy French accent—a characteristic typically associated with Haitian immigrants.

16. It is for this reason that some observers have relegated *vodú* to the status

of magical practices and a cobbling of rituals alone and not to the status of formal religion. Consider, for example, Simpson's definition of Haitian *vodou* as a "syncretistic cult based upon West African religious traits, Catholic theology and ritual, items from the storehouse of European witchcraft, and local innovations, [and] includes a wide range of magical beliefs and practices as well as a variety of religious ceremonies" (1954:395).

17. In Haiti, conversion saves followers from obligations to the *lwa*, even in death. Elizabeth McAlister (2002:109) notes that Protestant *zonbi* are not obliged to work for an *oungan* in need: "In Port-au-Prince there is a brotherhood and sisterhood among Vodouists that stipulates that if an *oungan* or *manbo* is in need, they may ask the spirits of the recently dead for mystical help in their work. The same is not true for Protestants. Those who converted and renounced the *lwa* will not work for Vodouists after death."

18. According to Labourt (n.d.), within Dominican *vodú* there are designated individuals called *desmontadors* (dismounters) or *liberador de espiritus* (spirit liberator) who may be called upon to expel an unwanted spirit.

Chapter 4. Christians Apart: Being and Becoming Pentecostal

1. Here I understand ritual in basic terms as "prescribed formal behavior for occasions not given over to technological routine, having reference to belief in mystical beings or powers" (Turner 1967:19).

2. "Evangelical" is a broad term used to describe a number of Protestant denominations loosely characterized as sharing an emphasis on the "literal" interpretation of the Bible and the importance of adult baptism and conversion. In the Dominican Republic, the terms "*evangélico*" and "*cristiano*" are indiscriminately applied to Protestants of all types and are almost always used to refer to Pentecostals (the term "*pentecostal*" is infrequently used by believers).

3. Being Dominican is very much tied to the country's Catholic heritage and a historical consciousness about its relationship with the rest of the world. As such, being Catholic in the Dominican Republic is a distinction that, among many Dominicans, carries little significance by itself since everyone, ostensibly, is thought to be Catholic by virtue of their Dominicanness. Despite the questionable merits of such an appraisal, the myth of national identity trumpets the republic's Catholic heritage as the primeval cultural gestalt that gave birth to the Dominican nation (see chapter 1).

4. Although conceding doctrinal differences with Seventh Day Adventists, for instance, members of IdD and IEP see these differences as superficial: what really matters, they claim, is that the church in question approximates a "true Christian church," and lives according to what they believe to be a literal inter-

pretation of the Bible. When they do make a distinction between "Christian churches," these differences usually focus on the relative strictness (discussed in terms of liberalness) of a given church's rules regarding the behavior of its congregants. For instance, people often make comparisons such as "our church is more conservative; the women over *there* are allowed to wear pants, *here* they are not," or "some churches are more liberal; we must wear skirts, we do not drink." "Liberal" here means more relaxed rules ("more modern," they would say), where congregants are allowed to dress more freely (women can wear pants and jewelry), perhaps drink a little wine on occasion, or maybe even dance from time to time. The Assemblies of God (*Asambleas de Dios*) is often referenced as a more permissive, "liberal" Pentecostal church in the eyes of members of IdD and IEP (which people considered more or less conservative or traditional on the whole). Even when differences are pointed out, care is usually taken to suggest that these differences are trivial and that what matters most is that true Christian churches abide by the Word and follow the teachings of Jesus Christ. That being said, often converts in the barrio find permissive churches to be unfavorable to the project of salvation that so many of them work tirelessly toward achieving. Only through unwavering obedience to the law of the gospel, by adhering strictly to abstinence and a rigid code of conduct, can converts ensure their entrance into heaven and be rewarded the gifts of grace promised to the faithful.

5. Even the verb "*creer*," or "to believe," implies action or the practice of actually *doing* something (as opposed to just having an opinion or "inactive" thoughts about something). For instance, it is not, as we saw in chapter 3, that Pentecostals do not believe in the power of local spirits; they do. But when they say that they do not believe in them it means that they do not turn to such powers in search of assistance, they do not build altars or light candles to local saints in the hope of securing favors or blessings. "Belief" in the vernacular is often taken to be what a person does (and how one does it) and not whether a person accepts a statement as true or takes a concept to be an empirical reality.

6. These rules include, for example, abstaining from alcohol, popular music (especially *bachata* and *reggaeton*), cursing, dancing, gambling, wearing certain clothing, and going to forbidden religious festivals.

7. For a helpful figure outlining the same prohibitions followed by Protestants in Colombia, and the reasons commonly given for following them, see Thornton (1984:31). In this publication, he suggests that *prohibiciones* (negative demands) along with *deberes*, or "duties" (positive demands), are important aspects of the ethical indoctrination of new converts. These negative demands were also identified as important markers of difference between Protestants and Catholics in Guatemala (Annis 1987:80).

8. Pentecostals in Villa are acutely aware that they are representatives of their faith, and they work hard to protect it by maintaining an enviable public image. Members are reprimanded if their transgressions are found to be particularly damaging to the image of the church. Offenses that occur in the public eye are dealt with swiftly and publicly in order to show others that the church disapproves of such transgressions. Disciplinary action is taken in order to demonstrate that the church has high standards that must be met. Such was the case with Diego, who was suspended from participation in church services indefinitely for "doing something that he should not have done" with a young woman at the church. After the incident, the young woman's mother (who was neither a member of the church nor a Christian convert) went to Pastor Ramón for answers as to why a member of his congregation had "done something that he should not have done" with her daughter. In order to demonstrate to members of the congregation, as well as to others in the neighborhood, that Diego's behavior was unacceptable to the church, Pastor Ramón was forced to punish him for his misbehavior. Diego was suspended from playing instruments in the church and taking part in the youth group as a result.

9. If members are found to be struggling with the demands of the faith, their status is downgraded to that of "being lost," or *descarriado*—a believer who has backslid and gone astray of his or her spiritual commitments. These individuals are considered to have "bad testimonies," an indication of insincere conviction that casts doubt on their claims to sanctity. Their example is taken to be harmful to the church's reputation.

10. Compare with the widespread West Indian notion of "talking bad" or "broken"—speaking styles associated with the street, the antithesis of church and household values, as distinguished from respectable behavior (Abrahams and Bauman 1971; Abrahams and Szwed 1983; Abrahams 1983:51, 54; see also chapter 7).

11. Words are thought to have potentially contaminating or polluting properties as well. This is the main reason behind the Pentecostal prohibition on listening to forbidden genres of music like *reggaeton* that discuss sex and violence.

12. By no means are evangelicals viewed as particularly stylish or fashionable (*la moda*). On the whole they are considered to dress conservatively and restrained. Although not made explicit, a convenient consequence of the Pentecostal's subdued style is the deflection of envy that would otherwise follow personal ostentation and threaten to bring ill fortune to the one against whom it is directed. A sentiment shared widely throughout African American cultures of the Caribbean, *envidia*, or "envy," like witchcraft and the evil eye, can function

as psychic powers of ill will that can imperil those who are prosperous if they are not careful.

13. See Anderson (2004:187–205) for a summary of what he calls a "theology of the Spirit"; see Wacker (2001:35–57) on the importance of speaking in tongues to the early Pentecostal church; see also Hollenweger (1972:3–20, 2004) for a discussion of whether a coherent Pentecostal theology even exists.

14. In many cases, the word "*charismata*" has come to denote the gifts of grace themselves, while the term "charisma" has been reserved for the more general state produced by reception of such gifts (see chapter 6).

15. See Robbins (2004a), who defines Pentecostal-charismatic Christianity as "the form of Christianity in which believers receive the gifts of the Holy Spirit"; see also Wacker (2001:40–44).

16. While believers experience Spirit baptism only once in a lifetime, they may continue to have access to spiritual power through the gifts of the Holy Spirit (Chesnut 1997:97). See Wacker (2001:44) for a distinction between the "sign" (spirit baptism) and the "gift" (*charismata*).

17. Wacker (2001:110) suggests that one of the effects of these practices is to make the transition between outside and inside more memorable, effecting such a significant emotional response from the baptized that backsliding becomes a far less likely scenario. See also Wilson (1994:108), who notes that water baptism usually follows indoctrination adjoining a sufficiently long enough probationary period as to ensure a neophyte's commitment to the group and assure the community of his or her sincerity.

18. The American preacher and evangelist Charles Fox Parham (1873–1929), a key figure in the development of Pentecostalism, is credited with the theological innovation connecting glossolalia with baptism in the Holy Spirit.

19. Of course, even at its best, the church cannot put a complete end to racism. Still, as Chesnut (1997:123) observes, Pentecostal ideologies are robust enough to insulate black Brazilians from the most insidious manifestations of racial discrimination.

Chapter 5. Youth Gangs, Conversion, and Evangelical Moral Authority

1. Etymology of the word "machete" was gleaned from the *Online Etymology Dictionary*.

2. I thought at the time that perhaps his faith was so strong that he considered himself invincible. I have since revised this consideration based on the fact that the Pentecostals whom I came to know rarely took chances that put themselves at risk. They do not believe that faith alone will protect them in all circumstances.

Anything can happen to anyone, and because evil lurks around every corner, one needs to be careful, ever vigilant of Satan's traps.

3. Perhaps it bears mentioning that I myself encountered no hostility in Villa from anyone during my fieldwork there. Even walking close to a mile many evenings sometimes as late as 11:00 or 12:00 at night through town in the dark just to take a *carro público* back to the capital, I never found myself a target of theft or harassment. I was of course seen and seen often. But it was also obvious with whom I spent most of my time. I cannot be certain that my association with the Pentecostals in town ensured my safety, but it is an intriguing thought in relation to some of the claims of my informants discussed here (see also Smilde [2007:72] for a parallel observation in Venezuela).

4. See Goldstein (2003:217), who submits that women may choose religious conversion as a form of oppositional culture in the favelas of Rio de Janeiro.

5. Symbolic role reversal is a performative cultural strategy of resistance not unfamiliar to creole cultures of the Caribbean (see Burton 1997).

6. See Frazier (1974:87) and Simpson (1978:239) for how this same idea has been applied to understanding the so-called black church in the United States.

7. Annis (1987) has argued that Protestantism in Guatemala draws impressively from those alienated from the traditional economy, stating "to those who are economically marginalized by an abject poverty or socially marginalized by increased entrepreneurial activity, Protestantism says: Come to me" (141).

Chapter 6. Residual Masculinity and Gendered Charisma

1. The notion of *tigueraje* in the Dominican Republic is complex, and little room exists here for a suitable treatment of such an important but equally slippery concept. For additional exposition, see Collado (1992), Krohn-Hansen (1996), Padilla (2007:132–140), and Derby (2009:184–194).

2. The division between *cristianismo* and *tigueraje* maps well onto the classic distinction between *la casa* and *la calle* found elsewhere in Latin America (Manners 1956; Mintz 1956; Scheele 1956) and also the opposing but complementary cultural values of respectability and reputation prevalent in the Caribbean as outlined by Wilson (1995). Similar comparisons may also be made with the incompatibility of "black churches" and "black clubs" in Bermuda as discussed by Manning (1973), and the discordant values of "the yard" and "the road" in St. Vincent as recorded by Abrahams (1983).

3. Despite my observations of several Pentecostal communities to the contrary, most people affiliated with the church would affirm that women tend to be more involved than men, and that women represent a greater percentage of most

congregations. This would support several statistical findings cited by Betances (2007:223) for the country as a whole.

4. This dynamic is not unique to urban barrios or even the Dominican Republic. See Brereton (1991) for a parallel account of male conversion narratives in the United States.

5. Schultze (1984:80) has suggested that the issue of whether personal testimonies are *literally* true is largely irrelevant in so-called oral cultures: "This is not to say that testimonies are fictional, or worse yet that they are intentional fabrication. Truthfulness resides in an oral culture, in the belief in the message, not in the literal components of the message."

6. Weber appears to have drawn inspiration for his idea of charisma, at least in part, from Le Bon's notion of prestige (Baehr 2008:111–112n.56; Le Bon 1952:129–140). Weber did not restrict his use of charisma to manifestations of divinity alone; sometimes he attributed the term to "extraordinary" individuals who do not necessarily understand their actions as being related to or motivated by divine inspiration (Shils 1965:200).

7. My definition of negative-charisma differs from Aberle's (1966), who understands it as the negative valuation of otherwise positively valued charismatic leaders. His paradigmatic example is Adolf Hitler, who was valued by those who endowed him with charisma, his supporters, and disvalued by his opponents and detractors. As Lewis (1986) has pointed out, the attribution of grace or of sin to an individual can shift, according to context. One person's savior is another's devil. I would add that the present case illustrates the fundamental relation between sin and sanctity, each necessary for the true expression of the other. That is to say, sanctity can only have meaning in a world of sin, and vice versa.

8. In other words, there should be no "superiors" because every believer, in theory, has equal access to the power of the Holy Spirit, and everyone is considered equal in the eyes of the Lord. Furthermore, salvation may only be achieved by and for oneself, it is the individual who must answer the call and accept Jesus Christ as his or her savior, and it is the individual who must choose a new life. Redemption cannot be achieved on another's behalf.

9. These Pentecostal leaders do not see themselves as objects of praise, but believe that their charisma should be understood as by and for the glory of God and not for their own exaltation. Personal authority is actively refuted in favor of crediting divine inspiration and leadership of the Word. Inquiring minds are told first to consult the Bible (believed to be the infallible word of God) before they seek the advice of church leaders. Even in prayer healings and the laying on of hands, it is never the believers themselves who heal, but rather it is God, through the Holy Spirit, who is thought to be the active restorative agent.

Chapter 7. Pentecostal Social Currency and the Search for Respect

1. Discussing the social dynamics of Pentecostal Christianity in Latin America generally, Wilson (1994:107), for example, observes that the approval of the larger community, "even if conceded reluctantly in the form of respect for persons with strong convictions," places members of evangelical churches "on a platform not generally available to unaffiliated Latin Americans."

2. For a compelling discussion on the politics of sound in negotiating religious group boundaries in the context of urban poverty, particularly as it relates to Pentecostalism, see Oosterbaan (2009).

3. For other arguments linking conversion with economic gain in Latin America, see Martin (1995), and in Zimbabwe see Maxwell (1998).

4. I am reluctant to suppose that Pentecostal membership enables any real economic social mobility in Villa; it is clear from the research elsewhere, however, that at least at the household level, there is probably a slight economic advantage (Brusco 1995). Anecdotally, at any rate, several of my informants four years after my initial fieldwork were doing noticeably better financially than they were when we first met. Nonetheless, the vast majority had made little perceptible economic advancement. Even considering those who had, it is difficult methodologically to attribute their success with any confidence to conversion alone without the requisite demographic data to compare community members as a whole against their neighbors, including group data on changes in household economics over time.

5. Consider, supplementarily, the curiously similar notion indexed by the English term "slackness" in the Anglophone Caribbean where, in Jamaica for example, it refers to acts and behaviors that are considered lewd or vulgar—conduct understood to be the opposite of respectable behavior.

6. Here we might even compare the *tíguere* with the "badman" folk hero of black communities in the United States. See, for example, Abrahams (1963:65–66) and Roberts (1989:171–219).

7. See Burton (1997:162) for a parallel schema concerning Wilson's oppositions between reputation and respectability. Abrahams has remarked about similar communities of the Caribbean that "the oppositions between such forces as good and evil, men and women, reputation and respectability, even life and death, are never played out to any sort of resolution. Rather such oppositions are seen to be the essence of life, and their enactment through dramatization can have no real conclusion, only temporary states of truce through a balancing of these contrarieties" (Abrahams in the foreword to *The Windward of the Land* by Jane Beck, 1979).

8. We might also note the implicit nature (*tíguere*) versus culture (*cristiano*) symbolic opposition at play; after all, Christianity's representatives have quite forcefully claimed the seat of culture (as in "cultured") since the conquest and have positioned the faith in hierarchical relation to other modes of moral conduct in the country, including, and particularly, *tigueraje*. It might be pertinent as well to note that the *tíguere* imagery—that of the urban tiger, of an aggressive wild animal—lends itself nicely to an analogy with the popular story of Christ sending his disciples out into the world as "sheep among wolves" (see Matthew 10:5–15), a caution to the faithful to be vigilant amid the wickedness that plagues *el mundo*.

9. Congregants who have experience in the gospel will likely explain their reasons for joining the church to be related to salvation; however, it is unlikely that they will join for that specific reason alone, or even at all. Most of the young congregants whom I got to know joined for myriad reasons, including to meet women, to escape gangs, to fulfill a *promesa*, et cetera, none of the reasons having to do specifically with sanctity or salvation per se.

Conclusion: The Politics of Christian Identity

1. Despite their resemblance to *propósitos*, *promesas* are understood by Pentecostals to be demonic. When intending to ask about *propósitos* one day while visiting with Denny and Josefina at their home, I used the term "*promesa*" and was promptly corrected. "No," Denny admonished, "those are not *promesas*. *Promesas* are diabolical, they are made to images and the Virgin. We do *propósitos*."

Works Cited

Aberle, David

1966   Religio-Magical Phenomena and Power, Prediction, and Control. *Southwestern Journal of Anthropology* 22(3): 221–230.

Abrahams, Roger

1963   *Deep Down in the Jungle: Negro Narrative Folklore from the Streets of Philadelphia*. Chicago: Aldine.

1970   Patterns of Performance in the British West Indies. In *Afro-American Anthropology: Contemporary Perspectives*, ed. Norman Whitten and John Szwed, 163–179. New York: Free Press.

1976   *Talking Black*. Rowley, Mass.: Newbury House Publishers.

1983   *The Man-of-Words in the West Indies: Performance and the Emergence of Creole Culture*. Baltimore: Johns Hopkins University Press.

Abrahams, Roger, and Richard Bauman

1971   Sense and Nonsense in St. Vincent: Speech Behavior and Decorum in a Caribbean Community. *American Anthropologist* 73(3): 762–772.

Abrahams, Roger, and John Szwed

1983   *After Africa: Extracts from British Travel Accounts and Journals of the Seventeenth, Eighteenth, and Nineteenth Centuries Concerning the Slaves, Their Manners, and Customs in the British West Indies*. New Haven, Conn.: Yale University Press.

Adams, Robert

2006   History at the Crossroads: Vodú and the Modernization of the Dominican Borderland. In *Globalization and Race*, ed. Kamari Maxine Clarke and Deborah Thomas, 55–72. Durham, N.C.: Duke University Press.

Albrecht, Daniel

1999   *Rites in the Spirit: A Ritual Approach to Pentecostal/Charismatic Spirituality*. Sheffield, England: Sheffield Academic Press.

Alegría-Pons, José Francisco

1993   *Gagá y Vudú en República Dominicana: Ensayos Anthropológicos*. Santo Domingo: Ediciones El Chango Prieto.

Alleyne, Mervyn

1980   *Comparative Afro-American: An Historical-Comparative Study of English-based Afro-American Dialects of the New World*. Ann Arbor, Mich.: Karoma.

Alvarez Vega, Bienvenido

1996   El Movimiento Pentecostal. In *Papeles: El Campo Religioso Dominicano en la Década de los 90's: Diversidad y Expansión*. Santo Domingo: Departamento de Estudios de Sociedad y Religion.

Anderson, Allan

2004   *An Introduction to Pentecostalism*. Cambridge: Cambridge University Press.

Andújar, Carlos

2006   *La Presencia Negra en Santo Domingo: un Enfoque Entohistórico*. Santo Domingo: Letra Gráfica Breve.

2007   *Identidad Cultural y Religiosidad Popular*. Santo Domingo: Letra Gráfica Breve.

Annis, Sheldon

1987   *God and Production in a Guatemalan Town*. Austin: University of Texas Press.

Aracena, Soraya

1999   *Apuntes Sobre la Negritud en Republica Dominicana*. Santo Domingo: Helvetas.

2000   *Los Imigrantes Norteamericanos de Samaná*. Santo Domingo: Helvetas.

Austin-Broos, Diane

1997   *Jamaica Genesis: Religion and the Politics of Moral Orders*. Chicago: University of Chicago Press.

2001   Jamaican Pentecostalism: Transnational Relations and the Nation-State. In *Between Babel and Pentecost: Transnational Pentecostalism in Africa and Latin America*, ed. André Corten and Ruth Marshall Fratani, 142–162. Bloomington: Indiana University Press.

Baehr, Peter

2008   *Caesarism, Charisma, and Fate: Historical Sources and Modern Resonances in the Work of Max Weber*. New Brunswick, N.J.: Transaction.

Bascom, William

1950   The Focus of Cuban Santería. *Southwestern Journal of Anthropology* 6(1): 64–68.

Bastian, Jean-Pierre

1993   The Metamorphosis of Latin American Protestant Groups: A Sociohistorical Perspective. *Latin American Research Review* 28(2): 33–61.

2001   Pentecostalism, Market Logic and Religious Transnationalisation. In *Between Babel and Pentecost: Transnational Pentecostalism in Africa and Latin America*, ed. André Corten and Ruth Marshall Fratani, 163–180. Bloomington: Indiana University Press.

Bastide, Roger

1971   *African Civilizations in the New World*. New York: Harper and Row.

1978   [1960] *African Religions in Brazil*. Baltimore: Johns Hopkins University Press.

Bastide, Roger, with Françoise Morin and Françoise Raveau

1974   *Les Haïtiens en France*. The Hague: Mouton.

Bayle, Constantino

1946　El campo propio del sacerdote secular en la evangelización Americana. *Missionalia Hispanica*, III.

Beck, Jane

1979　*To Windward of the Land: The Occult World of Alexander Charles.* Bloomington: Indiana University Press.

Besson, Jean

1993　Reputation & Respectability Reconsidered: A New Perspective on Afro-Caribbean Peasant Women. In *Women & Change in the Caribbean: A Pan-Caribbean Perspective*, ed. Janet Momsen, 15–37. Bloomington: Indiana University Press.

Betances, Emelio

2007　*The Catholic Church and Power Politics in Latin America.* Lanham, Md.: Rowman & Littlefield.

Bialecki, Jon, with Naomi Haynes and Joel Robbins

2008　The Anthropology of Christianity. *Religion Compass* 2(6): 1139–1158.

Boddy, Janice

1989　*Wombs and Alien Spirits: Women, Men, and the Zar Cult in Northern Sudan.* Madison: University of Wisconsin Press.

1994　Spirit Possession Revisited: Beyond Instrumentality. *Annual Review of Anthropology* 23:407–434.

Boudewijnse, Barbara, with André Droogers and Frans Kamsteeg, eds.

1998　*More Than Opium: An Anthropological Approach to Latin American and Caribbean Pentecostal Praxis.* Lanham, Md.: Scarecrow Press.

Bourgois, Philippe

1995　*In Search of Respect: Selling Crack in El Barrio.* Cambridge: Cambridge University Press.

Bourguignon, Erika

1952　Class Structure and Acculturation in Haiti. *Ohio Journal of Science* 52(6): 317–320.

2000　Relativism and Ambivalence in the Work of M. J. Herskovits. *Ethos* 28(1): 103–114.

2004　Suffering and Healing, Subordination and Power: Women and Possession Trance. *Ethos* 32(4): 557–574.

Bowen, Kurt

1996　*Evangelism and Apostasy: The Evolution and Impact of Evangelicals in Modern Mexico.* Montreal: McGill-Queen's University Press.

Brana-Shute, Gary

1979　*On the Corner: Male Social Life in a Paramaribo Creole Neighborhood.* Assen, The Netherlands: Van Gorcum.

Brenneman, Robert

2012　*Homies and Hermanos: God and Gangs in Central America.* Oxford: Oxford University Press.

Brereton, Virginia

1991   *From Sin to Salvation: Stories of Women's Conversions, 1800 to the Present.*
        Bloomington: Indiana University Press.

Brodwin, Paul

1996   *Medicine and Morality in Haiti: The Contest for Healing Power.* Cambridge:
        Cambridge University Press.

2003   Religion and the Production of Community in the Haitian Diaspora. *American Ethnologist* 30(1): 85–101.

Brotherton, David

2008   La globalización de los Latin Kings: criminología cultural y la banda transnacional. In *Otras Naciones: Jóvenes, Transnacionalismo y Exclusión*, ed. Mauro
        Cerbino and Luis Barrios, 27–39. Quito: FLACSO Ecuador.

Brotherton, David, and Luis Barrios

2009   Displacement and Stigma: The Social-Psychological Crisis of the Deportee.
        Crime Media Culture 5(1): 29–55.

2011   *Banished to the Homeland: Dominican Deportees and Their Stories of Exile.*
        New York: Columbia University Press.

Brusco, Elizabeth

1995   *The Reformation of Machismo: Evangelical Conversion and Gender in Colombia.* Austin: University of Texas Press.

2010   Gender and Power. In *Studying Global Pentecostalism: Theories and Methods*,
        ed. Allan Anderson, Michael Bergunder, André Droogers, and Cornelis Van
        Der Laan, 74–92. Berkeley: University of California Press.

Burdick, John

1993   *Looking for God in Brazil: The Progressive Catholic Church in Urban Brazil's
        Religious Arena.* Berkeley: University of California Press.

1998   *Blessed Anastácia: Women, Race, and Popular Christianity in Brazil.* New York:
        Routledge.

Burton, Richard

1997   *Afro-Creole: Power, Opposition, and Play in the Caribbean.* Ithaca, N.Y.: Cornell University Press.

Candelario, Ginetta

2007   *Black behind the Ears: Dominican Racial Identity from Museums to Beauty
        Shops.* Durham, N.C.: Duke University Press.

Cannell, Fenella

2006   The Anthropology of Christianity. In *The Anthropology of Christianity*, ed.
        Fenella Cannell, 1–50. Durham, N.C.: Duke University Press.

Cerbino, Mauro, and Ana Rodríguez

2008   La nación imaginada de los Latin Kings, mimetismo, colonialidad y transnacionalismo. In *Otras Naciones: Jóvenes, Transnacionalismo y Exclusión*, ed.
        Mauro Cerbino and Luis Barrios, 41–74. Quito: FLACSO Ecuador.

Chesnut, Andrew

1997   *Born Again in Brazil: The Pentecostal Boom and the Pathogens of Poverty.* New
        Brunswick, N.J.: Rutgers University Press.

2003   *Competitive Spirits: Latin America's New Religious Economy*. Oxford: Oxford University Press.

Chidester, David

2000   *Christianity: A Global History*. New York: HarperCollins.

Chireau, Yvonne

2003   *Black Magic: Religion and the African American Conjuring Tradition*. Berkeley: University of California Press.

Cleary, Edward

1997   Introduction: Pentecostals, Prominence, and Politics. In *Power, Politics, and Pentecostals in Latin America*, ed. Edward Cleary and Hannah Stewart-Gambino, 1–24. Boulder, Colo.: Westview Press.

Cleary, Edward, and Hannah Stewart-Gambino, eds.

1997   *Power, Politics, and Pentecostals in Latin America*. Boulder, Colo.: Westview Press.

Clifford, James

1997   *Routes: Travel and Translation in the Late Twentieth Century*. Cambridge, Mass.: Harvard University Press.

Collado, Lipe

1992   *El Tíguere Dominicano*. Santo Domingo: Editora Panamericana.

Conway, Frederick

1980   Pentecostalism in Haiti: Healing and Hierarchy. In *Perspectives on Pentecostalism: Case Studies from the Caribbean and Latin America*, ed. Stephen Glazier, 7–26. Lanham, Md.: University Press of America.

Corten, André, and Ruth Marshall-Fratani, eds.

2001   *Between Babel and Pentecost: Transnational Pentecostalism in Africa and Latin America*. Bloomington: Indiana University Press.

Courlander, Harold

1960   *The Drum and the Hoe: Life and Lore of the Haitian People*. Berkeley: University of California Press.

Cox, Harvey

1995   *Fire from Heaven: The Rise of Pentecostal Spirituality and Reshaping of Religion in the Twenty-First Century*. Cambridge: Da Capo Press.

Crick, Malcolm

1976   *Explorations in Language and Meaning*. London: Croom Helm.

1979   Anthropologists' Witchcraft: Symbolically Defined or Analytically Undone? *Journal of the Anthropological Society of Oxford* 10:139–146.

Csordas, Thomas

1997   *Language, Charisma, and Creativity: The Ritual Life of a Religious Movement*. Berkeley: University of California Press.

2007   Global Religion and the Re-enchantment of the World. *Anthropological Theory* 7(3): 295–314.

2011   Ritualization of Life. In *Practicing the Faith: The Ritual Life of Pentecostal-Charismatic Christians*, ed. Martin Lindhardt, 129–151. New York: Berghahn Books.

Cucchiari, Salvatore

1990   Between Shame and Sanctification: Patriarchy and Its Transformation in Sicilian Pentecostalism. *American Ethnologist* 17(4): 687–707.

Damboriena, Prudencio

1963   *El Protestantismo en America Latina.* Vol. 2. Bogotá: Oficina Internacional de Investigaciones Sociales de FERES.

Davis, Martha

1987   *La Otra Ciencia: el Vudú como Religión y como Medicina Popular.* Santo Domingo: Universidad Autónoma de Santo Domingo.

de Heusch, Luc

1962   Cultes de possession et religions initiatiques de salut en Afrique. *Annales du Centre d'Études des Religions.*

1989   Kongo in Haiti: A New Approach to Religious Syncretism. *Man* 24:290–303.

Deive, Carlos

1992   [1975] *Vodú y Magia en Santo Domingo.* Santo Domingo: Fundación Cultural Dominicana.

de Moya, Antonio

2002   Power Games and Totalitarian Masculinity in the Dominican Republic. In *Caribbean Masculinities: Working Papers,* ed. Rafael Ramírez, Victor García-Toro, and Ineke Cunningham, 105–146. San Juan: HIV/AIDS Research and Education Center, University of Puerto Rico.

d'Epinay, Christian

1969   *Haven of the Masses: A Study of the Pentecostal Movement in Chile.* London: Lutterworth.

Derby, Lauren

2009   *The Dictator's Seduction: Politics and the Popular Imagination in the Era of Trujillo.* Durham, N.C.: Duke University Press.

Derby, Lauren, and Richard Turits

1993   Historias de terror y los terrores de la historia: la massacre haitiana de 1937 en la Republica Dominicana. *Estudios Sociales* 26(92): 65–76.

Deren, Maya

1953   *Divine Horsemen: The Living Gods of Haiti.* New York: Thames & Hudson.

Desmangles, Leslie

1992   *The Faces of Gods: Vodou and Roman Catholicism in Haiti.* Chapel Hill: University of North Carolina Press.

Dominguez, Ivan, with Jose Castillo and Dagoberto Tejada

1978   *Almanaque Folklórico Dominicano.* Santo Domingo: Museo del Hombre Dominicano.

Droogers, André

1994   The Normalization of Religious Experience: Healing, Prophecy, Dreams, and Visions. In *Charismatic Christianity as a Global Culture,* ed. Karla Poewe, 33–49. Columbia: University of South Carolina Press.

Drummond, Lee
1980   The Cultural Continuum: A Theory of Intersystems. *Man* 15(2): 352–374.
Engelke, Matthew, and Matt Tomlinson
2006   Meaning, Anthropology, Christianity. In *The Limits of Meaning: Case Studies in the Anthropology of Christianity*, ed. Matthew Engelke and Matt Tomlinson, 1–38. New York: Berghahn Books.
Evans-Pritchard, E. E.
1976   *Witchcraft, Oracles, and Magic among the Azande.* Oxford: Clarendon Press.
Farmer, Paul
1990   Sending Sickness: Sorcery, Politics, and Changing Concepts of AIDS in Rural Haiti. *Medical Anthropology Quarterly* 4(1): 6–27.
Fennema, Meindert, and Troetje Lowenthal
1987   *La construcción de raza y nación en la República Dominicana.* Santo Domingo: Editora Universitaria—UASD.
Fernández Olmos, Margarite, and Lizabeth Paravisini-Gebert
2003   *Creole Religions of the Caribbean: An Introduction from Vodou and Santería to Obeah and Espiritismo.* New York: New York University Press.
Frazier, E. Franklin
1974 [1963] *The Negro Church in America.* New York: Schocken Books.
Geertz, Clifford
1973   *The Interpretation of Cultures.* New York: Basic Books.
Genovese, Eugene
1976   *Roll, Jordan, Roll: The World the Slaves Made.* New York: Vintage Books.
Geron, Candido
1980   *Sabana de Los Muertos: La Historia de Villa Altagracia.* Santo Domingo: Editorial Santo Domingo.
Glazier, Stephen, ed.
1980   *Perspectives on Pentecostalism: Case Studies from the Caribbean and Latin America.* Washington, D.C.: University Press of America.
Goldstein, Donna
2003   *Laughter Out of Place: Race, Class, Violence, and Sexuality in a Rio Shantytown.* Berkeley: University of California Press.
González, Justo L.
1969   *The Development of Christianity in the Latin Caribbean.* Grand Rapids, Mich.: W. B. Eerdmans.
Gooren, Henri
2010a   Conversion Narratives. In *Studying Global Pentecostalism: Theories and Methods*, ed. Allan Anderson, Michael Bergunder, André Droogers, and Cornelis Van Der Laan, 74–92. Berkeley: University of California Press.
2010b   *Religious Conversion and Disaffiliation: Tracing Patterns of Change in Faith Practices.* New York: Palgrave Macmillan.
Gregory, Steven
2007   *The Devil behind the Mirror: Globalization and Politics in the Dominican Republic.* Berkeley: University of California Press.

Guadeloupe, Francio

2008   *Chanting Down the New Jerusalem: Calypso, Christianity, and Capitalism in the Caribbean.* Berkeley: University of California Press.

Harding, Susan

1991   Representing Fundamentalism: The Problem of the Repugnant Cultural Other. *Social Research* 58(2): 373–393.

Harrison, Michael

1974   Preparation for Life in the Spirit: The Process of Initial Commitment to a Religious Movement. *Urban Life and Culture* 2(4): 387–414.

Haynes, Naomi

2012   Pentecostalism and the Morality of Money: Prosperity, Inequality, and Religious Sociality on the Zambian Copperbelt. *Journal of the Royal Anthropological Institute* 18:123–139.

Heredia, Aida

2003   *La Representación del Haitiano en las letras Dominicanas.* University, Miss.: Romance Monographs.

Herskovits, Melville

1937   African Gods and Catholic Saints in New World Negro Belief. *American Anthropologist* 39(4): 635–643.

1938   *Acculturation, the Study of Culture Contact.* New York: J. J. Augustin.

1946   Problem, Method and Theory in Afroamerican Studies. *Phylon* 7(4): 337–354.

1964 [1937] *Life in a Haitian Valley.* New York: Octagon Books.

1970 [1958] *The Myth of the Negro Past.* Gloucester, Mass.: P. Smith.

Hine, Virginia

1970   Bridge Burners: Commitment and Participation in a Religious Movement. *Sociological Analysis* 31(2): 61–66.

Hoetink, Harry

1970   The Dominican Republic in the Nineteenth Century: Some Notes on Stratification, Immigration, and Race. In *Race and Class in Latin America*, ed. Magnus Mörner, 96–121. New York: Columbia University Press.

1985   "Race" and Color in the Caribbean. In *Caribbean Contours*, ed. Sidney Mintz and Sally Price, 55–84. Baltimore: Johns Hopkins University Press.

Hollenweger, Walter

1972   *The Pentecostals: The Charismatic Movement in the Churches.* Minneapolis: Augsburg Publishing House.

2004   An Introduction to Pentecostalisms. *Journal of Beliefs & Values* 25(2): 125–137.

Howard, David

2001   *Coloring the Nation: Race and Ethnicity in the Dominican Republic.* Oxford: Signal Books.

Hurbon, Laënnec

1992   The Church and Afro-American Slavery. In *The Church in Latin America 1492–1992*, ed. Enrique Dussel, 363–374. New York: Orbis Books.

1995   American Fantasy and Haitian Vodou. In *Sacred Arts of Haitian Vodou*, ed.

Donald Cosentino, 181–197. Los Angeles: UCLA Fowler Museum of Cultural History.

2001a   Current Evolution of Relations between Religion and Politics in Haiti. In *Nation Dance: Religion, Identity, and Cultural Difference in the Caribbean*, ed. Patrick Taylor, 118–128. Bloomington: Indiana University Press.

2001b   Pentecostalism and Transnationalisation in the Caribbean. In *Between Babel and Pentecost: Transnational Pentecostalism in Africa and Latin America*, ed. André Corten and Ruth Marshall-Fratani, 124–141. Bloomington: Indiana University Press.

Hurston, Zora Neale

2009   [1938] *Tell My Horse: Voodoo and Life in Haiti and Jamaica*. New York: Harper Perennial.

Huxley, Francis

1966   *The Invisible Voodoo Gods in Haiti*. New York: McGraw-Hill.

Jacobson, C. Jeffrey

2003   '¿Espiritus? No. Pero la Maldad Existe': Supernaturalism, Religious Change, and the Problem of Evil in Puerto Rican Folk Religion. *Ethnos* 31(3): 434–467.

Jenkins, Philip

2002   *The Next Christendom: The Coming of Global Christianity*. New York: Oxford University Press.

Jiménez Lambertus, Abelardo

1981   Aspectos Históricos y Psicológicos del Culto a los Luases en República Dominicana. *Boletín del Museo del Hombre Dominicano* 9(15): 171–183.

Kamsteeg, Frans

1998   *Prophetic Pentecostalism in Chile: A Case Study on Religion and Development Policy*. Lanham, Md.: Scarecrow Press.

Khan, Aisha

2001   Journey to the Center of the Earth: The Caribbean as Master Symbol. *Cultural Anthropology* 16(3): 271–302.

Krohn-Hansen, Christian

1996   Masculinity and the Political among Dominicans: The Dominican Tiger. In *Machos, Mistresses, Madonnas: Contesting the Power of Latin American Gender Imagery*, ed. Marit Melhuus and Kristi Anne Stølen, 108–133. New York: Verso.

Labourt, José

N.d.   El exorcismo se practica con frecuencia en el pais. *CEPAE Boletín* 7:17–19.

Laguerre, Michel

1989   *Voodoo and Politics in Haiti*. New York: St. Martin's Press.

Lampe, Armando

1992   Christianity in the Caribbean. In *The Church in Latin America 1492–1992*, ed. Enrique Dussel, 185–200. New York: Orbis Books.

Le Bon, Gustave

1952 [1896] *The Crowd: A Study of the Popular Mind*. London: E. Benn.

Lehmann, David

1996   *Struggle for the Spirit: Religious Transformation and Popular Culture in Brazil and Latin America.* Cambridge: Blackwell.

Lemus, Francisco Javier, and Rolando Marty

2010   Creencias y prácticas de la religiosidad popular. In *Religiosidad Popular Dominicana*, ed. Francisco Javier Lemus, 13–75. Santo Domingo: Banco Popular.

Lewis, I. M.

1966   Spirit Possession and Deprivation Cults. *Man* 1(3): 307–329.

1971   *Ecstatic Religions: An Anthropological Study of Possession and Shamanism.* London: Penguin.

1986   *Religion in Context: Cults and Charisma.* Cambridge: Cambridge University Press.

Lewis, Linden

1990   Are Caribbean Men in Crisis? An Economic and Social Dilemma. *Caribbean Affairs* 3(3): 104–112.

2004   Caribbean Masculinity at the Fin de Siècle. In *Interrogating Caribbean Masculinities*, ed. Rhoda Reddock, 244–266. Kingston: University of the West Indies Press.

Lindhardt, Martin

2009   The Ambivalence of Power: Charismatic Christianity and Occult Forces in Urban Tanzania. *Nordic Journal of Religion and Society* 22(1): 37–54.

2011   Introduction. In *Practicing the Faith: The Ritual Life of Pentecostal-Charismatic Christians*, ed. Martin Lindhardt, 1–48. New York: Berghahn Books.

Lizardo, Fradique

1982   *Apuntes Investigacion de Campo para el Montaje del Espectaculo Religiosidad Popular Dominicana.* Santo Domingo: Museo del Hombre Dominicano.

Lockward, George

1982   *El Protestantismo en Dominicana.* Santo Domingo: Editora Educativa Dominicana.

Luhrmann, T. M.

2004   Metakinesis: How God Becomes Intimate in Contemporary U.S. Christianity. *American Anthropologist* 106(3): 518–528.

2012   *When God Talks Back: Understanding the American Evangelical Relationship with God.* New York: Alfred A. Knopf.

Lundius, Jan, and Mats Lundahl

2000   *Peasants and Religion: A Socioeconomic Study of Dios Olivorio and the Palma Sola Movement in the Dominican Republic.* London: Routledge.

Manners, Robert

1956   Tabara: Subcultures of a Tobacco and Mixed Crops Municipality. In *The People of Puerto Rico*, ed. Julian Steward, 93–170. Urbana: University of Illinois Press.

Manning, Frank

1973   *Black Clubs in Bermuda: Ethnography of a Play World.* Ithaca, N.Y.: Cornell University Press.

Mariz, Cecília Loreto

1994   *Coping with Poverty: Pentecostal and Christian Base Communities in Brazil.*
        Philadelphia: Temple University Press.

Mariz, Cecília Loreto, and María Campos Machado

1997   Pentecostalism and Women in Brazil. In *Power, Politics, and Pentecostals in
        Latin America,* ed. Edward Cleary and Hannah Stewart-Gambino, 41–54.
        Boulder, Colo.: Westview Press.

Martin, Bernice

1995   New Mutations of the Protestant Ethic among Latin American Pentecostals.
        Religion 25(2): 101–117.

2001   The Pentecostal Gender Paradox: A Cautionary Tale for the Sociology of Re-
        ligion. In *The Blackwell Companion to Sociology of Religion,* ed. Richard Fenn,
        52–66. Oxford: Blackwell.

Martin, David

1990   *Tongues of Fire: The Explosion of Protestantism in Latin America.* Cambridge:
        Blackwell.

1994   Evangelical and Charismatic Christianity in Latin America. In *Charismatic
        Christianity as a Global Culture,* ed. Karla Poewe, 73–86. Columbia: University
        of South Carolina Press.

2002   *Pentecostalism: The World Their Parish.* Oxford: Blackwell.

Martínez, Samuel

2003   Not a Cockfight: Rethinking Haitian-Dominican Relations. *Latin American
        Perspectives* 30(3): 80–101.

Martínez-Fernández, Luis

1995   The Sword and the Crucifix: Church-State Relations and Nationality in the
        Nineteenth-Century Dominican Republic. *Latin American Research Review*
        30(1): 69–93.

Martínez-Vergne, Teresita

2005   *Nation & Citizen in the Dominican Republic, 1880–1916.* Chapel Hill: Univer-
        sity of North Carolina Press.

Matibag, Eugenio

2003   *Haitian-Dominican Counterpoint: Nation, State, and Race on Hispaniola.* New
        York: Palgrave Macmillan.

Maxwell, David

1998   Delivered from the Spirit of Poverty? Pentecostalism, Prosperity and Moder-
        nity in Zimbabwe. *Journal of Religion in Africa* 28(3): 350–373.

Mayes, April

2014   *The Mulatto Republic: Class, Race, and Dominican National Identity.* Gaines-
        ville: University Press of Florida.

McAlister, Elizabeth

2002   *Rara! Vodou, Power, and Performance in Haiti and Its Diaspora.* Berkeley: Uni-
        versity of California Press.

McNeal, Keith

2011   *Trance and Modernity in the Southern Caribbean: African and Hindu Popular Religions in Trinidad and Tobago.* Gainesville: University Press of Florida.

Métraux, Alfred

1972   [1959] *Voodoo in Haiti.* New York: Schocken Books.

Meyer, Birgit

1998   Make a Complete Break with the Past: Memory and Postcolonial Modernity in Ghanaian Pentecostal Discourse. In *Memory and the Postcolony: African Anthropology and the Critique of Power,* ed. Richard Werbner, 182–208. London: Zed Books.

1999   *Translating the Devil: Religion and Modernity among the Ewe in Ghana.* Edinburgh: Edinburgh University Press.

Miller, Donald, and Tetsunao Yamamori

2007   *Global Pentecostalism: The New Face of Christian Social Engagement.* Berkeley: University of California Press.

Miniño, Manuel

1985   *¿Es el Vudú religion? El Vudú dominicano.* Santo Domingo: Editora Libros y Textos.

Mintz, Sidney

1956   Cañamelar: The Subculture of a Rural Sugar Plantation Proletariat. In *The People of Puerto Rico,* ed. Julian Steward, 314–417. Urbana: University of Illinois Press.

1989   [1974] *Caribbean Transformations.* New York: Columbia University Press.

Mintz, Sidney, and Richard Price

1992   [1976] *The Birth of African-American Culture: An Anthropological Perspective.* Boston: Beacon Press.

Mintz, Sidney, and Michel-Rolph Trouillot

1995   The Social History of Haitian Vodou. In *Sacred Arts of Haitian Vodou,* ed. Donald Cosentino, 123–147. Los Angeles: UCLA Fowler Museum of Cultural History.

Moya Pons, Frank

1978   *La Dominación Haitiana, 1822–1844.* Santiago: Universidad Católica Madre y Maestra.

1985   The Land Question in Haiti and Santo Domingo: The Sociopolitical Context of the Transition from Slavery to Free Labor, 1801–1843. In *Between Slavery and Free Labor: The Spanish-Speaking Caribbean in the Nineteenth Century,* ed. M. Fraginals, F. Moya Pons, and S. Engerman, 181–214. Baltimore: Johns Hopkins University Press.

Ochoa, Todd Ramón

2010   *Society of the Dead: Quita Manaquita and Palo Praise in Cuba.* Berkeley: University of California Press.

O'Neill, Kevin Lewis

2010   *City of God: Christian Citizenship in Postwar Guatemala.* Berkeley: University of California Press.

Oosterbaan, Martijn
2009   Sonic Supremacy: Sound, Space and Charisma in a Favela in Rio de Janeiro. *Critique of Anthropology* 29(1): 81–104.

Orces, Diana
2009   *World Views: "Political Monism" the Battle between Good and Evil.* Latin American Public Opinion Project, Insights Series, No. 17.

Padilla, Mark
2007   *Caribbean Pleasure Industry: Tourism, Sexuality, and AIDS in the Dominican Republic.* Chicago: University of Chicago Press.

Parsons, E. G.
1928   Spirit Cult in Hayti. *Journal de la Société des Américanistes* 20:157–179.

Parsons, Talcott
1964   [1937] *The Structure of Social Action: A Study in Social Theory with Special Reference to a Group of Recent European Writers.* New York: Free Press of Glencoe.

Patín Veloz, Enrique
1975   El Vudu y Sus Misterios (Referencias y Definiciones). *Revista Dominicana de Folklore* 141–161.

Pérez, Antonio Morillo
2003   *Focalización de la Pobreza en la República Dominicana (Segunda Edicion).* Santo Domingo: Secretariado Técnico de la Presidencia Oficina Nacional de Planificación.

Pérez Memén, Fernando
1984   *La Iglesia y el Estado en Santo Domingo, 1700–1853.* Santo Domingo: Editora de la UASD.
2008   El indio y el negro en la visión de la Iglesia y el Estado. *Mar Oceana* 24:77–93.

Platt, Dario
1981   *Nueva Esperanza para Santo Domingo.* Santo Domingo: Universidad CETEC.

Poewe, Karla
1994   The Nature, Globality, and History of Charismatic Christianity. In *Charismatic Christianity as a Global Culture,* ed. Karla Poewe, 33–49. Columbia: University of South Carolina Press.

Powdermaker, Hortense
1968   *After Freedom: A Cultural Study in the Deep South.* New York: Atheneum.

Price-Mars, Jean
1983   [1928] *So Spoke the Uncle.* Washington, D.C.: Three Continents Press.

Pritchard, Hesketh
1900   *Where Black Rules White: A Journey Across and About Hayti.* New York: Scribner's Sons.

Raboteau, Albert
1978   *Slave Religion: The "Invisible Institution" in the Antebellum South.* New York: Oxford University Press.

Rey, Terry, and Alex Stepick

2013   *Crossing the Water and Keeping the Faith: Haitian Religion in Miami*. New York: New York University Press.

Ripley, Geo

2002   *Imágenes de Posesión: Vudú Dominicano*. Santo Domingo: Cocolo Editorial.

Rivera, Luis

1992   *A Violent Evangelism: The Political and Religious Conquest of the Americas*. Louisville, Ky.: Westminster/John Knox Press.

Robbins, Joel

2003a   What Is a Christian? Notes toward an Anthropology of Christianity. *Religion* 33:191–199.

2003b   On the Paradoxes of Global Pentecostalism and the Perils of Continuity Thinking. *Religion* 33:221–231.

2004a   The Globalization of Pentecostal and Charismatic Christianity. *Annual Review of Anthropology* 33:117–143.

2004b   *Becoming Sinners: Christianity and Moral Torment in a Papua New Guinea Society*. Berkeley: University of California Press.

2007   Continuity Thinking and the Problem of Christian Culture: Belief, Time, and the Anthropology of Christianity. *Current Anthropology* 48(1): 5–38.

2010   Anthropology of Religion. In *Studying Global Pentecostalism: Theories and Methods*, ed. Allan Anderson, Michael Bergunder, André Droogers, and Cornelis van der Laan, 156–178. Berkeley: University of California Press.

Roberts, Bryan

1968   Protestant Groups and Coping with Urban Life in Guatemala City. *American Journal of Sociology* 73(6): 753–767.

Roberts, John

1989   *From Trickster to Badman: The Black Folk Hero in Slavery and Freedom*. Philadelphia: University of Pennsylvania Press.

Rodríguez León, Mario

1992   Invasion and Evangelization in the Sixteenth Century. In *The Church in Latin America 1492–1992*, ed. Enrique Dussel, 43–54. New York: Orbis Books.

Rosenberg, June

1979   *El Gaga: Religion y Sociedad de un Culto Dominicano, Un Estudio Comparativo*. Santo Domingo: Universidad Autónoma de Santo Domingo.

Safa, Helen

1995   *The Myth of the Male Breadwinner*. Boulder, Colo.: Westview Press.

2002   Questioning Globalization: Gender and Export Processing in the Dominican Republic. *Journal of Developing Societies* 18(2–3): 11–31.

Sagás, Ernesto

1993   A Case of Mistaken Identity: Antihaitianismo in Dominican Culture. *Latinamericanist* 29(1): 1–5.

2000   *Race and Politics in the Dominican Republic*. Gainesville: University Press of Florida.

Schaffler, Yvonne
2004   Dominican Folk Catholicism—Healing Spirits Away from Tourism. In *Vien-nese Ethnomedicine Newsletter*, 6–13. Vienna: Institute for the History of Medicine, Medical University of Vienna, Austria.

Scheele, Raymond
1956   The Prominent Families of Puerto Rico. In *The People of Puerto Rico*, ed. Julian Steward, 418–462. Urbana: University of Illinois Press.

Schultze, Quentin
1994   Orality and Power in Latin American Pentecostalism. In *Coming of Age: Protestantism in Contemporary Latin America*, ed. Daniel Miller, 65–116. Lanham, Md.: University Press of America.

Scott, James
1990   *Domination and the Arts of Resistance: Hidden Transcripts*. New Haven, Conn.: Yale University Press.

Seabrook, William
1929   *The Magic Island*. New York: Harcourt, Brace.

Shils, Edward
1965   Charisma, Order, and Status. *American Sociological Review* 30(2): 199–213.

Simmons, Kimberly Eison
2009   *Restructuring Racial Identity and the African Past in the Dominican Republic*. Gainesville: University Press of Florida.

Simpson, George Eaton
1940   Haitian Magic. *Social Forces* 19(1): 95–100.
1945   The Belief System of Haitian Vodun. *American Anthropologist* 47(1): 35–59.
1954   Magical Practices in Northern Haiti. *Journal of American Folklore* 67(266): 395–403.
1978   *Black Religions in the New World*. New York: Columbia University Press.

Smilde, David
1997   The Fundamental Unity of Conservative and Revolutionary Tendencies in Venezuelan Evangelicalism: The Case of Conjugal Relations. *Religion* 27:343–359.
2007   *Reason to Believe: Cultural Agency in Latin American Evangelicalism*. Berkeley: University of California Press.

Smith, M. G.
1960   Social and Cultural Pluralism. *Annals of the New York Academy of Sciences* 83(5): 763–785.
1965   *The Plural Society in the British West Indies*. Berkeley: University of California Press.

Steigenga, Timothy, and Edward Cleary, eds.
2007   *Conversion of a Continent: Contemporary Religious Change in Latin America*. New Brunswick, N.J.: Rutgers University Press.

Stewart, Charles
1991   *Demons and Devil: Moral Imagination in Modern Greek Culture*. Princeton, N.J.: Princeton University Press.

Stoll, David
1990   *Is Latin America Turning Protestant? The Politics of Evangelical Growth.* Berkeley: University of California Press.
Synan, Vinson
1997   [1971] *The Holiness-Pentecostal Tradition: Charismatic Movements in the Twentieth Century.* Grand Rapids, Mich.: W. B. Eerdmans.
Taylor, Charles
2007   *A Secular Age.* Cambridge, Mass.: Harvard University Press.
Thompson, Dondrea
2002   The Politics of Display or the Display of Politics? Cultural Policy and the Museo del Hombre Dominicano. *Museum Anthropology* 25(2): 38–49.
Thornton, Brendan Jamal
2012   Public Participation in an Urban Barrio: Collective Social Action from the Streets to the Pulpit. Paper presented at the Annual Meeting of the Caribbean Studies Association, Le Gosier, Guadeloupe, May 28.
Thornton, W. Philip
1984   Resocialization: Roman Catholics Becoming Protestants in Colombia, South America. *Anthropology Quarterly* 57(1): 28–38.
Todorov, Tzvetan
1982   *The Conquest of America: The Question of the Other.* New York: HarperCollins.
Torres-Saillant, Silvio
1998   The Tribulations of Blackness: Stages in Dominican Racial Identity. *Latin American Perspectives* 25(3): 126–146.
Toulis, Nicole
1997   *Believing Identity: Pentecostalism and the Mediation of Jamaican Ethnicity and Gender in England.* Oxford: Berg.
Trouillot, Michel-Rolph
2003   *Global Transformations: Anthropology and the Modern World.* New York: Palgrave Macmillan.
Turits, Richard Lee
2002   A World Destroyed, A Nation Imposed: The 1937 Haitian Massacre in the Dominican Republic. *Hispanic American Historical Review* 82(3): 589–635.
Turner, Victor
1967   *The Forest of Symbols: Aspects of Ndembu Ritual.* Ithaca, N.Y.: Cornell University Press.
Vigil, James Diego
2003   Urban Violence and Street Gangs. *Annual Review of Anthropology* 32:225–242.
Villamán, Marcos
1993a   *El Auge Pentecostal: Certeza, Identidad, Salvación.* Mexico City: Centro Antonio de Montesinos.
1993b   Perfil Religioso en el Caribe Hispano-Parlante: el Caso de la República Dominicana in Perfiles. *Latinoamericanos* 2:51–83

2002   La vuelta de lo sagrado religión y dinámica social. *Ciencia y Sociedad* 27(4): 504–548.

Wacker, Grant

2001   *Heaven Below: Early Pentecostals and American Culture*. Cambridge, Mass.: Harvard University Press.

Weber, Max

1963 [1922] *The Sociology of Religion*. Boston: Beacon Press.

1992 [1930] *The Protestant Ethic and the Spirit of Capitalism*. New York: Routledge.

Wedenoja, William

1980   Modernization and the Pentecostal Movement in Jamaica. In *Perspectives on Pentecostalism: Case Studies from the Caribbean and Latin America*, ed. Stephen Glazier, 27–48. Washington, D.C.: University Press of America.

Whitten, Norman, Jr.

1973   Contemporary Patterns of Malign Occultism among Negroes in North Carolina. In *Mother Wit from the Laughing Barrel: Readings in the Interpretation of Afro-American Folklore*, ed. Alan Dundes, 402–418. Jackson: University Press of Mississippi.

Wiarda, Howard

1965   The Changing Political Orientation of the Catholic Church in the Dominican Republic. *Journal of Church and State* 7(2): 238–254

Willems, Emílio

1967   *Followers of the New Faith: Cultural Change and the Rise of Protestantism in Brazil and Chile*. Nashville, Tenn.: Vanderbilt University Press.

1968   Culture Change and the Rise of Protestantism in Brazil and Chile. In *The Protestant Ethic and Modernization: A Comparative View*, ed. S. N. Eisenstadt, 184–210. New York: Basic Books.

Wilson, Everett

1994   The Dynamics of Latin American Pentecostalism. In *Coming of Age: Protestantism in Contemporary Latin America*, ed. Daniel Miller, 89–116. Lanham, Md.: University Press of America.

Wilson, Peter

1995 [1973] *Crab Antics: A Caribbean Case Study of the Conflict Between Reputation and Respectability*. Prospect Heights, Ill.: Waveland Press.

Wipfler, William

1966   *The Churches of the Dominican Republic in the Light of History: A Study of the Root Causes of Current Problems*. Cuernavaca: Centro Intercultural de Documentacion.

Wirkus, Faustin, and Taney Dudley

1931   *The White King of Gonave*. Garden City, N.Y.: Garden City Publishing.

Wolseth, Jon

2008   Safety and Sanctuary: Pentecostalism and Youth Gang Violence in Honduras. *Latin American Perspectives* 35(4): 96–111.

2011   *Jesus and the Gang: Youth Violence and Christianity in Urban Honduras.* Tucson: University of Arizona Press.

Wucker, Michele

1999   *Why the Cocks Fight: Dominicans, Haitians, and the Struggle for Hispaniola.* New York: Hill and Wang.

Zane, Wallace

1999   *Journeys to the Spiritual Lands: The Natural History of a West Indian Religion.* Oxford: Oxford University Press.

Index

BRENDAN JAMAL THORNTON is an
anthropologist and associate professor
of religious studies at the University of
North Carolina at Chapel Hill.

Printed in the USA
CPSIA information can be obtained
at www.ICGtesting.com
LVHW091032281024
794670LV00004B/113